FROM INITIAL EDUCATION TO WORKING LIFE

MAKING TRANSITIONS WORK

OECD

ORGANISATION FOR ECONOMIC CO-OPERATION AND DEVELOPMENT

ORGANISATION FOR ECONOMIC CO-OPERATION AND DEVELOPMENT

Pursuant to Article 1 of the Convention signed in Paris on 14th December 1960, and which came into force on 30th September 1961, the Organisation for Economic Co-operation and Development (OECD) shall promote policies designed:

- to achieve the highest sustainable economic growth and employment and a rising standard of living in Member countries, while maintaining financial stability, and thus to contribute to the development of the world economy;
- to contribute to sound economic expansion in Member as well as non-member countries in the process of economic development; and
- to contribute to the expansion of world trade on a multilateral, non-discriminatory basis in accordance with international obligations.

The original Member countries of the OECD are Austria, Belgium, Canada, Denmark, France, Germany, Greece, Iceland, Ireland, Italy, Luxembourg, the Netherlands, Norway, Portugal, Spain, Sweden, Switzerland, Turkey, the United Kingdom and the United States. The following countries became Members subsequently through accession at the dates indicated hereafter: Japan (28th April 1964), Finland (28th January 1969), Australia (7th June 1971), New Zealand (29th May 1973), Mexico (18th May 1994), the Czech Republic (21st December 1995), Hungary (7th May 1996), Poland (22nd November 1996) and Korea (12th December 1996). The Commission of the European Communities takes part in the work of the OECD (Article 13 of the OECD Convention).

Publié en français sous le titre :
DE LA FORMATION INITIALE A LA VIE ACTIVE
Faciliter les transitions

© OECD 2000
Permission to reproduce a portion of this work for non-commercial purposes or classroom use should be obtained through the Centre français d'exploitation du droit de copie (CFC), 20, rue des Grands-Augustins, 75006 Paris, France, Tel. (33-1) 44 07 47 70, Fax (33-1) 46 34 67 19, for every country except the United States. In the United States permission should be obtained through the Copyright Clearance Center, Customer Service, (508)750-8400, 222 Rosewood Drive, Danvers, MA 01923 USA, or CCC Online: http://www.copyright.com/. All other applications for permission to reproduce or translate all or part of this book should be made to OECD Publications, 2, rue André-Pascal, 75775 Paris Cedex 16, France.

FOREWORD

In late 1996 the OECD's Education Committee launched a Thematic Review of the Transition from Initial Education to Working Life. Fourteen OECD countries took part: Australia; Austria; Canada; the Czech Republic; Denmark; Finland; Hungary; Japan; Norway; Portugal; Sweden; Switzerland; the United Kingdom; and the United States. The review stemmed from countries' desire to gain a better understanding both of how young people's transitions changed during the 1990s, and of the types of national policies and programmes associated with successful transition outcomes. The Thematic Review took a broad perspective of its brief. Within a lifelong learning framework it was concerned with the transition outcomes of all young people: those who enter working life after tertiary study as well as those who enter it after upper secondary education; those who take general education pathways as well as students in vocational education programmes; those who appear to make successful transitions as well as those who struggle to get a secure foothold in the labour market. It was concerned not only with education policies, but with employment and labour policies and welfare and social policies, as well as with the interaction between these policy domains.

The Thematic Review has had several outputs in addition to this summary comparative volume. Each of the participating countries produced a national Background Report. Against a common framework countries used these reports to describe national transition arrangements, to discuss key concerns and problems in the transition, and to set out recent initiatives, wherever possible supported by data from evaluation studies. Each of the countries was then visited by an expert team consisting of OECD Secretariat members and international experts. The contribution of these review team members to the study must be acknowledged with thanks as a vital element in its success. The team visits formed the basis of Country Notes that summarised the review teams' views and suggestions for action. The national Background Reports and the national Country Notes have been published on the Education and Training web site (*http://www.oecd.org/els/edu/index.htm*). Also available on the site is the interim report produced in late 1998 after the first six countries had been reviewed.

The organisation of the national visits by the review teams, as well as the writing of the national Background Reports, was made possible by national co-ordinators and national steering committees in each of the participating countries. Thanks are owed to all of these for their efforts in making both the national studies and the overall comparative study a possibility. Within the OECD Secretariat, Mme Marianne Durand-Drouhin, Mr Phillip McKenzie and Mr Richard Sweet were responsible for the study. Under Mr Abrar Hasan, Head of Division, administrative support was provided by Ms Carola Miras and Ms Sabrina Leonarduzzi. This report is published under the responsibility of the Secretary-General of the OECD.

© OECD 2000

TABLE OF CONTENTS

Preface	7
Executive Summary	9
Chapter 1. **Introduction**	23
1.1. Why have OECD Members conducted a Thematic Review of the transition to working life?	23
1.2. How was the Thematic Review conducted?	24
1.3. What do we mean by "the transition from initial education to working life"?	26
Chapter 2. **Transition Outcomes**	29
2.1. How can outcomes be related to the processes and context of transition?	29
2.2. Does a healthy economy lead to healthy transition outcomes?	37
2.3. How equitable are transition outcomes?	43
2.4. Is optimism justified?	48
Chapter 3. **The Transition Process**	57
3.1. Transition pathways	57
3.2. The length of the transition	67
3.3. A more uncertain transition?	77
Chapter 4. **Key features of Effective Transition Systems**	83
4.1. Well organised pathways	83
4.2. Workplace experience combined with education	91
4.3. Tightly woven safety nets	107
4.4. Good information and guidance	116
4.5. Effective institutions and processes	123
4.6. Putting the jigsaw together	133
Chapter 5. **How Can the Transition Phase Promote Learning Throughout Life?**	137
5.1. Structural approaches to promoting lifelong learning	138
5.2. Learner-centred approaches to promoting lifelong learning	143
Chapter 6. **Conclusion**	149
References	151
Appendix 1. **National Co-ordinators and Review Team Members**	159
Appendix 2. **Consultants' Papers**	163
Appendix 3. **Statistical Tables**	165
Appendix 4. **Using Labour Market Indicators of Transition Outcomes in Comparative Studies**	185
Appendix 5. **A Comprehensive Framework for Indicators of the Transition from Initial Education to Working Life**	195
Appendix 6. **Low Education Levels and Labour Market Disadvantage**	199
Appendix 7. **The Availability of Indicators of Key Transition Goals**	201
Appendix 8. **Country Codes Used in Tables and Charts**	203

© OECD 2000

PREFACE

The OECD's *Thematic Review of the Transition from Initial Education to Working Life* was launched by the OECD's Education Committee in November 1996. Within a lifelong learning framework it has been concerned with two basic issues:
- How has young people's transition from initial education to working life been changing during the 1990s?
- What policies and programmes – education, employment, and social – deliver effective transition outcomes for young people?

The Thematic Review has involved 14 of the OECD Member countries: Australia; Austria; Canada; the Czech Republic; Denmark; Finland; Hungary; Japan; Norway; Portugal; Sweden; Switzerland; the United Kingdom and the United States. These countries are diverse in terms of their institutional arrangements to support the transition, their levels of economic development, their stages in the economic cycle at the time of the review, and their traditions and cultures.

This publication describes the key trends and conclusions that have emerged from the Thematic Review. It is organised in six chapters:

Chapter 1 introduces the Thematic Review, explains the reasons that it was initiated by the OECD membership, describes the methodology used to conduct it, and sets out its conceptual framework.

Chapter 2 focuses upon transition outcomes. It first examines ways in which transition outcomes can be related to the processes and the context of transition, and then examines the relationship between economic conditions and transition outcomes. An examination of the relationship between equity and transition outcomes is followed by an overall assessment of whether or not an optimistic view of young people's transition outcomes seems to be justified.

Chapter 3 looks at the transition process. It begins by describing the major upper secondary pathways that young people take between initial education and work, tertiary study or both; examines why the length of the transition differs between countries and has grown over time; and then describes some ways in which the transition appears, in some countries and for some young people, to have become both more blurred and more uncertain during the 1990s.

Chapter 4 looks at some of the key features of effective transition systems: well organised pathways; workplace experience combined with education; tightly woven safety nets for those at risk; good information and guidance; and effective institutions and processes.

Chatper 5 asks how the transition phase can promote learning throughout life, and looks at two complementary approaches: one concentrating upon educational institutions and structures; and learner-centred approaches.

Chapter 6 looks at some key policy challenges for the future.

© OECD 2000

EXECUTIVE SUMMARY

Why and how was the Thematic Review conducted?

The *Thematic Review of the Transition from Initial Education to Working Life* has been stimulated by a wide range of concerns in OECD countries. These range from concerns about youth unemployment and those at risk in the transition; to concern for what appears to be the growing length of the transition; to a concern to understand how the transition phase can lay a better foundation for learning throughout life, as well as for initial labour market entry.

Within a lifelong learning context the Thematic Review has focused upon two broad questions:
- How has young people's transition to working life been changing during the 1990s? and
- What sorts of policies and programmes are effective in delivering successful transition outcomes for young people?

Two key questions have guided the Thematic Review.

Within the framework of these questions the Thematic Review has adopted a broad approach: focusing upon labour and social policies as well as education policies; focusing upon a broad range of young people. It has included 14 countries: Australia; Austria; Canada; the Czech Republic; Denmark; Finland; Hungary; Japan; Norway; Portugal; Sweden; Switzerland; the United Kingdom and the United States. These differ widely in their transition frameworks, as well as in their economic context, population, geographical size, and forms of government.

The Thematic Review has taken a broad approach to these questions.

Participating countries have prepared Background Reports setting out national trends and issues against a common set of questions. Each country has been visited by a team of expert reviewers. These country visits have led to Country Notes which both describe national transition arrangements for the benefit of a wider audience, and set out the review team's views on key issues and their policy suggestions. Background Reports and Country Notes are available on the Thematic Review's web site: (http://www.oecd.org/els/edu/index.htm).

The transition to working life is just one of the transitions that young people must make on the way to adulthood. For many, other transitions – to economic independence, establishing a household, personal development, family formation – will be more important to them at particular points in their lives. In a lifelong learning context the transition from initial education – whether upper secondary education or tertiary education – is seen as simply the first of many transitions between work and learning that young people will experience throughout their lives. The substantive task of the Thematic Review has been to combine qualitative and quantitative insights in order to understand the

From Initial Education to Working Life

ways in which national transition contexts and transition processes relate to transition outcomes.

Some basic goals for all transition policies are suggested, and multiple indicators have been used to judge how well these goals are met.

Within this framework some basic goals are suggested that all transition policies should aim for. These include:

- High proportions of young people completing a full upper secondary education with a recognised qualification for either work, tertiary study or both.
- High levels of knowledge and skill among young people at the end of the transition phase.
- A low proportion of teenagers being at the one time not in education and unemployed.
- A high proportion of those young adults who have left education having a job.
- Few young people remaining unemployed for lengthy periods after leaving education.
- Stable and positive employment and educational histories in the years after leaving upper secondary education; and
- An equitable distribution of outcomes by gender, social background and region.

In judging the extent to which these goals are met, multiple transition indicators have been used. The set of key indicators that has been adopted spans both education and labour market outcomes, both for teenagers and for young adults. Use of multiple indicators rather than single indicators reveals the complexity of transition outcomes. Within any one country, for example, outcomes can be high for teenagers but not for young adults, and *vice versa*; or education outcomes can be high but not labour market outcomes, and *vice versa*.

How has young people's transition to work changed during the 1990s?

Cautious optimism about outcomes seems justified... with some reservations.

During the 1990s young people's transition from initial education to working life appears to have improved on a number of dimensions. Participation in initial education has risen, although in some countries rates of underqualification remain high among young adults. In absolute terms the proportion of teenagers who are unemployed is quite small in many OECD countries, particularly when only non-student job seekers are taken into account. On the other hand in many countries young adults are significantly more likely to experience unemployment than are teenagers, and the problems of those young adults who have low qualifications are particularly high. Since the mid-1970s there has been a significant reduction in youth to adult unemployment ratios across OECD countries. This suggests an improved ability of young people to compete for work with adults, perhaps in large part due to the rising education levels of new labour market entrants. The rate of improvement, however, was much greater prior to the 1990s than during the 1990s. During the 1990s there was a slight worsening of the overall disadvantage suffered by teenagers in the labour market across countries participating in the Thematic Review, perhaps as a function of the growing concentration of early school leavers among those teenagers in the labour force. Among young adults, however, there has been no obvious trend for their labour market situation to worsen relative to that of adults. The incidence of long term youth unemployment has

© OECD 2000

shown no overall tendency to rise during the 1990s, although there are some countries participating in the Thematic Review in which it has grown. On the other hand in some of the Nordic countries long term unemployment as a share of total youth unemployment has been falling during the 1990s.

By themselves falling youth employment rates, which have been common in OECD countries, are not a good indicator of young people's overall labour market situation, as they are associated with and often caused by rising educational participation. A more important measure is the proportion of young people who are neither in education nor in work, and this showed improvement between the mid 1980s and the late 1990s.

In virtually all countries young workers have experienced declines in earnings relative to older workers during the 1990s. In some countries there is evidence that this has been associated with an increasing concentration of young workers in low-skilled jobs and in low paying industries. This is a particularly worrying development, as the age group is becoming increasingly well educated and well qualified.

The length of the transition from the end of compulsory education to working life varies widely between countries, but there has been a general tendency for it to rise during the 1990s. Across 15 OECD countries the average duration of the transition rose by nearly two years between 1990 and 1996. The reasons are complex and varied. They lie both in the nature of pathways through education, and in what happens to young people after they leave initial education.

The transition from initial education to working life is commonly taking longer.

In some cases longer transitions are the result of young people delaying the transition from compulsory education to upper secondary education. This is either because they move into a "holding pattern" to increase their chance of gaining a place in more prestigious pathways, because they are reluctant to commit themselves at an early age to quite specific occupational preparation pathways, or because employers are reluctant to hire them as apprentices at too early an age. This delay in moving from one level of education to another can also be seen between upper secondary and tertiary education. At times the delay at this level is because of bottlenecks caused by a shortage of tertiary places. At other times it is because young people simply want to have time off, for work or travel, before embarking upon the next stage of their lives. Their ability to make such choices is strengthened by rising national wealth and strong currencies.

Part of the explanation for longer transitions lies in the pathways through education.

Part of the explanation for a longer transition to work is that increasing proportions of young people are now completing a full upper secondary education, rather than dropping out after compulsory schooling or part way through their upper secondary schooling. Closely related to this is an increase in the proportion of young people who continue on to tertiary study after the end of upper secondary education, a tendency that is likely to increase as countries create more bridges between vocational education and tertiary study and create new non-university institutions and courses. Part of the explanation for longer transitions lies in countries extending the average duration of upper secondary education: for example from two years to three years. And part of the explanation lies in young people "double dipping", completing more than one course at the same level, or, in a related trend, completing tertiary courses at non-university level after completing a degree. An important if insufficiently understood factor appears to be interactions between tuition costs, student

© OECD 2000

financing arrangements, access to and the conditions attached to part-time work and the taxation system, which in some countries act together to create incentives for tertiary students to delay course completion.

Part of it is due to increasing delays in settling into work after leaving initial education.

In some countries there has been a rise during the 1990s in the time that it takes young people to settle into work after leaving initial education. In some of these countries the explanation lies in more difficult labour market circumstances. However it can also be related to young people's attitudes and values: to a desire to travel or otherwise postpone settling into work; and to a belief in the importance of satisfying work rather than work for its own sake.

Patterns of participation in upper secondary pathways are changing, often for similar reasons to those that explain why the transition is lengthening.

Patterns of participation in the pathways that young people take between compulsory education and work have been changing in many countries during the 1990s. Although there are a number of exceptions, a common trend has been for participation in upper secondary vocational education pathways to fall, particularly those not linked to tertiary study. At the same time participation has risen in those pathways, whether vocational or general education, that provide a bridge to tertiary study. These shifts are related to a number of factors: young people "working the system" in order to maximise their outcomes; the changing labour market rewards that are associated with the different pathways; the changing patterns of demand for skill and qualifications that often underlie these changing rewards; and changing attitudes on the part of young people and their parents are among these. These changes focus policy attention increasingly upon the importance of creating more flexible and supple pathways that allow young people to gain solid combinations of general and vocational education, and of education and workplace experience, during the transition from initial education to working life. The arguments for such combinations apply as much within tertiary education as within upper secondary education. The trends also focus attention upon difficult issues posed by young people's apparent desire to delay specific preparation for working life in a rapidly changing labour market in which increasing emphasis is being placed upon generic workplace skills.

The transition is becoming more blurred, and for some increasingly uncertain.

Compared to the mid 1980s, young people are now more likely to combine their studies with work during the transition phase. This is partly the result of participation in apprenticeship and the like, but also the result of students having part-time and summer jobs. Education systems are increasingly encouraging this blurring between the classroom and the workplace through school-organised workplace experience programmes such as co-operative education. This means that for many young people the transition from being a student to being a full-time worker is now less sharp and sudden than once it was.

Some dimensions of the transition to adult life appear to have become more difficult during the 1990s. Young people in some countries are now leaving the parental home at a later age, largely because of cost factors, and the earnings of those who are in work on average have been falling relative to adult earnings.

Longer transitions have both benefits and costs.

Longer transitions should not be seen as an altogether negative phenomenon. They have both benefits and costs. The short transitions that result from early school leaving certainly carry high and by now well understood costs for both individuals and governments. A more highly educated population and labour force requires more extended periods of education. The combination of work and study, to the extent that it contributes to longer initial study can improve the conditions of labour market entry, and some of the activities in which young people engage in order to delay the transition, such as travel abroad, can contribute in a positive way to their personal development. On the other hand long periods spent looking for work, in labour market programmes, or out of either education or work, are poor indicators of future labour market success, particularly if they occur in the immediate post-school period. Similarly, longer transitions through initial education can be the result of pathways being too narrow or too inflexible, requiring young people to backtrack, sidetrack or wait for study places if they want to obtain the mix of skills, experience, knowledge and qualifications demanded in the labour market. Such negative reasons for prolonged transitions from initial education to working life should be the object of policy concern.

When young people do leave initial education for work, a high proportion of their jobs are likely to be part-time and temporary, in many cases poorly paid. In some countries a clear pattern can be detected of young people "swirling" through a sequence of such jobs, interspersed with periods of unemployment, participation in labour market programmes, or inactivity. This type of early career instability needs to be clearly distinguished from the type of "job shopping" in the early period after leaving initial education that can improve the fit between young people's skills and employer requirements. Many of those who are at risk in the transition are not included within formal definitions of unemployment, and as a result are often not included in programmes of assistance. Broader definitions of those who are at risk, to include those who are inactive or trapped in cycles of low-skilled and insecure work, are needed.

New ways of defining who is at risk in the transition are needed.

The key features of effective transition systems

The Thematic Review has highlighted a parsimonious set of key ingredients of successful transition systems. These are:
- A healthy economy.
- Well organised pathways that connect initial education with work and further study.
- Widespread opportunities to combine workplace experience with education.
- Tightly knit safety nets for those at risk.
- Good information and guidance; and
- Effective institutions and processes.

Effective transition systems are characterised by a limited number of key ingredients.

A well functioning economy is perhaps the most fundamental factor to shape young people's transition from initial education to work. Sound transition outcomes are easier to achieve when national wealth is high and rising, and when overall unemployment is low. Where jobs are plentiful, they are more likely to be shared with the young. If unemployment is falling for adults, it will generally fall for youth as well. Where overall unemployment is low, the need for expenditure upon remedial labour market programmes for youth without work is reduced. The same resources are able to be used for effective mainstream education and for preventative programs that reduce the risk of early school leaving. Economies in which national wealth is high or increasing can afford to invest more in the education of the young. Extended participation

i) A healthy economy.

in schooling, in training-intensive employment or in tertiary education for entire cohorts of young people largely depends upon economies creating sufficient wealth to invest in longer periods of initial education. Economies in which productivity is rising through more efficient use of capital, investment in new technologies or more effective ways of managing and organising work are more likely to eliminate jobs for the lesser skilled and poorly qualified, and to create more interesting and skill-enhancing work that requires higher levels of education and training.

Good transition outcomes are also more likely to be achieved when labour markets are youth friendly: providing ample opportunities for young people to be trained within enterprises under wage arrangements and employment contracts that encourage their recruitment and training; providing ample opportunities for them to gain experience of paid work while they are students; and limiting the restrictions that are attached to hiring them.

Compared to the impact of overall economic conditions the effects of the types of education and employment policies discussed here on young people's transition may appear to be of secondary importance. Nevertheless, education, employment and social policies can make a significant difference in laying effective foundations for lifelong learning, in dealing with the transition problems of those most at risk of being excluded, and in enhancing both economic effectiveness and social equity. This can be illustrated in several ways. In the first place, at any given level of GDP or of overall unemployment there are wide differences between national transition outcomes. Second, a healthy economy and low unemployment will not by themselves ensure that all types of transition outcomes will be effective. In the United States, for example, solid employment growth during the 1990s and high GDP per capita are associated with high employment rates for young adults and a low incidence of long term youth unemployment. Yet there, young people find it more difficult to compete for work with adults than in many other OECD countries, apparent upper secondary graduation rates are relatively low, relatively few young people achieve high literacy standards, and those young people with low qualifications struggle harder to find work than in many other countries.

Third, while it is relatively easy to achieve good outcomes for young people when economic and labour market conditions are favourable, the absence of strong institutional arrangements to support the transition makes it more likely that poor outcomes will result when economic conditions worsen. A more difficult test for national transition frameworks is their ability to protect young people from the effects of worsening economic conditions. Despite more difficult economic and labour market conditions for much of the 1990s, compared to the previous decades, youth unemployment to population ratios in Japan remained low in the late 1990s, employment rates for young adults remained high, and school participation and graduation rates have remained high. In Sweden, an inclusive upper secondary school system and well organised locally managed safety nets for early leavers have together helped to prevent unemployment among teenagers rising during the 1990s in step with overall unemployment, despite a very marked decline in overall employment levels.

Finally, it is important to stress that effective national institutions appear better able to support the transition of teenagers during times of economic difficulty than the transition of young adults, whose chances of being unemployed are more directly a function of overall labour market conditions than are those of teenagers.

No one type of pathway – whether apprenticeship, school-based vocational or general education – appears to hold the key to successful transition outcomes. Excellent transition outcomes for young people can be found in different countries, regardless of which pathway predominates. However the chances of solid transition outcomes being achieved are higher where young people have available to them learning pathways and qualification frameworks that are clearly defined, well organised and open, designed and developed in a lifelong learning perspective, with effective connections to post school destinations, whether work or further study. Countries in which the connections between pathways and their destinations are embedded in solid institutional frameworks seem more likely to demonstrate successful initial transition outcomes, and are less likely to demonstrate poor transition outcomes, than are countries in which the connection is more loosely coupled. These features appear to be more important than the particular nature of the pathway itself.

ii) Well organised pathways that connect initial education with work, further study or both.

Countries in which young people are evenly spread over all three of the principal pathways, rather than concentrated in one or two, appear to have advantages in achieving good transition outcomes. In these instances young people can be offered wider choices. There can be greater potential flexibility in movements between pathways to suit individual needs, although often this does not occur in practice. A mix of pathways makes it more likely that young people will have available to them a wide variety of general, technical and vocational education options, developing both work-related competencies and personal and social skills. A broad mix helps to ensure that the developing vocational interests of adolescents are able to be met by the curriculum, and that a broad range of talents and achievements can be recognised by qualifications systems.

Well organised connections between upper secondary pathways and tertiary study, as well as between upper secondary pathways and jobs, are important. In some countries, particularly those with occupationally organised labour markets, those graduates from upper secondary general education pathways who have not qualified for tertiary study are thought to have particular difficulties in the labour market.

Pathways are becoming more flexible as policy makers respond both to the wishes of young people and their parents, and to perceived changes in the nature of work. The following developments can be observed:

- More links are being created between vocational pathways and tertiary study.
- The vocational content of general education pathways is increasing.
- The entry points to vocational education pathways are becoming fewer but broader, with specialisation being delayed.
- The general education content of vocational pathways is being increased.
- Modular curriculum structures are becoming more common, allowing young people greater choice in the ways in which they can combine different areas of study.
- In some cases the one pathway is being offered in more than one type of institutional setting; and
- Non-university tertiary programmes are being created or expanded.

A number of issues arise from attempts to increase the relevance and flexibility of pathways:

- Raising the amount and the level of the general education content of vocational pathways, or their level of abstraction, in order to improve links to tertiary study can cause motivation problems among lower achievers.

- In a related way, there can be problems in motivating the lowest achievers in countries in which general education pathways are large and dominant. Ways need to be found to make learning applied, relevant and contextual, and to clearly link school performance to jobs.

- Attempts to broaden the vocational content of general education pathways can suffer from lack of clarity about the purpose of the changes: to provide full occupational qualifications; to provide credit towards such qualifications; to develop generic work skills; or to improve career awareness and decidedness. This confusion is not made easier by the fact that some segments of the labour market in the countries concerned are tightly coupled to occupational qualifications, whereas others are not.

- Attempts to broaden the entry points of vocational pathways, making their content more generic to a number of related occupations or industries, can be difficult to implement if teachers have only specialised expertise, and if schools' physical facilities have not been constructed to meet the needs of more broadly defined pathways. These factors are often not taken into account sufficiently when reforms are being planned.

- It is not easy to halt or reverse the falling status of upper secondary vocational education. However the Thematic Review does point to some important lessons. These include:

    • Avoid making it a residual and dead-end pathway, linked to poor quality jobs and directed at the lowest achievers.

    • Provide institutionalised bridges between vocational education and apprenticeship and tertiary education and ensure that significant proportions of students and apprentices do take this pathway.

    • Design vocational education and training programmes for less successful young people as part of safety nets rather than as ordinary vocational programmes, and make sure that safety net programmes prepare young people for participation in mainstream vocational education and training; and

    • Pay attention to the financial costs and benefits for individuals and firms, for instance by providing support to employers training young people in safety net programmes and by ensuring that participants in vocational education and training programmes are not disadvantaged in terms of income support and rights to welfare programmes.

- By themselves modular curriculum structures might result in little real change in young people's actual choices and flexibility without changes to organisational factors such as school facilities and the school timetable. And they can run the risk of encouraging young people to leave education with only partial skills and qualifications.

Workplace experience combined with education can be important for a number of reasons. It aids matching between employers and young people; it improves the quality of learning by making it more applied and relevant; it develops important work-related knowledge and skills; and it can have a positive impact upon the firm as a learning organisation. Workplace experience and education can be combined in a number of ways. Apprenticeship is the best known of these. Other ways that the two can be combined include school-organised workplace experience, of which the best known model is co-operative education, but also shorter periods within the workplace integrated into school programmes; and students' part-time and holiday jobs. Each of these ways of combining work and education can vary widely both within and between countries in their purposes, nature and organisation. The dimensions along which they vary have a strong impact both upon the extent to which they are learning-intensive, and upon the demands that they make upon the enterprise. As a result their benefits to the parties can vary widely.

iii) Workplace experience combined with education.

There are several reasons for growth in the proportion of young people who combine their education with workplace experience. In some cases it is due to rising participation in apprenticeship, although this has not been the most common experience, particularly in countries that have for many years had fairly large apprenticeship systems. Many countries have invested substantial effort during the 1990s in attempting to increase the availability of school-organised workplace experience. And in a number of countries the incidence of part-time work by students has grown strongly.

The impact of workplace experience upon transition outcomes is not always easy to assess, as it is often combined with many other features that are associated with good national transition outcomes, with their effects being difficult to disentangle. It is also not easy to isolate the impact of the selection effects which lead to those of differing abilities taking different transition pathways that involve varying amounts of workplace experience, and that are associated with sectors of the labour market with varying employment opportunities. Nevertheless comparative data shows a clear correlation between the opportunities for teenagers to combine their study with work, in whatever way, and employment rates among young adults. Careful studies of the impact of apprenticeship show that it is associated with good outcomes for many young people even if the particular features of it that cause these outcomes are not always clear. Despite the positive message that emerges from such studies, considerable caution should be attached to too enthusiastic suggestions that apprenticeship is a model that can readily be transplanted. It is particularly difficult to transplant apprenticeship to countries that are unwilling or unable to make some of the necessary and difficult institutional changes that are part of the reason for its apparent success.

There is consistent evidence from several countries that students' part-time and holiday employment is associated with positive transition outcomes. More mixed messages emerge from evaluations of co-operative education and other forms of school-organised workplace experience. If school-organised alternatives to apprenticeship are to be more effective, more careful attention to their quality is needed. The Thematic Review has highlighted some lessons about the conditions under which this quality can be raised. There are parallels between these and some of the features of successful apprenticeship programmes: careful attention to quality control, for example through screening of employers who train young people; shared ownership by the key parties rather than token consultation; and the existence of mutual benefits. Employer participation is a key to the quality of school-organised workplace experience programmes, and this is easier when it is supported by appropriate institutional arrangements, both from employer organisations and from school systems, rather than left to the individual school or the individual firm. The organisation of the school so that these programmes can form a normal part of their operation is important. Effective school organisation to support workplace experience programmes is made easier by well developed national policy frameworks.

iv) Tightly knit safety nets for those at risk.

Countries with effective transition outcomes actively seek to achieve high rates of participation in, achievement during and completion of upper secondary education. High rates of upper secondary achievement and completion help to reduce the numbers who are most at risk in the transition because of low levels of skill and qualifications. High rates of upper secondary completion are also important in helping to reduce disparities in outcomes between social groups: achieving outcomes that are high for all is one way to ensure that they are more equitable across social groups. High rates of upper secondary achievement and completion are also important in making safety nets for those who do drop out of school early more affordable. Such safety nets are one way in which societies can develop inclusive transition systems.

During the 1990s some of the Nordic countries have developed impressive safety net mechanisms designed to rapidly re-insert early leavers into the mainstream of education so that they can gain an upper secondary qualification for work or further study. Their success in part is because they have achieved a degree of policy coherence: through resolving a tension between immediate employment or education and training qualifications as the goal of intervention to assist those at risk; and through coherence between education, employment and income support policies. The second key ingredient in their success has been the development of local delivery mechanisms that can co-ordinate practical assistance across several policy domains and several levels of government, and tailor this assistance to the needs of individual young people. Safety nets have been accompanied by explicit or implicit guarantees that give all young people an entitlement to an upper secondary education. These rights have been balanced by obligations on the part of the young person to actively participate in order to receive income support. The implementation of these safety nets has been accompanied by evidence in support of their effectiveness in reducing the labour market difficulties of teenagers, although their success in achieving the same results for young adults has not been as evident, partly because young adults have less commonly or only more recently been targeted by them. Recent policy initiatives in a number of other countries have some of the features of the Nordic safety nets.

v) Good information and guidance.

Good information and guidance become increasingly important as the education and employment choices that face young people change and become more complex. Change and complexity arise not only from changes in jobs and career patterns, but also from the growing flexibility of the pathways that link education to working life. This change and complexity constitute strong grounds for the information and guidance that assist young people in the transition shifting away from an approach that tries to "match" their abilities and interests to particular jobs or courses, and towards an approach that places far more emphasis upon active career planning and personal and career development.

Information and guidance should not be expected to steer young people in particular directions to satisfy labour force planning requirements: for example to reverse trends away from vocational education and training at the upper secondary level, or to convince significantly larger numbers of females to choose vocational education and training in traditional "male" occupations. An emphasis upon the adjustment of supply and demand through improvements to working conditions and wages and through better signalling systems are more appropriate policy responses to shortages and surpluses of labour, although accurate information can play an important role in this process. Information and guidance, important as they are, cannot by themselves overcome a lack of equivalence between vocational and general education in current social and economic contexts, nor overturn deep-seated occupational hierarchies and gender differences in the labour market. A condition for effective information and guidance is continuing improvement to the ways in which education and employment systems are aligned, and to the linkages between initial and further education and training.

Countries differ in their characteristic approach to guidance, partly as a result of the nature of their dominant transition pathways. In many countries excellent examples can be found of innovation and good practice: for example in the use of computerised self assessment and job and course information tools.

Despite excellent examples and impressive individual innovations, in most countries a systematic approach to information and guidance during the transition phase is lacking. Wide variation can be observed within countries in most of the basic dimensions of information and guidance: for example whether or not it is mandatory; who provides it and their qualifications and training; and the nature and level of resources that are provided. Too often information and guidance services are marginal within the priorities of schools. This suggests a lack of policy coherence.

A key challenge for policy makers is how universal access to high quality information and guidance services can be provided at an affordable cost. Traditional classroom-based and counsellor-based models both have weaknesses in meeting this objective. They both have difficulty in adapting rapidly enough to changing course and job requirements: and the counsellor-based model in particular is too expensive if access is to be universal and the full range of young people's information and guidance needs are to be met. A more open and comprehensive strategy for the provision of information and guidance services that is able to meet greatly expanded needs for high quality information and guidance should be based around a number of key elements: the production of high quality job and course information by specialist organisations; wide use by students of self-directed techniques of personal assessment and job and course information, including computerised and on-line techniques; mandatory career education within the school curriculum; opportunities for all students to undertake periods of experience in real work settings; and systematic involvement by community members such as employers, parents and alumni.

Countries that consistently achieve good transition outcomes are characterised by strong institutional frameworks to support the transition, normally developed over an extensive period. The nature of these institutions can vary widely: from Japan's tightly woven links between schools and individual firms to lay down clear ground rules for school leaver recruitment; to the vocational

vi) Effective institutions and processes.

education and training systems that have a strong industry involvement that characterise countries where apprenticeship is strong. Such institutional frameworks appear to be most effective when they are able to combine central regulation with local flexibility.

Effective policy processes are needed to support effective institutions.

Effective policy processes are needed to support effective transition institutions. Effective policy implementation needs to be given as much attention as policy design. The involvement of key stakeholders in the on-going management of transition frameworks, not simply in their design, is important. National and local, bottom-up and top-down approaches need to be balanced. Effective transition policy implementation requires learning to be built in as a key feature. Monitoring and evaluation, the deliberate use of pilot projects, and using successful local initiatives as a model for wider policies and programmes are ways in which this can be done. Coherent policy development also requires attention to be paid to the resources needed to bring new frameworks into effect. These include financial resources, human resources, and physical and capital resources. Comprehensive reforms are to be preferred to isolated and piecemeal reforms.

Effective relationships are also important.

Sound transition outcomes also require effective personal relationships between the key parties, as well as good relationships between representative organisations. These help to improve the quality of information sharing, to build mutual obligations, and to promote trust and sharing. Better local tracking of the destinations of school leavers, and feedback of the results of such tracking to school systems and the local community, can be an important way of building local networking and information sharing in support of the transition.

Many countries are trying to encourage local partnerships between educational institutions, employers and communities as a way of strengthening these relationships and improving the transition. This can be observed particularly where the organised involvement of employers and trade unions in education and training has traditionally been weak. In many instances these partnerships have formed spontaneously at the local level in response to locally perceived needs. Such partnerships can be a way to marshal employer support for and involvement in career education programmes, and to extend opportunities for work placements and contextual and applied learning. Effective partnerships require adequate resourcing by educational institutions; they work best when both employers and schools obtain benefits; and they require genuine shared ownership, not just token consultation. Building and maintaining local partnerships is easiest when they are supported by a strong institutional framework, on the part of both employer organisations and school systems.

A related trend has been for governments to stimulate the creation of intermediary bodies to act as brokers between educational institutions and employers in order to improve the transition. These can benefit young people by spreading training over a wider number of firms, thus both extending the breadth of training and experience and widening the network of firms providing training. They can assist firms through their recruitment expertise and young people through their specialised labour market knowledge. It is, however, important not to over-complicate such partnerships, and to ensure that they do not have competing and poorly co-ordinated roles. Governments have an important role to play in monitoring the impact of partnerships and intermediary bodies and in helping to ensure that quality outcomes are achieved by them.

These key ingredients of effective transition systems can work in different ways and in different circumstances to achieve success. National cultures, traditions and institutions will all influence the particular combinations that are effective.

There is no single answer to effective transition systems...

Countries face quite different policy challenges in attempting to improve the transition from initial education to working life. For example countries where problems are concentrated among teenagers and early school leavers face quite different policy issues to countries in which problems are concentrated among young adults. Countries with large apprenticeship systems face quite different challenges to countries with large general education systems. In the former group of countries issues such as the need for broader entry points to apprenticeship and the need for better links to tertiary study will be more pressing. In the latter countries, the problem of motivating lower achieving students by building better bridges between general education pathways and work will be more important.

... nor is there a single problem.

Some of the key features of effective transition systems are difficult to transplant across national borders without modifications to key labour market institutions: for example regulating labour markets so that particular types of occupational qualifications are required for entry to particular types of jobs; or requiring all employers to belong to economic chambers. However other key features do not appear to be closely dependent upon the nature of national labour market institutions. In particular safety nets for those at risk in the transition and career information and guidance appear to be able to be introduced or improved in a wide variety of different national contexts.

Although institutional frameworks differ, all effective transition systems appear to have one thing in common: underlying them are societies that assume responsibility for young people's transition from education to work. In different ways these societies make focused efforts to ensure that national transition arrangements are inclusive, so that as few young people as possible fall through the cracks. It is the fact that special arrangements – whether apprenticeships, safety nets, or efficient recruitment systems – are in place, rather than necessarily the specific means by which a priority for youth comes to be expressed, which appears to be one of the most important lessons to have emerged from the Thematic Review.

A commitment to youth is a common feature of all societies with effective transition systems.

Promoting learning throughout life during the transition phase

Lifelong learning has been a powerful notion in the reform of transition policies during the 1990s. Two basic approaches can be detected in countries' attempts to use the transition phase to lay a stronger basis for learning throughout life:

- Structural approaches that concentrate upon changing educational institutions; and
- Learner-centred approaches that focus upon the teaching and learning process.

Promoting lifelong learning has been a powerful stimulus for reforms to the transition phase.

A number of approaches have been adopted to increase the continuity of learning pathways beyond compulsory education. One has been to open up tertiary education to adults. Another, within apprenticeship countries, can be seen in highly respected post-initial qualifications such as Austria's and Switzerland's

Modifying educational structures is one approach.

Meister and Techniker qualifications, as a way of adding value to apprenticeship qualifications. Another approach, exemplified by the United Kingdom, has been to try to develop unified national qualification frameworks, able to include learning in both classrooms and other settings within the one qualification framework, to allow equivalence between qualifications awarded within initial and within further education, and organising learning in modular systems to allow the accumulation of credits over time. Whilst conceptually coherent, such an approach in practice raises questions about the solidity of young people's foundations for further learning, and about transparency and quality standards. The extent to which it genuinely encourages young people to return over time to accumulate credits and upgrade qualifications remains to be tested.

A complementary approach focuses upon the learner.

Many learner-centred approaches have been initiated for reasons other than or in addition to the development of lifelong learning habits during the transition phase: improving student motivation; making learning more interesting and relevant; and preventing school dropout are among the reasons. Nevertheless there has been a strong belief in many countries that if young people can be encouraged to take more responsibility for their own learning, to apply their learning in community and workplace settings other than the classroom, to bring learning from these settings back into the classroom, to centre their learning around problems rather than known solutions, and to develop generic skills that can be applied in many settings, then they will have laid a good foundation for learning throughout their lives beyond their initial education.

Many excellent initiatives of this sort exist in countries participating in the Thematic Review. The key policy challenge is how such initiatives can move beyond the pilot project and the single institution and have a wider application across education systems. The organisation of the educational institution, assessment practices and the conditions that govern teachers' work are at the heart of this challenge. Encouraging examples can be found in which some of these issues have been addressed on a system-wide basis in order to encourage whole education systems to organise students' learning in a more flexible way to promote better learning habits.

Emerging transition patterns pose particular challenges in laying a basis for lifelong learning in the transition phase.

Transition patterns have changed sharply in the last 20 years. In fewer and fewer countries is it now the norm for young people to permanently leave education at the end of compulsory schooling in order to enter work. As participation in upper secondary education approaches the universal in more and more countries, upper secondary education is increasingly challenged to find ways to motivate and raise the achievement levels of the weaker achievers. Providing all young people with a high quality upper secondary education that develops general, personal and work-related knowledge and skills, and providing all with opportunities for learning outside of the classroom is a key challenge in the ability of upper secondary education to lay a better foundation for lifelong learning during the transition phase.

A spreading of education over a wider period of working life is one of the logical consequences of lifelong learning becoming a reality. In some countries we can see this emerging quite early: in the transition phase. These new and emerging transition patterns are sufficiently common for us to ask whether, in 20 years time, we will be able to look back on present transition patterns and see them as being as unusual as we now regard the transition patterns of young people 20 years ago.

Chapter 1

INTRODUCTION

1.1. Why have OECD Members conducted a Thematic Review of the transition to working life?

Concern about youth unemployment, and about those young people at risk of unemployment and social exclusion, is ongoing in OECD countries. In some cases this concern has increased as growth in upper secondary completion rates has focused attention upon the relative disadvantage of the declining number of early leavers. In many countries growing social and regional inequalities during the 1990s have heightened concerns about the impact of these upon transitions to work by the young. These concerns have been reflected in OECD work over a 20 year period (OECD, 1977*a* and *b*; OECD, 1989; OECD, 1996*b*), and more particularly during the 1990s in the *Jobs Study* (OECD, 1994*c*) and in the Youth Initiative which was launched in a major conference held in February 1999 (OECD, 1999*b*). Complementary work has been conducted on vocational and technical education (OECD, 1994*a* and *d*; OECD, 1998*d*) and on the transition from school to work (Stern and Wagner, 1999).

Young people at risk are an ongoing concern.

In all countries the labour market is changing, creating new patterns of demand for skill and competence. Demand for unskilled work and for work in manufacturing has fallen, and employment has risen in service industries and in technical and professional occupations. In some countries concerns exist about shortages of workers with appropriate skills and qualifications. Policy makers want to know how the transition phase can best prepare young people for a changing economy, and contribute to future prosperity.

A growing interest in lifelong learning has led policy makers to ask themselves how the transition phase can lay the basis for learning throughout life and for long term participation in a knowledge-intensive economy. Preparing young people to get their first job after leaving school or to enter tertiary study is no longer seen to be enough.

In many countries the transition period is becoming longer, and transition patterns are becoming less defined and less certain than they once were. There is concern about dropout rates from both secondary and tertiary education. Young people seem increasingly to be charting their own pathways, and these do not always coincide with those that policy makers have developed. The costs and benefits – to young people, industry and society at large – of these new transition patterns need to be better understood.

Almost everywhere upper secondary and tertiary education systems have been changing. Many of these changes have been designed to improve young people's transition in a changing world. Almost all of them have affected the opportunities available to young people as they make the transition. There has

© OECD 2000

been a steady rise in educational aspirations, particularly for tertiary education (OECD, 1998e).

There is a concern to understand what works.

In the face of a growing interest in lifelong learning, new transition patterns, a changing labour market and changed educational opportunities all countries wish to increase their understanding of those policies and programmes that can make young people's transition to working life effective.

1.2. How was the Thematic Review conducted?

Key questions: change and effectiveness.

Launched by the OECD's Education Committee in November 1996, the Thematic Review has focused upon two broad questions:

– How has young people's transition to working life been changing during the 1990s? This focuses upon the impact of changing economic and labour market circumstances, changes in education systems, and changes in the attitudes and expectations of young people and their parents.

– What sorts of policies and programmes are effective in delivering successful transition outcomes for young people? This aspect of the Thematic Review focuses upon employment and social policies as well as education policies, and upon the ways in which these separate policy domains work together.

This broad policy focus reflects both the social and the economic dimensions of young people's transition from initial education to working life. A number of key concerns and questions arise:

– How can young people's motivation and interest in learning be increased?

– How can more learning opportunities in real work settings be created?

– What information and guidance do young people need?

– How can employers, trade unions and communities work with governments, locally and nationally, to improve young people's transition to stable employment?

– How can young people be helped to settle more quickly into work once they leave secondary and tertiary education?

A wide focus.

The Thematic Review has focused upon all young people: those who make the transition to work from tertiary study; those who enter work directly from upper secondary vocational or general education programmes; and those who have particular difficulties in making the transition to work successfully. It has spanned an age range from the end of compulsory education to the late 20s. The review has seen transition as an issue for all young people, not just those at risk or those of school leaving age. Its focus has nevertheless been more upon the transition from upper secondary education than upon the transition from tertiary study. In part this reflects the fact that an OECD review has recently been conducted of the early years of tertiary education (OECD, 1998e), and in part it reflects the priorities of the participating countries on transition issues.

A wide range of countries.

The Thematic Review has included 14 countries which illustrate quite diverse approaches to young people's transition: Australia, Austria, Canada, the Czech Republic, Denmark, Finland, Hungary, Japan, Norway, Portugal, Sweden, Switzerland, the United Kingdom, and the United States. This allows rich comparisons not only between quite different countries but also within apparently similar groups of countries: for example Canada and Australia as well as the United Kingdom and the United States within Anglo-Saxon countries; Austria, Switzerland and Denmark within countries that rely heavily upon apprenticeship; and a number of Nordic countries – Denmark, Finland, Norway and Sweden.[1]

The review has included countries at different levels of economic development, countries at quite different points in the economic cycle, and countries with quite different levels of economic performance during the 1990s. Table 1.1 summarises some of these indicators.

The 14 countries differ markedly in population size, geographical area, forms of government, and reform strategies adopted over the last two decades. They include large and sparsely populated countries such as Australia and Canada, as well as small and densely populated countries such as Denmark and the Czech Republic. They include countries which have federal forms of government such as Switzerland and the United States, as well as countries which do not, such as Japan and Sweden.

The Thematic Review has attempted to gain an understanding of transition trends and issues within the participating countries from a number of perspectives, both quantitative and qualitative (LeTendre, 1999). Guided by a national steering committee and managed by a national co-ordinator, Background Reports have been prepared by each country against a common framework of questions and issues (OECD, 1998i). These reports have set the context for teams of expert reviewers who have visited each country and talked with young people, teachers, employers and parents, as well as government officials and researchers. In total 39 external experts from 19 OECD Member countries and four members of the OECD secretariat have participated in the 14 visits. This has added a rich set of perspectives and national backgrounds against which to assess countries' experiences, and assisted countries to learn from one another. Details of national co-ordinators and members of the review teams may be found in Appendix 1.

The Thematic Review's methodology.

The qualitative assessments and judgements of the review teams have been supplemented by analysis of statistics and documents both supplied by participating countries and from OECD and other sources. The Thematic Review has been able to build upon a rich international literature on transition that has developed during the 1990s as scholars have explored it in a richer conceptual and empirical way. Some of these scholars have been drawn upon as consultants to the Thematic Review and their contributions are listed in Appendix 2. These analyses and judgements have been combined to produce a Country Note for each participating country. The Country Notes written by the review teams, as well as national Background Reports, have been heavily drawn upon, although not individually cited, in the writing of this publication. They can be found on the Thematic Review's web site,[2] and offer rich contextual material on each of the countries, with the Country Notes

1. However only Portugal among those Southern European countries which in many respects have somewhat different transition patterns to other countries (Planas, 1999; Ryan, 1999) was able to be included.
2. http://www.oecd.org/els/edu/index.htm.

© OECD 2000

providing the review teams' assessments and recommendations. The interim report (OECD, 1998i) produced after the first six countries had been reviewed can also be found on the web site.

In adopting a comparative methodology, and in deciding to include as many as 14 countries, some clear trade-offs have been involved. In particular the balance between depth and breadth needed to be considered. A more intensive and detailed analysis of each country would have greatly limited the number of countries able to be included in the review. A focus simply upon quantitative analysis would have lost the opportunity to gather the qualitative insights that are essential in trying to explain quantitative patterns and to reach policy relevant conclusions. The methodology that has been adopted has several advantages. It allows a rich set of qualitative insights to be combined with quantitative analysis. Data can be gathered within a timeframe short enough to allow useful comparative assessments to be made. This allows lessons from countries' experience to be considered before national circumstances have changed sufficiently to invalidate these assessments.

Another trade-off is that between country-specific perspectives and consistency. The way in which the Thematic Review has been conducted has given participating countries substantial ownership over the process. As a result the selection of issues to be dealt with in-depth in Background Reports and in the visits by review teams reflects those of uppermost interest to the countries concerned. At times these advantages are traded off against loss of comparability and loss of a degree of depth in which particular issues are covered in some countries. On the other hand this has assisted their policy development process, and has ensured that the Thematic Review has focused upon issues that are of real current interest to policy makers, and has not just been an academic exercise or relied simply upon quantitative analysis.

1.3. What do we mean by "the transition from initial education to working life"?

The transition as a multi-dimensional process.

The transition from dependent student to working life is an important milestone in all young people's journey to adulthood. As well as the transition to work, young people must establish economic independence, establish an independent household, and begin family formation. Each is a necessary rite of passage in all industrialised societies. Each of these transition dimensions affects the others, and young people will arrange their lives to give different priorities to each at different times. For many young people establishing an identity as an adult, pursuing leisure interests, or personal relationships will at certain times take a higher priority in their lives than the transition to stable employment (Dwyer and Wyn, 1998). It makes sense to see the transition as a multi-dimensional process, and not as a single event at one point in time.

Is "the transition rom initial education to working life" still a useful term?

The term "the transition from initial education to working life" can be taken to imply that young people have completed their preparation for working life. This tends to perpetuate a front-end model of education The transition from initial education to working life, through whatever route, is not the only transition between education and work, or between work and education, that today's young people will make. Increasingly it will become normal for them to intersperse working life with periods of learning, and for working life itself to become learning-rich. For many young adults in OECD countries this is already a reality. For increasing numbers of young people initial education extends beyond upper secondary education, and involvement in working life begins well before the end of either upper secondary education or the first phase of tertiary education. If institutional and funding arrangements make it possible for education to be more easily interspersed with work, the notion of the transition having a clear ending point becomes less meaningful. In a lifelong learning context the concern of the Thematic Review is with the first transition from education to working life, regarded as the first of many moves between and combinations of work and learning that young people will experience throughout their lives.

Young people's transition from initial education to working life takes place within a social, economic and educational *context*: the way that labour markets are organised; the nature and structure of education systems; institutional relationships between key actors such as employers, schools and governments; national values and traditions are among the factors that can describe these different national contexts.

A conceptual framework of the Thematic Review.

The transition can be analysed in terms of a *process*: the nature of the pathways that young people pass through in their transition from student to worker; the ways in which work and education are combined; the nature of the flows that exist over time between different levels of education, the labour market and other activities; the length of the stay within each of these activities, and the frequency of changes between them are among the ways of describing this process.

The transition from initial education to working life results in *outcomes*, both for individuals and for cohorts as a whole: educational qualifications; employment; earnings; unemployment and activity neither in education nor in the labour market are among these. Many of these outcomes can be used as key criteria to judge the relative effectiveness of the transition: rates of early school leaving, unemployment to population ratios, employment rates and qualification rates. Other outcomes are more difficult to evaluate in this sense. Temporary work, for example, can be seen either as a positive first step into permanent work, or as a barrier that is hard to surmount. The match between the programme completed and the occupation entered is also difficult to evaluate. It can be seen either as evidence of the effectiveness of the education and training system if high, or as evidence of its flexibility if low, depending in large part upon the nature of national labour markets. Chapter 2 elaborates upon transition outcomes.

The substantive task of the Thematic Review has been to *describe* and *understand* the ways in which national transition *contexts* and *processes* relate to transition *outcomes*. Transition indicators are a key tool in this task, and gaining a better understanding of their strengths and gaps has been a theme of the Thematic Review. Appendix 4 discusses the strengths and weaknesses of labour market indicators of transition outcomes. Appendix 5 sets out a framework for transition indicators.

The publication commences with a description and analysis of transition outcomes, attempting to relate these to the ways in which countries characteristically organise the pathways that link initial education to employment and tertiary study, to national economic and labour market performance, and to

The structure of the publication.

© OECD 2000

gender equity. The following chapter examines the transition process: patterns; pathways; and duration. It then describes five key features of effective transition frameworks that have emerged from the Thematic Review: well organised pathways; workplace experience; effective relationships and processes; tightly woven safety nets for those at risk; and good information, guidance and counselling. Closely related to these, it then asks how the transition phase can lay a basis for lifelong learning. The concluding chapter looks at some key policy challenges for the future.

Chapter 2
TRANSITION OUTCOMES

2.1. How can outcomes be related to the processes and context of transition?

Substantial effort has been devoted by transition researchers to attempts to characterise countries by "models", or "ideal types" of transition arrangements. These bring together within the one conceptual framework a number of dimensions of the transition: the structure and organisation of education and training pathways and qualification systems; the operation of youth labour markets; the nature of the links between education and employment systems; national policy approaches to improving the school-to-work transition; national decision making patterns among key actors; and transition processes and outcomes.

Country typologies have frequently been used by researchers to understand the transition.

McKenzie (1998), for example, after Hannan, Raffe and Smyth (1996), contrasts countries that have "tightly connected" links between the education and training system and the labour market with those in which the connections are "loosely coupled". The former are said to be characterised by: occupationally organised labour markets; strong central tripartite involvement in education and employment decision making; vertical segmentation and differentiation of the education and training system; strongly institutionally based pathways; and nationally standardised curriculum and certification arrangements. The latter are said to be characterised by: internal labour markets and selection based upon broad employability and trainability, often as evidenced by general education results rather than specific occupational qualifications; education that is horizontally segmented by level but relatively undifferentiated by institutional type at each level; individually constructed pathways between education and work; and wide regional and local variation in curricula and certification.

Müller and Shavit (1998), in a somewhat narrower typology, differentiate between what they call "qualificational spaces" and "organisational spaces" within which the transition to work takes place. The former are said to be characterised by an emphasis upon specific vocational preparation, stratified education systems that maintain a clear difference between academic and vocational tracks, and standardised national curricula. The latter are said to be characterised by an emphasis upon academic or general education, skill acquisition on-the-job after leaving school rather than within educational institutions, and substantial variation in curriculum and certification arrangements between regions and school types. Other typologies can be found in Ryan and Buechtemann (1996), OECD (1998*i*) and Hannan and Werquin (1999).

Such typologies typically pay attention to education and training arrangements at upper secondary level and to their relationship to the labour market. Less frequently do they take detailed account of important contextual factors

But they have weaknesses as explanatory devices.

© OECD 2000

in the transition to work: national economic circumstances, population size and density, geographical size, typical forms of government, the structure and role of tertiary education in occupational preparation, and national cultures and traditions. They can provide valuable rough guides in attempting to identify major differences between countries, particularly when the number of countries is relatively large. But they tend to over-simplify, both when describing the nature of transition contexts and processes, and when describing transition outcomes.

The value of such typologies as explanatory devices, within the conceptual framework adopted by the Thematic Review, can be limited if they include both transition processes and contexts on the one hand, and transition outcomes on the other. They frequently gloss over important differences between countries that are perceived to be similar. For example there are important differences between Anglo-Saxon countries in the role of apprenticeship arrangements and hence of occupational regulation of the labour market (Gospel, 1994), as there are within countries in the extent to which qualifications and certificates govern access to different jobs. For example within the United States, often characterised as a country in which specific educational qualifications play a minor role in occupational entry, large segments of the labour market, including health, education and legal occupations, are covered by occupational licensing and certification requirements at the state level, and it has been estimated that 55% of all workers need qualifying training to get their jobs, roughly half of this occupationally specific or technical training (Amirault, 1992).

A multi-dimensional approach is preferred.

When we look in detail at differences between countries in transition outcomes, as is done below, it soon becomes clear that no one typology holds the answer. Nor will any single indicator, or too narrow a set of indicators, explain the ease or difficulty with which young people move into the labour market. Single typologies or single indicators will be insufficient to assess the complexity of the transition process or to arrive at a judgement on the effectiveness of national transition arrangements. The Thematic Review therefore looks at the ways in which various dimensions of transition outcomes relate to the context and the processes of transition within and across the countries reviewed.

A broad set of indicators is needed.

"Successful" transitions can be defined in many ways and from many perspectives. In a lifelong learning context transition outcomes must be seen more broadly than the immediate job after leaving school. They include both education and labour market outcomes, as well as other aspects of social, economic and cultural integration. In a lifelong learning context literacy and qualification levels are important outcomes, as they influence both the quality of jobs obtained after initial education and opportunities for further education and career development. Not all transition outcomes can be measured by static or cross-sectional indicators, at a single point in time. Some become apparent only when young people's patterns of activity are monitored over an extended period.

There are additional reasons for using multiple indicators of transition outcomes: some are often available only for limited numbers of countries; and some that are widely available can be misleadingly imprecise (for example unemployment rates and employment to population ratios that fail to distinguish between students and non-students). More relevant and precise indicators are often available only for limited numbers of countries.

There are some basic goals that all transition policies should aim for, and Appendix 7 outlines the availability of outcome indicators for each of these for countries participating in the Thematic Review. They include:

- High proportions of young people completing a full upper secondary education with a recognised qualification for either work, tertiary study or both.
- High levels of knowledge and skill among young people at the end of the transition phase.[1]
- A low proportion of teenagers being at the one time not in education and unemployed.
- A high proportion of those young adults who have left education having a job.[2]
- Few young people remaining unemployed for lengthy periods after leaving education.
- Stable and positive employment and educational histories in the years after leaving upper secondary education; and
- An equitable distribution of outcomes by gender, social background and region.

Clearly desirable transition goals are common to all countries.

There are, of course, a number of other important goals of national transition policies, many of which are either difficult or impossible to measure across large numbers of countries given the present state of the art. These include young people feeling that they have become successful members of the economy and of society, individual job satisfaction, utilisation in work of individual skills and talents and, from a wider perspective, the absence of skill shortages and the delivery of successful policies and programmes at an affordable cost.

While typologies have some problems as explanatory devices, it is nevertheless helpful to group countries according to their common characteristics along key dimensions of the transition context and process. Given the importance that the notion of a pathway plays in the study of transitions to work, countries have been grouped in terms of their dominant upper secondary pathways. This method of organising data looks at one of the key contextual dimensions of the transition to work that is particularly relevant to policy makers. Using the three basic types of pathways identified by the Thematic Review,[3] countries can be grouped into four categories:

Outcomes can be examined by countries' dominant upper secondary pathways.

- *Apprenticeship countries* are defined as those in which greater than 50% of young people participate in apprenticeship-type arrangements. Germany and Switzerland satisfy this criterion.
- *Mixed pathway countries* are defined as those in which greater than 20% but less than 50% of young people participate in apprenticeship-type arrangements, and in which less than 50% are found in general education programmes. Typically such countries have the most diverse mix of pathway types. Four countries satisfy these criteria: Austria; Denmark; the Netherlands; and Norway.

---

1. See Caspi *et al.* (1998), Marks and Fleming (1998*a*, 1998*b*) and OECD (1997*b*) on the relationship between literacy levels and labour market outcomes.
2. And preferably this should exclude involuntary temporary or part-time work.
3. Apprenticeship-type pathways, school-based vocational pathways and general education pathways are described in OECD (1998*i*), and are discussed in more detail in Section 3.1.

- *School-based vocational countries* are defined as those in which more than 50% of young people participate in vocational programmes but in which 20% or less are found in apprenticeships or the like.[4] Belgium, the Czech Republic, Finland, France, Hungary, Italy, Poland, Sweden and the United Kingdom satisfy these criteria.
- *General education countries* are defined as those in which more than 50% of young people take part in general education programmes. Ten countries satisfy this criterion: Australia; Canada; Greece; Ireland; Japan; Korea; New Zealand; Portugal; Spain and the United States.[5]

A *complex picture emerges of transition outcomes within and across countries.*

Table 2.1a summarises 14 indicators of transition outcomes for 25 OECD countries, grouped, as indicated above, according to their dominant upper secondary pathways.[6] Countries have been ranked on each of the indicators, and the table shows the countries falling into the top (most effective outcomes) and the bottom (least effective outcomes) quartiles of the OECD on each.[7] The table includes a wide range of OECD countries in order to show the outcomes profile of Thematic Review participants compared to other OECD countries.

Taken together the indicators that have been chosen allow a picture to be drawn of: the relative difficulty that young people experience in the early stage of the transition; the relative success that they have in settling into work as young adults, including the extent to which they are able to compete with adults for employment; education and knowledge outcomes from the transition; and the extent to which the poorly qualified struggle in the labour market.

A first message to emerge from Tables 2.1 is that "success" in the transition can look quite different when seen from different perspectives.

- Very rarely do all indicators point in the one direction within any one country. Norway, for example, appears to have successful transition outcomes on several criteria (low long term youth unemployment, high apparent upper secondary graduation rates, few low qualified young adults) yet has a high youth to adult unemployment ratio. Canada has a relatively high incidence of teenage unemployment, relatively high numbers of early leavers, low apparent upper secondary graduation rates, and those young adults with low educational qualifications suffer from relatively high disadvantage in the labour market. Yet literacy levels among young people are high, as is the proportion of young people with tertiary qualifications.
- Outcomes for teenagers can differ from outcomes for young adults. For example Belgium and France each have low proportions of their teenagers seeking work, but poor outcomes for young adults (high unemployment to population ratios, high long term unemployment, or low

---
4. These countries often combine their school-based programmes with periods of training or experience in enterprises, but most typically these periods are relatively brief compared to apprenticeships. In most cases they do not involve either an employment relationship or a contractual relationship.
5. In some of these – notably Australia, Canada, and the United States – student participation in the labour force is high. In 1996 it ranged from 48% in Australia to 37% in the United States among 15-19 year-olds.
6. Table 2.2 gives the data used to classify the 25 countries into these four categories.
7. For example where 24 countries are ranked, the top six constitute the top quartile and the bottom six the bottom quartile. Table 2.1a gives the actual values used to rank the countries.

employment rates). Australia has a high proportion of its teenagers seeking work, and yet a high proportion of its young adults in employment.
- Within any one age group some outcomes can be positive yet others unsatisfactory. In Finland for example the incidence of long-term unemployment is low among young adults, yet high numbers of 20-24 year olds are seeking work. Portugal has relatively large numbers of poorly qualified young adults, and yet their relative labour market disadvantage is low.
- Labour market and education outcomes can suggest different messages about the effectiveness of the transition. Austria, for example, has effective labour market outcomes for young adults, as has the Czech Republic, yet both have a low proportion of their 25-29 year olds with tertiary qualifications. Sweden has few early school leavers, few young adults with low levels of education, and high literacy levels among 16-25 year-olds. Yet it has relatively high unemployment among both teenagers and young adults.

In countries in which the incidence of under-qualification is low such as the Czech Republic and the United Kingdom,[8] those who have not completed upper secondary school are substantially over-represented among the unemployed. On the other hand in countries that have a high proportion of young people with less than an upper secondary level of education, those with low qualifications either suffer relatively little disadvantage in the labour market compared to those who have completed upper secondary education or, as in Greece, Italy and Portugal, can have a positive advantage in the labour market when compared to those who have completed upper secondary education.

Low qualification levels are associated with labour market disadvantage – but its extent varies across countries.

In those countries that have relatively few young adults with low qualification levels there is a substantial spread of labour market disadvantage. It ranges at one extreme from the Czech Republic where it is very high, to Norway and Sweden where it is quite modest. This suggests that it is by no means inevitable that as the incidence of early school leaving falls the labour market disadvantage of the low qualified will rise. (Appendix 6 presents more details of the relationship between rates of under-qualification and the relative labour market disadvantage experienced by the low qualified.) The data by themselves do not explain these differences. Among Thematic Review participants, compared to countries where the low qualified have greater labour market difficulties, both Norway and Sweden are characterised by safety nets that actively attempt to reintegrate young early school leavers into education so that they can complete an upper secondary education (see Section 4.3). Both Norway and Sweden also make substantial efforts to ensure that unemployed young adults can access labour market assistance – education, training or subsidised employment.

However this disadvantage is not inevitable.

---

8. Each of these countries has very flexible upper secondary qualification systems which allow young people to leave upper secondary education with qualifications that can be associated with widely different periods of study, and hence which can have widely different labour market values. The incidence of leaving following relatively short-cycle upper secondary programmes appears to be greater in the United Kingdom than in the Czech Republic.

In most cases better education pays handsomely.

Within-country evidence cannot easily answer questions about which types of transition pathways and programmes lead to the best outcomes. Very large selection effects result in the most able and the least able young people being strongly concentrated in different pathways. Furthermore, different pathways and programmes often provide preparation and qualifications for relatively exclusive areas of the labour market. As a result it is often hard to separate effects caused by different patterns of labour market demand by occupation or industry from effects due to the nature of the pathways or programmes themselves (Ryan, 1998).

Nevertheless it is clear in nearly all countries taking part in the Thematic Review that those young people who obtain tertiary qualifications[9] have superior labour market outcomes to those who do not. Their unemployment rates are normally lower, their employment rates are usually higher, and their relative earnings are generally higher. And in general those who complete upper secondary education achieve better outcomes than those who do not. Table 2.3 and Figure 2.1 summarise relevant evidence for 13 of the Thematic Review participants: for those aged 25-29 in the case of unemployment and employment measures, and for those aged 30-44 in the case of earnings.

The picture depends in many ways upon which measure of labour market outcomes is used: unemployment, employment, or earnings. The greatest differences between countries in the relative outcomes of those with higher levels of education emerge if unemployment rates are used as the measure of labour market advantage. Differences between countries are substantially less if earnings are used as the measure, and somewhat less again if employment to population ratios are used.

There are significant differences between Thematic Review countries in the relative labour market advantage conferred by higher levels of education. Taking the three measures and the three pairs of education achievement levels as a whole, the gap in outcomes between the highly educated and the poorly qualified is greatest in the Czech Republic, the United States, Hungary, and the United Kingdom.

On balance the gap in outcomes is least, among Thematic Review participants, in Austria and in three Nordic countries: Norway, Sweden and Denmark. In the Nordic countries this seems to arise in part because of deliberate policies to reduce wage differentials as a function of education levels. However such policies have been much less a feature of wage bargaining in Austria (Pichelmann and Hofer, 1999).

Portugal provides an intriguing variation on these trends. As in some other southern European countries, unemployment and employment measures of relative labour market advantage show that those with higher levels of education have relatively little advantage in the labour market compared to those with lower levels. Indeed on some measures those with lower levels of education are better off than the more highly educated. However when earnings are examined, it is clear that those with higher levels of education are substantially better off in Portugal than are those with lower levels of education, and are substantially better off in relative terms than are those with comparable levels of education in other countries. This suggests that whilst the Portuguese economy is able to provide relatively large numbers of jobs for young people with low

---

9. In most but not all cases this is after taking general education programmes in upper secondary education.

Figure 2.1. **Three comparisons of relative labour market advantage by level of education**

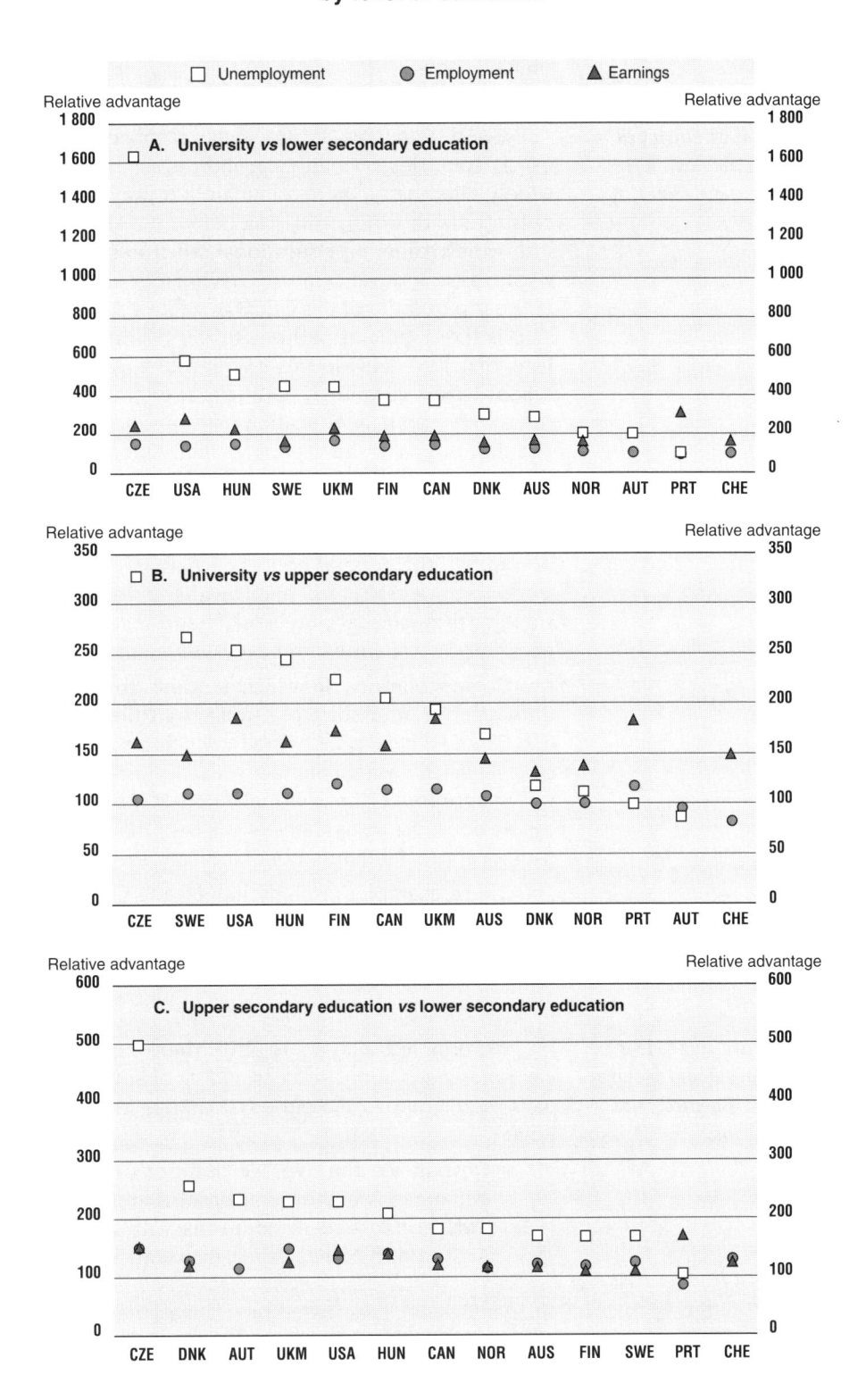

☐ Unemployment ● Employment ▲ Earnings

A. University *vs* lower secondary education

B. University *vs* upper secondary education

C. Upper secondary education *vs* lower secondary education

Source: See Table 2.3.

qualifications, these are relatively poorly paid compared to the earnings that upper secondary and tertiary graduates are able to command.[10] Findings such as this raise the question of whether high employment rates, regardless of the nature and quality of the employment, should be seen as a goal of transition policies.

Quite different types of countries can have excellent outcomes.

Good outcomes, in the sense of those falling within the top quartile of OECD countries on particular indicators, can be observed in countries with widely differing types of dominant pathways between education and work, in countries with widely differing labour market arrangements, and in countries with widely differing educational structures. Looking at OECD countries as a whole, among those countries having four or more of the indicators used here in the top quartile of the OECD in Table 2.1*a* we find two in which apprenticeship is the dominant pathway to work (Germany and Switzerland), two countries that have a wide mix of pathways (Austria and Norway), two in which school-based vocational pathways predominate (Belgium and Sweden), and three where general education pathways occupy the majority of young people (Japan, Korea and the United States). Among OECD countries as a whole, the highest number of successful transition indicators, of the sample used here, is found in the case of Switzerland, Norway and Korea. Apprenticeship is the predominant pathway in Switzerland, and is strong and growing in Norway. In Korea, in contrast, the general education pathway predominates, comparatively few students appear to have contact with the workplace either through apprenticeships or through part-time work,[11] and recent attempts to introduce apprenticeships do not appear to have been markedly successful (Jeong, 1995).

Some countries in which student contact with the workplace, either through apprenticeships or through part-time work, is low (such as Italy, Spain and Greece), have poor overall transition outcomes. But there are other countries in which student contact with the workplace seems to be quite low and where apprenticeship is virtually non-existent, such as Japan and Korea, which can demonstrate comparatively few unsatisfactory transition outcomes combined with an appreciable number of indicators of effective outcomes.

These examples strongly suggest the need to broaden thinking beyond a faith in single solutions, such as student contact with the workplace or strong vocational pathways, when attempting to understand the mysteries of effective transition systems.

There are some clear messages about factors underlying successful transitions.

Nevertheless all is not relative. There are some common patterns, and some clear messages about success and its absence, that emerge from the analysis of a wide group of countries, including those taking part in the Thematic Review.

– On balance the average number of indicators of effective transition outcomes is higher in apprenticeship countries such as Germany and Switzerland and in countries with a wide mix of pathways such as Austria and Norway than in countries in which general education or

---

10. Portugal is characterised by relatively high rates of under-qualification among 20-24 year-olds.
11. Some 40% of upper secondary students are in vocational programmes, and they are required to spend periods that can range between one month and one year at industrial sites during their three-year programme of study. The quality and duration of these placements appears to be highly variable (OECD, 1998*f*).

school-based vocational pathways predominate. (Although examples can be found of countries in the latter categories that have many indicators of effective outcomes – such as Belgium, Korea, Japan and the United States.) Indicators of effective transition outcomes are fewest in Hungary, Italy, Poland, the United Kingdom, Greece, New Zealand and Portugal.

– Indicators of unsatisfactory transition outcomes are absent or virtually absent in apprenticeship countries such as Switzerland and Germany, and in countries with mixed pathways such as Austria, Denmark and Norway. Indicators of unsatisfactory transition outcomes are more frequent in countries where school-based vocational or general education pathways dominate.

– Unsatisfactory transition outcomes are most likely to be found in Italy, Greece and Spain. Countries in which school-based vocational pathways predominate have the lowest average number of indicators of successful outcomes and a high average number of indicators of unsatisfactory outcomes.

– Low apparent upper secondary graduation rates and relatively high rates of early school leaving are concentrated more heavily in countries in which general education pathways predominate such as Canada, Greece and Spain than they are in countries in which other types of pathways and pathway mixes are dominant.

– Countries in which the gap in outcomes between the poorly educated and the highly educated are high appear somewhat less likely to have many indicators of successful transition outcomes than do those countries in which the gap in outcomes between the poorly educated and the highly educated is lower such as Austria, Norway and Denmark.

The explanatory task is to account both for common patterns and for the exceptions, and to try to understand the circumstances under which particular policy and programme mixes can be effective. While not all countries that achieve successful transition outcomes were included in the Thematic Review, and a number who perform poorly were not included, the sample of participating countries is sufficiently wide to provide rich insights into the ways in which transition institutions, contexts and processes influence transition outcomes.

2.2. Does a healthy economy lead to healthy transition outcomes?

Many factors influence transition outcomes, and the overall health of the economy is one of the more important. GPD per capita is one key indicator of the overall state of an economy. The chances of young people achieving good transition outcomes are higher in prosperous countries. For example Figure 2.2 shows that the relationship between GDP per capita and the proportion of 20-24 year-olds who are in work is quite strong.[12] However there can be wide variation in outcomes at any given level of GDP. The Czech Republic and Portugal have roughly comparable levels of GDP per capita. Yet the proportion of 20-24 year-olds in work is some 10 percentage points higher in the former than in the latter. GDP per capita in Sweden and Finland is close to that in

Higher GDP is associated with better transition outcomes... but not always.

---
12. A similar relationship can be illustrated using a wide range of transition outcome indicators. The employment to population ratio among 20-24 year-olds has been chosen for illustrative purposes as it is a key indicator of the success of the transition towards its end point.

From Initial Education to Working Life

Figure 2.2. **GDP per capita and percentage of 20-24 year-olds in work[1] (Thematic Review countries), 1998**

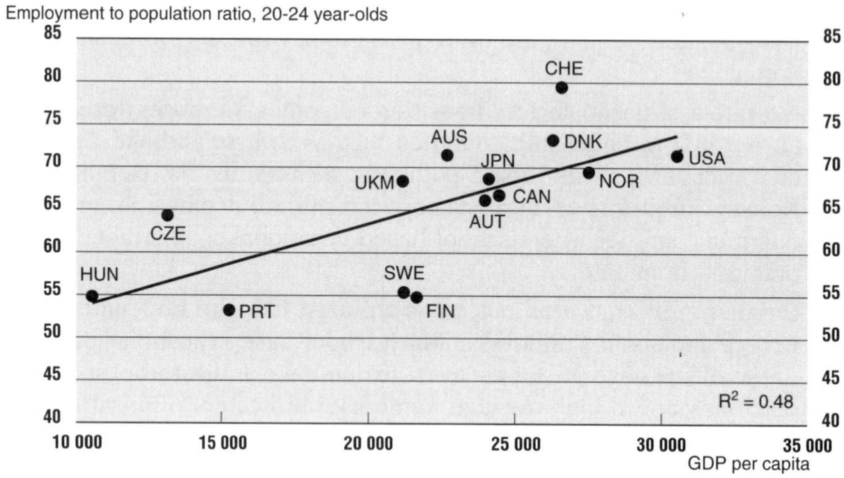

Employment to population ratio, 20-24 year-olds

$R^2 = 0.48$

1. This will be inflated in those countries such as Denmark and Canada in which significant numbers of students of that age are in the labour force.
Sources: 1998 GDP per capita in US dollars at Purchasing Power Parities; *OECD Observer*, July 1999; 1998 employment to population ratios, OECD labour force database. Austria 1997, Portugal and Switzerland 1996.

Australia and the United Kingdom, and yet the proportion of 20-24 year-olds in work in Australia and the United Kingdom is substantially higher than in Sweden and Finland. Switzerland has a higher proportion of its young adults in work than Norway, despite a similar level of GDP per capita.

Low overall unemployment is also associated with better transition outcomes, but again, not always.

The total unemployment rate is another key indicator of the overall state of the economy. The chances of young people achieving good transition outcomes are higher in countries in which overall unemployment is low. Figure 2.3 shows that the relationship is quite a strong one. However at any given level of total unemployment there can be wide variation in transition outcomes for young people. In 1998 Portugal, Denmark and the United States had comparable overall levels of unemployment. Yet only slightly more than half of Portugal's young adults had a job, compared to closer to three quarters in Denmark and the United States. Unemployment levels were similar in Australia and Hungary, yet the proportion of young adults with a job in Australia was over 70%, compared to only 55% in Hungary. Canada and Sweden had similar unemployment rates, yet two thirds of Canada's young adults were in work, compared to 55% of Sweden's.

The sensitivity of youth unemployment to economic cycles also varies across countries and age groups.

Previous OECD work (OECD, 1996b) based upon analysis of the 15-24 year-old age group has highlighted both the sensitivity of youth unemployment to overall levels of unemployment, and the variation between countries in the extent of this sensitivity. Table 2.5 explores this for ten of the countries participating in the Thematic Review and nine other OECD countries.[13] It shows that

13. The countries are those for which relatively long time series data is available.

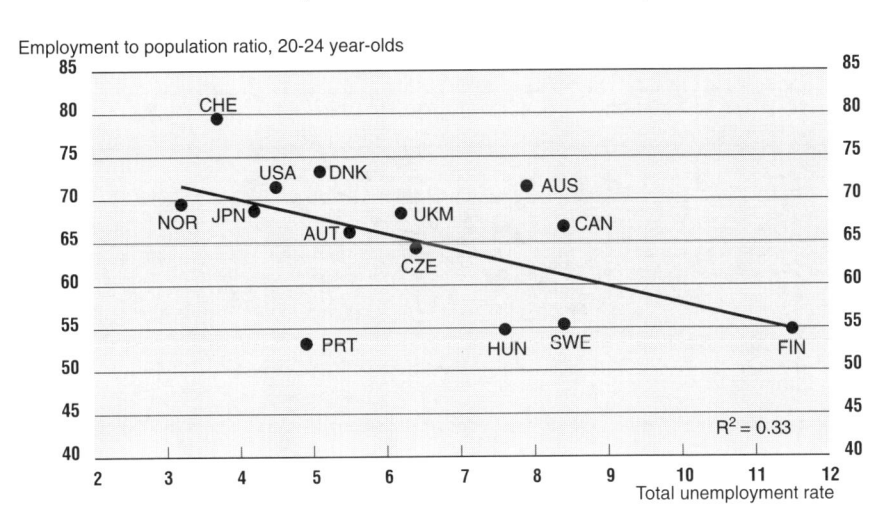

Figure 2.3. **Total unemployment rate and percentage of 20-24 year-olds in work[1] (Thematic Review countries), 1998**

Employment to population ratio, 20-24 year-olds

[Scatter plot showing countries CHE, USA, DNK, NOR, JPN, AUT, UKM, AUS, CAN, CZE, PRT, HUN, SWE, FIN against total unemployment rate (x-axis, 2-12) and employment to population ratio (y-axis, 40-85). $R^2 = 0.33$]

1. This will be inflated in those countries such as Denmark and Canada in which significant numbers of students are in the labour force.
Sources: OECD labour force database. Employment to population ratios as for Figure 2.2.

the strength, and shape, of the relationship between adult (25-54 year-olds) and youth unemployment can vary markedly between countries, as well as between age groups. In general the relationship is much stronger for young adults (20-24 year-olds) than it is for teenagers (15-19 year-olds): unemployment among young adults is more likely to move directly with adult unemployment than is teenage unemployment. Differences between countries are also much greater in the case of teenagers than in the case of young adults.

In some countries youth and adult unemployment generally move together in a linear fashion, in the same direction and at around the same rate. In other countries youth unemployment at times moves at a faster rate than adult unemployment, and at times moves more slowly, so that the relationship over time is better described as curvilinear. Figure 2.4 illustrates these differences, contrasting 20-24 year-olds in the United States and 15-19 year-olds in Sweden.

A number of factors could explain these results:

- Policy interventions designed to influence the transition outcomes of youth, and to shield them from the effects of decline in the demand for labour, are more often targeted at teenagers than at young adults, and country differences in policy approaches to the transition are more evident for teenagers than for young adults.
- Interventions designed to shield youth from rising unemployment may be more effective in some countries than in others.
- A greater proportion of 15-19 year-olds than of 20-24 year-olds are in education rather than in the labour force.
- There are significant compositional differences between the teenage and young adult labour forces. The former contains a higher proportion of those with low education levels and of students. The student and non-student sectors of the labour force behave differently in some respects,

Figure 2.4. **Relationship between youth and adult unemployment**

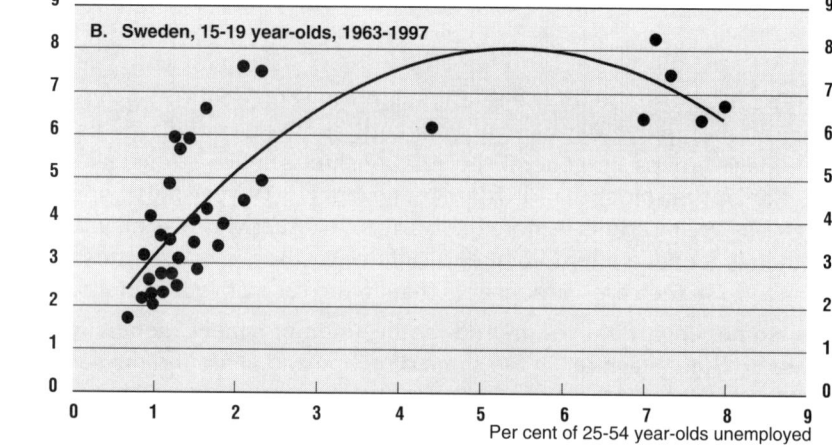

Per cent of 20-24 year-olds unemployed

A. United States, 20-24 year-olds, 1957-1997

Per cent of 25-54 year-olds unemployed

Per cent of 15-19 year-olds unemployed

B. Sweden, 15-19 year-olds, 1963-1997

Per cent of 25-54 year-olds unemployed

Source: OECD labour force database.

and countries differ widely in the proportion of students who participate in the labour force. For example unemployment rates for teenagers are generally lower among students than among non students (Appendix 4).

– Increases in school participation in response to rising unemployment may not always be matched by corresponding falls in school participation when unemployment falls.

– When economies emerge from recessions younger labour force members may gain jobs at a different rate from other age groups as the result of changes in patterns of demand for skills and qualifications during recessions; and

– EFFECTS may be lagged over time.

At the margins transition policies and labour market institutions can influence transition outcomes, over and above the overall state of the economy or the overall health of the labour market.

Policies and institutions influence transition outcomes.

Sweden's experience during the 1990s provides a good illustration of this. The fact that teenage unemployment has not risen during the 1990s, despite a very large rise in adult unemployment and a sharp fall in overall employment levels, for both youth and adults, can be explained by two factors. First, the Swedish upper secondary school system has been able to provide a diverse and flexible curriculum, able to meet the needs and interests of a wide range of youth. It is a highly inclusive system that pays particular attention to the needs of weaker students. Together these have encouraged many of those who might otherwise have been tempted to enter the labour market to remain in education until the age of 19. This has helped to reduce the supply of youth labour. In particular it has kept many of those who are most vulnerable to unemployment within upper secondary school at a time of high overall unemployment. Second, Sweden has an effective locally managed follow-up service which ensures that those who drop out of upper secondary school are quickly re-inserted into education, with a strongly individualised approach to ensuring that they can complete a full upper secondary education. Together these policy measures have been effective in reducing the incidence of unemployment among teenagers.[14] Neither policy measure has directly applied to young adults in Sweden throughout most of the 1990s, and the proportion of 20-24 year-olds unemployed has risen largely in proportion to the rise in adult unemployment.

The case of Sweden during the 1990s provides a good illustration of this...

The United States has a higher level of employment among young adults than does Portugal, even though both countries have similar overall unemployment levels. They also have widely differing incidences of long term unemployment among the young adults. In the United States only 11% of unemployed 20-24 year-olds had been unemployed for six months or more in 1998. In Portugal the corresponding figure was 56%. Blanchard and Portugal (1998) have argued that such differences arise from higher employment protection in Portugal than in the United States, creating greater difficulties for new labour market entrants.

... so do differences in outcomes between Portugal and the United States.

Recent research analysing the 20-29 year-old age group suggests that strict employment protection legislation (EPL) can increase the burden of unemployment that is borne by youth (OECD, 1999a). An examination of the relationship between the strictness of employment protection legislation and the incidence of long term unemployment among unemployed 15-19 year-olds suggests a modestly strong relationship between the two. Where EPL is strict, a higher proportion of unemployed teenagers seem to remain unemployed for six months or more (Figure 2.5). This finding is consistent with theoretical predictions about the impact of strict EPL (Layard, Nickell and Jackman, 1991). Strict EPL is likely not to be a "youth friendly" institution for several reasons: it reduces unemployment outflows and increases unemployment duration, so that new labour market entrants have to wait longer to get a job; and it might reduce the youth employment to population ratio and might increase the youth unemployment rate.

Effective transition arrangements appear to reduce the negative consequences for teenagers of strict employment protection legislation.

Figure 2.5 suggests that the incidence of long term teenage unemployment can be reduced, even where EPL is relatively high, by appropriate

---

14. There has also been no worsening in the proportion of unemployed teenagers who have been unemployed for six months or more, despite a substantial worsening of the overall labour market situation.

© OECD 2000

Figure 2.5. **Employment protection legislation and long term teenage unemployment**

Per cent of 15-19 year-old unemployment lasting six months or more

$R^2 = 0.27$

Strictness of employment protection legislation, late 1990s

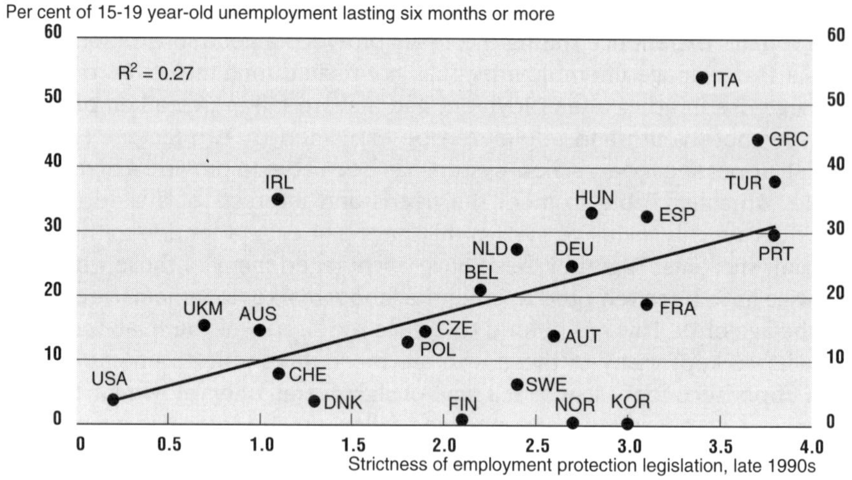

Sources: OECD labour force database and OECD (1999a).

transition policies and programmes.[15] Among those countries participating in the Thematic Review in which the level of long term teenage unemployment is lower than would be expected on the basis of their level of EPL (in other words where the value falls below the regression line in Figure 2.5) Switzerland, Austria and Denmark have strong apprenticeship systems and close institutional relationships between education and the labour market. Denmark, Sweden and Norway have strong safety nets for early school leavers (see Section 4.3), and Finland requires those under the age of 18 to participate in education, training or labour market measures in order to qualify for income support. Such a requirement is one of the features of the more comprehensive safety nets that can be observed in other Nordic countries.

In countries participating in the Thematic Review that fall above the regression line (Australia, the United Kingdom, Hungary) these features have been less highly developed in the past. However both the United Kingdom's New Deal and Australia's recently introduced Common Youth Allowance share some of the characteristics of this more active approach to the provision of income support to youth without work.

Labour markets can be made more "youth friendly".

There are several ways in which labour markets can be made more "youth friendly". One is through widespread opportunities for young people to be trained within firms in arrangements such as apprenticeship, as in countries such as Austria, Denmark and Switzerland. Such arrangements require appropriate contracts and wages to be struck, as well as agreement on the way in which educational qualifications will be used to regulate entry to employment. This requires close co-operation between employers, trade unions and governments, as well as close co-operation between schools and enterprises. As

---

15. It should be noted that a number of Mediterranean countries – such as Spain, Greece and Italy – combine high long-term teenage unemployment and relatively strict EPL with a number of other indicators of poor transition outcomes, summarised in Table 2.1a.

Section 2.1 has shown, transition outcomes are generally better in countries where such arrangements exist. However they require institutional settings that many countries may not find acceptable or desirable given different national cultures and institutional arrangements. Faced with these institutional difficulties some countries are experimenting with other forms of in-firm training and experience for young people, such as the unpaid work placements for school students being adopted in Australia, Finland and Sweden.

Widespread opportunities for young people to get after-school, weekend and holiday jobs when they are students are also important in assisting labour markets to be "youth friendly". These opportunities are the outcome both of labour market arrangements (for example the creation of appropriate temporary or casual employment contracts and the striking of appropriate wage rates), and of the capacity and willingness of school timetables to accommodate them. Such short-term employment is an important feature of young people's transition in Australia, Denmark, Sweden, the United Kingdom and the United States. Figure A4.2 (Appendix 4) shows that there is a strong positive relationship between rates of student participation in the labour force by teenagers and the proportion of 20-24 year-olds in work.

Japan provides an interesting example of a labour market that has many features which help to make it "youth friendly", although using somewhat different institutional arrangements from those described above. Schools have a formal role in the job placement of graduates. To assist the placement and recruitment of school leavers close relationships are built between individual firms and individual schools. These relationships are underpinned by implicit or semi-formal contracts. The recruitment of school leavers is based upon well understood criteria of academic achievement, with firms trusting schools to maintain the standards that they require (Kariya, 1999; Rosenbaum, 1999).

Japan provides an interesting example.

The wages of young people tend to be more sensitive to economic fluctuations than the wages of older workers in Japan. Age-wage profiles there are steeper than in many other OECD countries. Relatively low entry level wages are supported by strong internal labour markets, by intense on-the-job training of newly recruited school leavers, and by age- and skill-based wage systems (Mitani, 1999).

These examples underscore the importance of the interaction between national institutional frameworks and transition policies on the one hand and the overall health of the economy and of the labour market on the other in shaping national transition outcomes.

2.3. How equitable are transition outcomes?

The equity of transition outcomes has been an enduring focus of research on the transition from school to work. The fundamental issue has been the extent to which the structural features of national transition systems either support and reinforce or work to counteract inequalities that are a function of social class and gender. National transition policies in varying ways reflect these concerns. In Australia for example national education and training policies commonly include requirements for the needs of equity groups such as Indigenous Australians to be given particular attention. In the Nordic countries educational resourcing policies commonly have as one of their goals the minimisation of regional disparities in both access to and the outcomes of schooling. In Switzerland the particular disadvantages that young women and

Equity is an enduring concern in work on the transition.

young people from ethnic minorities suffer in access to the more prestigious training opportunities has, in recent years, become a substantial policy concern. In Hungary the worsening position of gypsies during the 1990s is an issue of concern for many policy makers.

While the interaction between both family background and gender and the transition are of concern, consistently defined comparative indicators of family background or social class are rare. They have not been available for many of the countries participating in the Thematic Review, and are not readily able to be related in a systematic way to the key transition indicators used in the Thematic Review. Analysis of micro-data from large national surveys is an approach that has been used in the recent literature (Shavit and Müller, 1998), but consistency of definitions remains a problem, as does the recency and comparability of such data over time. Within the context of the Thematic Review, countries have taken widely differing and not always consistent approaches to the analysis and description of the relationship between family background and transition outcomes. Information on gender is, however, almost universally available for transition indicators, and is available for all 14 of the key transition indicators discussed in Section 2.1 and set out in Table 2.1a.

Indexes of gender equity in transition outcomes have been constructed.

The relationship between gender and transition outcomes has been examined as follows. Differences between males and females were obtained for all countries on each of the 14 key indicators of transition outcomes shown in Table 2.1a. The relative difference between males and females was then calculated, using the ratio of the score on the indicator of the gender with the highest value divided by the score on the indicator of the gender with the lowest value on that indicator.[16] Two indices were then calculated using these ratios:

---

16. This method has several advantages compared to using absolute differences between the genders, and compared to using either males or females in all cases as the numerator when calculating ratios:
    – It takes account of differences in the location of scores along a scale. For example the difference between a 10% unemployment rate for males and a 20% unemployment rate for females is not treated numerically in the same way as a difference between an 80% employment rate for males and a 90% employment rate for females. The method chosen treats the first case as twice as unequal, but the second as 13% more unequal, rather than treating each difference equally as would be the case if absolute differences had been used.
    – It leads to values with a common interpretation across all indicators. Values of the ratio will be 1.0 when the two genders are equal on an indicator, no matter how it is scaled originally: for example as percentages that can have a maximum value of 100 as in unemployment to population ratios, or as values that can exceed 1.0 as in youth to adult unemployment ratios.
    – The extent to which the ratio exceeds 1.0 will have a common meaning, in terms of the of the extent to which outcomes for males and females are unequal, across all indicators. For example a value of 1.5 will always indicate that one gender is 50% higher than the other on an indicator, and a value of 1.8 that one gender is 80% higher than the other.
    – Its value does not depend upon whether males or females are arbitrarily chosen as the numerator of the index. For example scores of 45% and 35% for males and females would lead to a ratio of 1.29 if males were used as the numerator and .78 if females were used. In the first instance the inequality between the two groups would be shown as 29%, but in the second as 21%.
    – The index does not show whether it is males or females that are highest on a particular indicator, but this can be determined by inspection.

- An index of gender equity in educational transition outcomes. For each country this is the average of its relative equity ratios on indicators 9-12 and 14 in Table 2.1*a*; and
- An index of gender equity in labour market transition outcomes. For each country this is the average of its relative equity ratios on indicators 1-8 and 13 shown in Table 2.1*a*.

Figures 2.6 and 2.7 plot OECD countries on these two indices, showing countries participating in the Thematic Review separately from other countries.

Figure 2.6. **Index of gender equity in educational transition outcomes**

Source: See Table 2.6.

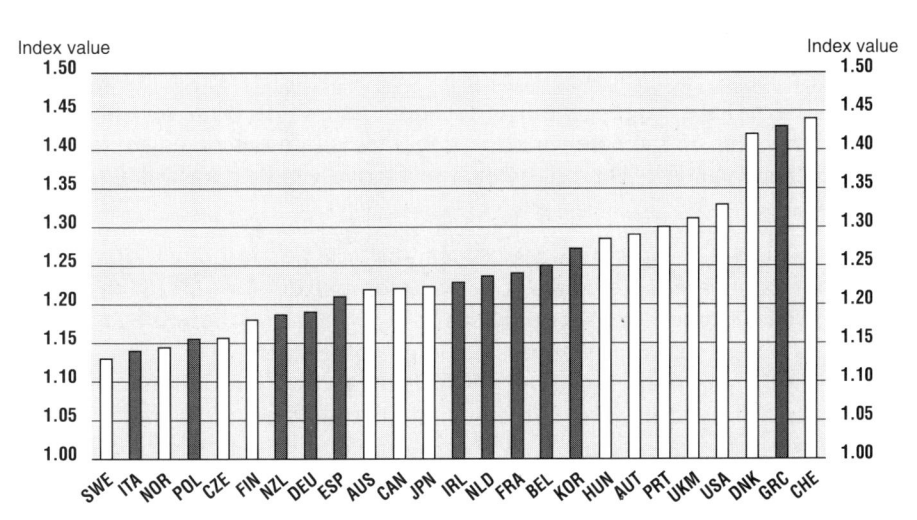

Figure 2.7. **Index of gender equity in labour market transition outcomes**

Source: See Table 2.6.

These show clear differences between countries.

There are substantial differences between countries in the extent to which transition outcomes are equal for males and females. Confining our attention to countries participating in the Thematic Review:

- Educational transition outcomes appear to be most equal between males and females in Sweden, Japan, the USA and then in Canada, Finland, Norway and Denmark. They appear to be least equal in Switzerland, Portugal, Australia and the Czech Republic.
- Labour market transition outcomes appear to be most equal between males and females in Sweden and Norway, and least equal in Switzerland, Denmark, the United States, Austria, Portugal, the United Kingdom and Hungary.

These differences appear to be related to some features of national transition systems.

These differences in transition outcomes between males and females appear to be related to some features of national education and transition systems. For example while Japan's education system is relatively segmented, both vertically and horizontally, one of its strengths has been its inclusiveness. Considerable effort is devoted to minimising dropout at each of the principal transition points: for example between compulsory school and secondary school.

Sweden places considerable emphasis upon equity in access and in outcomes in its educational policies. National policies require schools to emphasise improving the achievements of weaker students and achieving equality of outcomes between males and females. Despite a significant decentralisation of responsibility for educational decision making and financing during the 1990s, central guidelines ensure that regional differences in educational resources are minimised. Counties are funded according to formulae that take into account the proportion of disadvantaged and at-risk groups that they contain: for example recently arrived migrants or welfare recipients. Decentralisation has been accompanied by a system of steering by goals which requires local school systems to regularly report their progress in achieving national goals, including equity goals. One result of such policies has been very little regional variation in rates of access to upper secondary education. These features are associated with low differences between males' and females' transition outcomes.

Some features of national transition pathways appear, on the basis of this evidence, not to be strongly related to the equality of transition outcomes between males and females. For example Australia, Canada and the United States each have large general education pathways. However differences between males and females in educational transition outcomes are relatively low in Canada and the United States, yet relatively high in Australia.

The direction of the difference differs among countries and does not consistently favour either males or females.

Where differences between males and females in educational transition outcomes are large, there is no common pattern for differences in outcomes to favour one gender or the other. In Switzerland there is a consistent pattern, across most indicators, of young women achieving poorer educational outcomes than young men.[17] In Hungary it is predominantly young men who achieve the worst outcomes. In Australia and Portugal it is in most cases but not always young men, depending upon the indicator chosen. In

---

17. Although more recently young women have represented a majority of those completing the Maturité exam.

the Czech Republic the direction of the relative advantage is quite variable. In Australia the relatively poorer educational outcomes of young males is a significant national policy issue. It is also in Canada, although in comparative terms the disparity in outcomes between males and females appears to be relatively low.

Labour market outcomes suggest some particular problems that countries with large apprenticeship and vocational education systems, combined with occupationally organised labour markets, have in achieving equitable transition outcomes. In Switzerland, Austria and Denmark the differences between males' and females' labour market transition outcomes are high, and in each case it is young women who achieve, on balance, the poorest transition outcomes. Recent research (Müller and Shavit, 1998; Buchmann and Sacchi, 1998) indicates that transition systems which combine a high degree of vocational specificity with a high degree of stratification are likely to support and reinforce a differentiation of transition outcomes by social class. Austria, Denmark and Switzerland have each been marked by a significant horizontal stratification of upper secondary education and training with mutually isolated pathways, a high degree of vocational specificity in the pathways available to young people, and labour markets that are occupationally organised. To the extent that stratification and vocational specificity in the education and training system channel young men and young women into different pathways that are linked to labour market outcomes of differing prestige and differing rewards, national transition systems can act to reinforce gender inequalities in transition outcomes.

Disparities in transition outcomes between males and females in Austria, Denmark and Switzerland generally work against females. However differences

Distinct problems in achieving equal outcomes appear to exist in countries whose labour markets are tightly occupationally organised.

Figure 2.8. **Employment to population ratios and relative difference between male and female employment to population ratios, 20-24 year-olds, 1998**

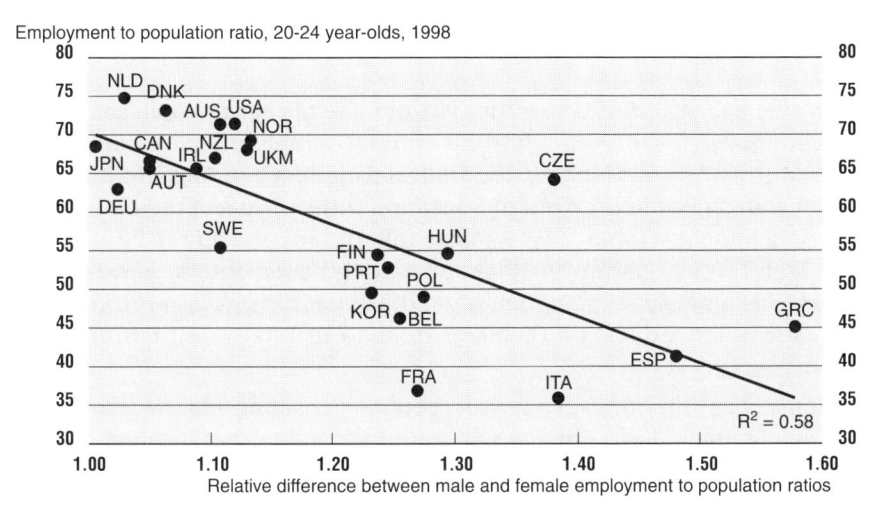

Source: OECD labour force database.

From Initial Education to Working Life

in labour market transition outcomes between males and females in Hungary, the United Kingdom and the United States generally favour females.[18]

Achieving higher outcomes for all appears to be one way to achieve more equal outcomes.

Poor overall transition outcomes appear to be associated with large differences between the outcomes of females and males. One way in which differences between the transition outcomes of particular groups can be reduced is to raise outcomes for all. This can be illustrated using the employment to population ratio for 20-24 year-olds. Figure 2.8 shows that in countries in which a high proportion of all 20-24 year-olds are employed, differences between the employment rates of males and females are low. This is to be expected, as the scope for differences to arise between females and males is greatly reduced by high overall employment rates. What is less predictable is that differences between the employment rates of females and males should be wider where overall employment rates are lower. While the scope for any differences to arise is greater, it need not follow that these differences should be unevenly distributed across genders.

2.4. Is optimism justified?

What are some of the lessons from country differences and trends over time?

In this section we look at whether differences between countries and over time in transition indicators on balance encourage an optimistic or a pessimistic view of young people's transition outcomes. We consider educational participation and achievement, the incidence and duration of unemployment, young people neither in education nor in work, young people's labour market situation relative to that of adults, and relative earnings.

Educational participation rose significantly during the 1980s and 1990s.

The 1980s and 1990s saw a steady rise in young people's educational participation in OECD countries, at both upper secondary and tertiary levels. Between 1984 and 1997 the proportion of 18 year-olds in education and training rose from an average of 57% to an average of 75% across 17 OECD countries for which data is available, and the proportion of 22 year-olds in education or training rose from 21% to 36% (Figure 2.9). This increasing educational participation has been associated with a steady fall in the number of young adults without a completed upper secondary education (OECD, 1998h). Policy concern for those without qualifications has risen as their numbers have fallen. This should not detract attention from the significant achievement represented by falling numbers of early school leavers.

Most young people continue in education after compulsory schooling, but many young adults have low qualifications.

In over half of all OECD countries 90% or more of young people continue in education for at least a year after the end of compulsory schooling. In only four countries (Spain, Hungary, the United Kingdom and Mexico) do 20% or more of young people drop out of education within a year of the end of compulsory schooling (Table 2.4). Against this, however, should be set relatively high rates of under-qualification among young adults. Across OECD countries as a whole some one in four 20-24 year-olds have not completed upper secondary education (Figure 2.10), and in Turkey and Portugal over half have not.

Some countries however have succeeded in ensuring that the great majority of young adults have obtained an upper secondary qualification: notably

---

18. With the exception of employment to population ratios which are almost universally lower for females in the 20-24 age group.

© OECD 2000

Figure 2.9. **Participation in education and training by 18 and 22 year-olds, 1984 and 1997**

□ 1997   ● 1984

Source: OECD (1999b). Data are averaged over 17 countries and are derived from national Labour Force Surveys.

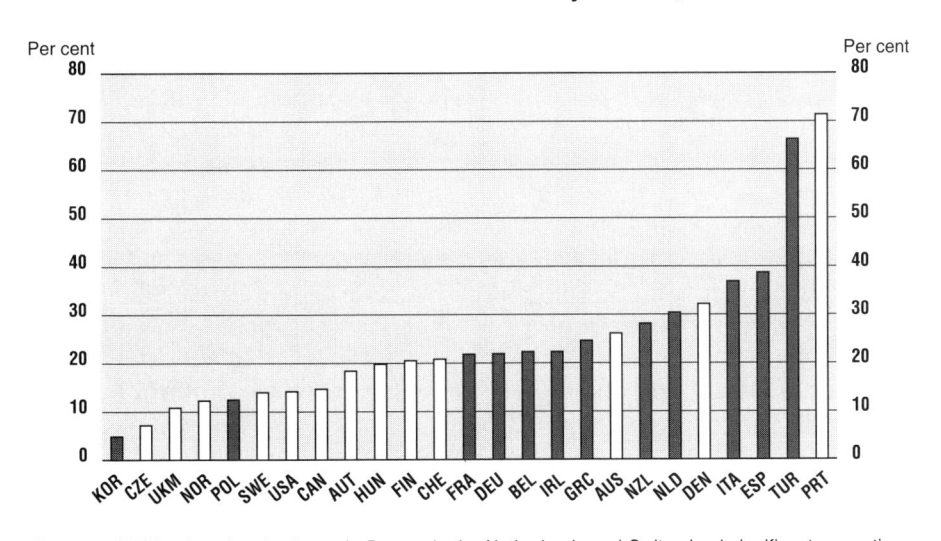

Figure 2.10. **Proportion of 20-24 year-olds whose highest level of education is lower secondary school, 1996**

Source: OECD education database. In Denmark, the Netherlands and Switzerland significant proportions of 20-24 year-olds are still enrolled in upper secondary education.

Korea, the Czech Republic, Austria, the United Kingdom,[19] Norway and Poland, but also Sweden, the United States and Canada. Among Thematic Review

---

19. For the United Kingdom and the Czech Republic see footnote 8 in Section 2.1. In countries such as Denmark where many 20-24 year-olds are still taking part in upper-secondary education the proportion with upper secondary qualifications appears artificially low.

From Initial Education to Working Life

participants such as Norway, Sweden, the United States and Canada this is the outcome not only of national rates of initial upper secondary graduation, but also of the existence of national second-chance and safety net mechanisms through which those who have dropped out of school are subsequently able to obtain an upper secondary qualification. For example in the United States 44% of high school dropouts complete high school within two years after the normal high school graduation date, and more than 60% complete high school at some stage. In the majority of cases this is through obtaining a high school equivalency certificate such as the GED, or Test of General Education Development (Rumberger and Lamb, 1998). In Sweden and Norway national safety net arrangements, discussed in greater detail in Section 4.3, help to ensure that early school leavers can be quickly re-inserted into education and complete upper secondary school.[20]

In most OECD countries the proportion of those under the age of 20 who are seeking work is quite small...

In absolute terms the proportion of teenagers who do not make a successful transition from initial education to working life appears to be quite small in many OECD countries. Even using those standard unemployment measures which exaggerate the scale of the problem by including students who are seeking work, only five per cent or less of all 15-19 year-olds are unemployed in close to half of all OECD countries. Only in Australia and Spain were ten per cent or more of this age group looking for work in 1998 (Table 2.7).

... and is even smaller when students seeking work are excluded.

When unemployment to population ratios include only non-students among the unemployed, the scale of the problem appears even smaller. 1996 data shows that over a group of 15 countries the proportion of all 15-19 year-olds seeking work falls from an average of seven per cent to an average of four per cent if only non-students are included in the numerator when calculating unemployment to population ratios (see Appendix 4). In Norway 80% of 16-19 year-olds recorded as unemployed in the labour force survey in 1996 were students seeking part-time work, as were one in four of 20-24 year-olds. In Australia, one of the countries which appears to have a relatively high proportion of unemployed 15-19 year-olds, the proportion of that age seeking work falls by half when only non-student job seekers are considered.

In many countries the problem of unemployment is much greater among young adults than among teenagers.

The scale of the transition problem appears substantially higher among young adults than among teenagers. Across 25 OECD countries in 1998 an average of six per cent of all 15-19 year-olds but ten per cent of 20-24 year-olds were seeking work (Table 2.7). In ten of these countries the proportion of 20-24 year-olds looking for work was twice or more the proportion of 15-19 year-olds. Yet even so, some countries have managed to keep the proportion of 20-24 year-olds seeking work low. Among Thematic Review participants these include Austria, Denmark and Switzerland, where it is below five per cent,[21]

---

20. In countries such as Denmark and Switzerland significant proportions of 20-24 year-olds are still enrolled in upper secondary education. In the case of countries such as Switzerland and Sweden the proportion of this age group without upper secondary qualifications is also influenced by the number of recently arrived migrants of this age with lower educational qualifications than the native born of the same age.
21. Some key Swiss labour force data provided to the OECD does not separately indicate 15-19 year-olds and 20-24 year-olds. In this instance 1996 data from an INES Network B 1998 special transition collection is the source. It, however, shows the Swiss estimate of 3.8% to be subject to high sampling variability. See OECD (1998a), Table D1.1.

© OECD 2000

and Japan, Norway, the United States, the Czech Republic and Hungary,[22] where it is below seven per cent.

While on average across the OECD the proportion of those seeking work is significantly higher among young adults than among teenagers, there are a number of countries in which 15-19 year-olds experience higher unemployment to population ratios than 20-24 year-olds. Among Thematic Review participants this includes the United States, the United Kingdom, Denmark, Norway, Australia, Austria and Canada, in each of which the unemployment to population ratio for young adults is lower than that for teenagers. On the other hand in Japan, Portugal, Hungary, Sweden and Finland the proportion of young adult job seekers is significantly higher than the proportion of teenage job seekers.

For the small group of young people under the age of 20 who have left education and who are without work the problems of unemployment and labour market integration tend to be severe. These problems are also severe for young adults who lack an upper secondary level of education. Across 13 countries participating in the Thematic Review, 20-24 year-olds with less than an upper secondary level of education represented an average of 22% of the population in 1996, yet they accounted for 30% of the unemployed. Their representation among the unemployed ranged from two and a half times their representation in the population in the Czech Republic to 20% more in Switzerland. Only in Portugal did they have a somewhat lower share of unemployment among the age group than would be expected from their share of the population (Figure 2.11).

The disadvantage of early leavers is high.

Figure 2.11. **20-24 year-olds with less than upper-secondary education as a percentage of the population of the same age and as a percentage of the unemployed of the same age, 1996**

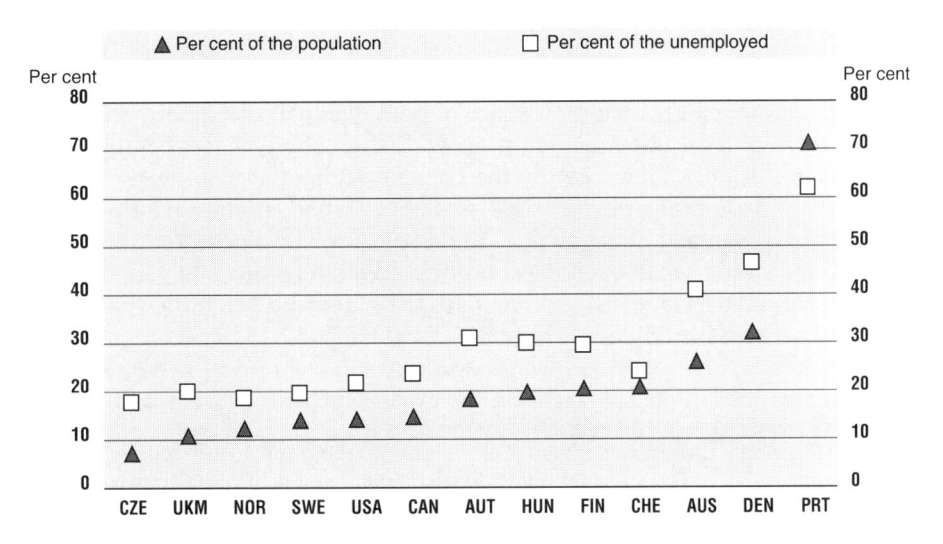

Source: OECD education database.

22. However the Hungarian Country Note shows that in 1997 the number of this age who were inactive (neither in education nor in the labour market) was nearly three times the number who were unemployed.

Trends in youth to adult unemployment ratios suggest that the relative position of young people in the labour market has improved over time...

Simple changes in unemployment rates, or ratios, among young people over time tell us little about whether their overall position in the labour market has been improving or worsening relative to other age groups. For this we need to take account of trends within the labour market as a whole. Looking at youth to adult unemployment ratios is one way to do this. Unemployment rates and ratios express something of the difficulty that young people experience in the labour market when competing with one another for work. But they also compete with adults for the available jobs. The ratio of the unemployment rate among youth to the unemployment rate among adults is one indicator of their success in this competition, and hence of the openness of labour markets to young new entrants.

Between the mid 1970s and the early 1990s the ratio of youth to adult unemployment rates fell, and in many cases by substantial orders of magnitude, in nearly all OECD countries (OECD, 1994c). This relative improvement in young people's position in the labour market appears to be in large part a result of rising educational levels among new labour market entrants. It has also been attributed to an easing of demographic pressures, increasing and prolonged enrolments in education having reduced the supply of youth labour, and the operation of labour market measures.

... but not as rapidly in the 1990s as in previous decades.

During the 1990s the trend for youth to adult unemployment ratios to fall has not been as strong, and trends in different countries have varied. There was only a very slight additional overall improvement in young people's labour market competitiveness relative to adults, across countries taking part in the Thematic Review, between 1990 and 1998.[23] In 1990 the youth to adult unemployment ratio averaged 2.6 across these countries, and 2.4 in 1998. In Canada, Norway, the United Kingdom and the United States it has in fact shown a tendency to rise during the 1990s. On the other hand, the trend in the youth to adult unemployment ratio has been downwards in Finland, Japan, Sweden and Switzerland (Table 2.8).

Another way to examine trends in the situation of youth relative to the situation of the labour force as a whole is to calculate young people's share of total unemployment in relation to their share of total employment. This ratio will be less than 1.0 if their share of total unemployment is less than their share of total employment, 1.0 if their share of both is equal, and greater than 1.0 if their share of total unemployment exceeds their share of total employment Trends in this ratio show whether the concentration of unemployment among young people is changing over time, and hence trends in their relative labour market disadvantage or advantage. Table 2.9 shows this index for the 1990-98 period for a wide range of OECD countries, separately for 15-19 year-olds and 20-24 year olds.[24] Figure 2.12 summarises the index for 13 countries participating in the Thematic Review.

---

23. As measured by the ratio of the unemployment rate among 15-24 year-olds to the unemployment rate among 25-54 year-olds.
24. Increasingly these two segments of the youth labour force have widely differing characteristics. The fall in labour force participation rates that has been associated with rising educational participation has resulted in the full-time 15-19 year-old labour force increasingly consisting of early school leavers. And the growth of student participation in the labour force in many countries has resulted in this part of the teenage labour force increasingly consisting of students either working part-time or seeking part-time jobs. On the other hand the 20-24 year-old labour force contains a smaller proportion of those who are still in education, a smaller proportion of early school leavers, and a higher proportion with upper secondary and tertiary qualifications.

Figure 2.12. **Relative labour market disadvantage of youth (13 Thematic Review countries), 1990-1998**

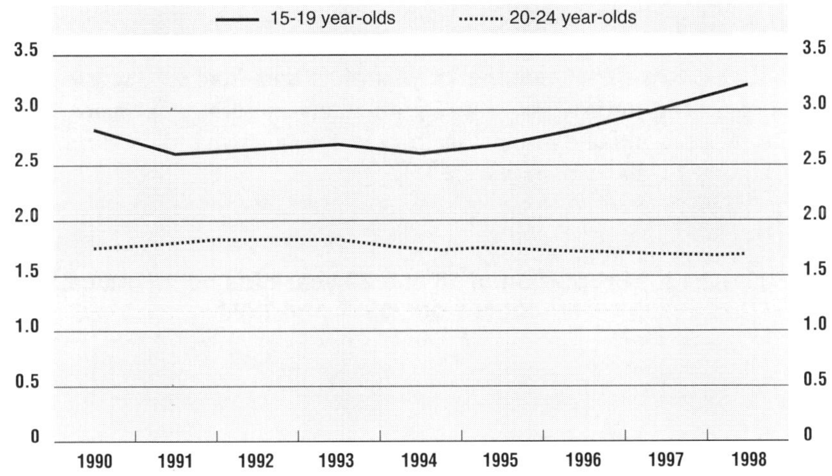

Source: OECD labour force database.

Across OECD countries as a whole, as well as among countries participating in the Thematic Review, the relative labour market disadvantage of teenagers is greater than that of young adults (and there is much greater variation between countries in the index for teenagers than in the index for young adults[25]). During the 1990s the labour market disadvantage of teenagers worsened slightly across OECD countries as a whole as well as among countries participating in the Thematic Review. However the relative disadvantage of young adults remained stable. The increase in the relative labour market disadvantage of teenagers is likely to be related to the increasing concentration of early school leavers among those teenagers who are in the labour force.[26]

There has been a slight worsening in the overall labour market disadvantage of teenagers in the 1990s...

Although in overall terms the relative labour market disadvantage of teenagers worsened somewhat during the 1990s, there are some notable exceptions among countries participating in the Thematic Review: in Finland, Japan and Sweden their relative disadvantage fell somewhat. In Denmark and Finland there was also a slight fall in the relative labour market disadvantage of young adults, but in general the index was stable for this age group in all countries participating in the Thematic Review.

... although there are some exceptions.

There has been a general tendency for young people's labour force participation and employment rates to fall among OECD countries during the 1980s and 1990s (OECD, 1996b; OECD 1999b). This is closely associated with a steady rise in educational participation among young people over the period, and

The number of young people neither in education nor in work has fallen.

---

25. Across 24 OECD countries the standard deviation calculated on all 1990-98 values is 1.1 for teenagers and 0.7 for young adults.
26. It is unlikely to be the result of an increasing concentration of students in the 15-19 year-old labour force, as the unemployment rates of students are generally lower than those of non-students. See Appendix 4.

From Initial Education to Working Life

cannot be regarded as indicating a worsening in young people's overall situation. A more important measure is the proportion of young people who are neither in education nor in work. This indicator shows a significant improvement between 1984 and 1997, measured among 18 and 22 year-olds across 15 OECD countries (OECD, 1999b). The average proportion neither in work nor in education fell from 17% to 11% among 18 year-olds, and from 23% to 18% among 22 year-olds. The improvement was particularly large among young women, with the proportion falling from 19% to 11% among 18 year-olds and from 29% to 20% among 22 year-olds (Figure 2.13).

Figure 2.13. **Proportion of 18 and 22 year-olds not in education and not in work, 1984 and 1997**

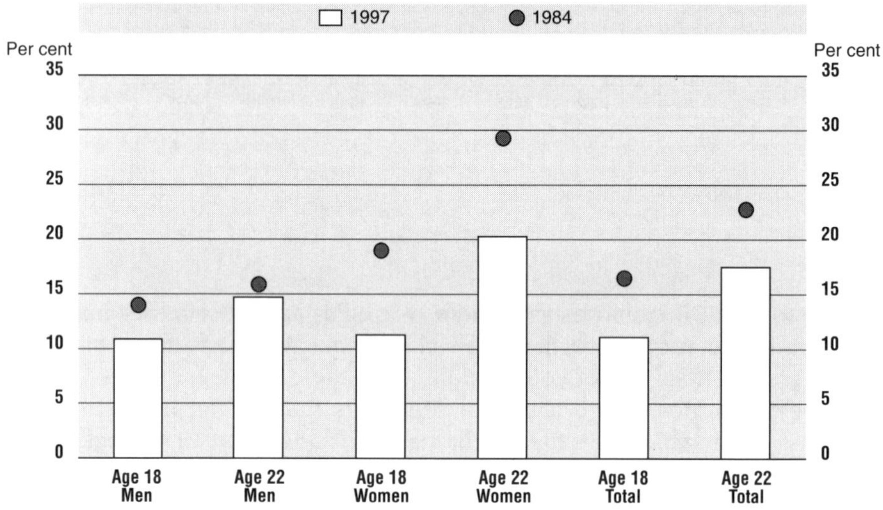

Source: OECD (1999b).

Long-term youth unemployment is a key policy concern.

Long term youth unemployment is another indicator of the extent to which young people experience problems in the labour market. It is a particular concern for policy makers. This concern is reflected in the European Community's 1997 employment strategy, which requires member states to offer assistance to the unemployed who are under the age of 25 within six months of them becoming unemployed (European Communities, 1999a).

Its share of total youth unemployment has remained stable on balance, falling in some countries, and rising in others.

The share of the long term unemployed[27] among unemployed youth varies widely. Among countries participating in the Thematic Review, for teenagers it was lowest in Denmark, Finland, Norway and the United States in 1998, and highest in Australia, Austria, Hungary and Portugal. For young adults it was lowest in Austria, Denmark, Norway and the United States, and highest in Hungary and Portugal (Table 2.10).

Across OECD countries as a whole there has been no tendency for the share of the long term unemployed among unemployed youth to rise during

---

27. Here defined as those unemployed who have been unemployed for six months or more.

the 1990s.[28] However among countries participating in the Thematic Review there have been widely differing experiences. During the 1990s Denmark and Norway have seen substantial falls in the share of the long term unemployed among unemployed teenagers, and Denmark, Finland and Norway have seen the share fall among 20-24 year-olds.[29] On the other hand the proportion of teenage unemployment lasting for six months or more has risen in Australia, Austria, Hungary and the United States among teenagers, and in Austria, the Czech Republic, Hungary and the United States among 20-24 year-olds.

In virtually all countries for which data is available, young workers experienced declines in earnings relative to older workers during the 1990s (OECD, 1996b; OECD, 1999b). These falls have occurred despite national differences in wage fixation mechanisms, despite a common pattern of decline rather than increase in the size of the youth cohort, and despite an increase in the education levels of young people. In part this is associated with an increase in student participation in the labour force, as the great majority of their jobs are part-time and therefore low-paid compared to full-time jobs. However Australian research (Wooden, 1998) reveals a decline in the relative earnings of 15-19 year-olds within both full-time jobs and part-time jobs. This has been associated with an increasing concentration of their jobs, both part- and full-time, in low paying industries. At the same time there has been an increasing concentration of employed 20-24 year-olds in low-skilled jobs (Wooden, 1999). This is a particularly disturbing development, as the age group is becoming increasingly well educated.

Relative earnings have fallen for young people.

Differences between countries provide grounds both for optimism and for concern. So do changes over time. On balance there is no need to be gloomy or pessimistic about overall transition outcomes across countries taking part in the Thematic Review. Educational participation has been rising. In many countries the proportions of teenagers who are seeking work is very low indeed. Many countries can demonstrate solid and positive outcomes for young people. Many indicators have not worsened over the 1990s, despite difficult labour market conditions. Some improvements over time can be detected in other indicators. We can and should learn from these successes.

In summary, cautious optimism on transition outcomes, tempered with concern, appears justified.

At the same time young people experience substantial transition difficulties in some countries. These difficulties, both in countries where overall outcomes are good and in countries where they are not, are heavily concentrated among young people with low qualifications and poor basic skills. While the transition problems of teenagers in many countries on balance are fairly small in scale, there is greater cause for concern about the difficulties that young adults experience in securing work. The falling income levels of young people in recent years is also a cause for concern in so far as it raises potentially disturbing questions about the quality of the jobs that an increasingly educated generation is able to find.

---

28. Very often long term unemployment among young people is less common than repeated spells of unemployment, although the latter is much more difficult to measure.
29. Section 4.3 relates these trends to policies and programmes in these countries.

Chapter 3
THE TRANSITION PROCESS

3.1. Transition pathways

The pathways concept has considerable value for describing the ways in which education, training and youth labour markets are organised and related to each other in different countries, as well as for analysing change in patterns of transition within countries. The concept establishes a link between the routes by which young people move between education and training programmes, the content of these programmes, the qualifications to which the programmes lead, and the destinations to which the qualifications provide entry – be they educational destinations, labour market destinations, or both. As Raffe puts it in referring to the "metaphor of travel" that is often used in discussing young people's transitions:

"Pathway" is a key organising concept in understanding the transition to work.

> "We talk of students' origins and destinations, and the itineraries that link them. We describe tracks and streams, royal roads and alternative routes, one-way streets and dead-ends, and ladders and bridges. We apply terms such as 'parking lot' to schemes where there is little progress. The pathways approach ... presents systems as networks of interconnected pathways, which may vary in the way that the pathways are structured and in the nature of their interconnections" (Raffe, 1998, p. 375).

The pathways approach sees the qualitative and quantitative features of transition systems being determined by three main groups of actors: governments, employers (at times in partnership with trade unions) and young people and their parents. Governments attempt to steer and regulate the provision of and participation in different types and levels of education and training, and to facilitate young people's transition to the labour market. In this process public and private education and training providers as well as enterprises (in their roles as both training providers and employers) can be partners in determining the rules according to which programmes can be organised, financed and certified, as well as the conditions under which young people are employed. On the other hand they can be the object of bureaucratic regulation. In most countries reality is situated somewhere in-between these extremes.

Transition pathways are shaped by governments and employers, but also by young people and their parents.

Young people and their parents are also decisive actors in shaping the nature of pathways. Through their educational choices they can confirm the objectives associated with existing or reformed pathways systems: for instance by choosing new or revived vocational pathways at the upper secondary stage. Or they can signal diverging interests by "voting with their feet", choosing pathways other than those that are of priority to policy makers, or combining pathways in ways not foreseen by pathways designers. Pathways systems are thus a result of an interaction between pathways design and reform by policy makers

© OECD 2000

(or the lack thereof) on one hand, and of decisions by young people and their families on the other. This interaction is a process in which the main actors continuously signal their changing needs and intentions and, at the same time, respond to the signals received.

Three principle types of pathways can be distinguished:

Three principal types of pathways through upper secondary education and training and beyond it to work or tertiary study can be distinguished:

– **General education,**

– *General education pathways.* In broad terms these have as their principal purpose the preparation of young people for tertiary study.[1] Among countries participating in the Thematic Review participation in general education pathways is highest in Australia, Canada, Japan and the United States, where they account for some three quarters of all young people, and in Portugal, where they account for nearly two thirds (Table 2.2). General education pathways can vary in the extent to which they are tightly coupled to tertiary education. For example in Austria and the Czech Republic, where the general education pathway is relatively small, only ten per cent or less of those who take it appear not to proceed directly from it to tertiary study. On the other hand in Australia and Norway perhaps one in two of those who complete a general education programme do not move directly to tertiary study.[2] General education pathways also vary widely in the degree to which students are free to choose what they study. For example in Sweden's two main upper secondary general education pathways 85% of students' time is spent on centrally determined subjects, and they have little choice over either their combination or their sequencing. On the other hand relatively few restrictions on choice of subjects, either their combination or their sequencing, apply in many of the general education tracks in the United States.

– **School-based vocational,**

– *School-based vocational pathways.* In almost all cases these have as their principal goal the provision of an upper secondary level occupational qualification followed by labour market entry.[3] Practical work forms a substantial part of students' programme of study, and generally this occurs in school workshops or other facilities, rather than in the workplace. Nevertheless in many cases short periods of workplace experience are included within programmes. This is discussed in more detail in Section 4.2. Among countries participating in the Thematic Review,

---

1. There are, however, some exceptions: for example in the United States a large "General" track exists alongside a "College preparation" track in most high schools, with the former qualifying those who take it neither for work nor for tertiary study; and in some Australian states it is possible for those taking a general education programme to take combinations of subjects that do not qualify them for tertiary study at the university level.
2. However in each case a significant proportion of this group appears to enter tertiary study at a later stage.
3. A significant exception is Denmark's HHX and HTX programmes and the Austrian Technical and Vocational Colleges (BHS), which share many of the characteristics of general education programmes, and which lead to a qualification for tertiary study rather than an occupational qualification in the Danish case, and to a qualification for both in the Austrian case. In Sweden very few sectors of the labour market are occupationally regulated, and as a result the link between the qualifications awarded to those in school-based vocational programmes and particular occupations is relatively loose.

participation in school-based vocational pathways is greatest in the Czech Republic and Hungary where it accounts for 68% and 82% respectively of all upper secondary students, in Sweden where it accounts for some 60% of all students, and in Austria and Finland where it accounts for close to 40% or more (Table 2.2). In some school-based vocational education pathways – for example those in Austria – the majority of students' time is devoted to vocational education subjects. In others – for example those provided in Japan and Sweden – roughly half of students' time is devoted to general education subjects and half to vocational education subjects. The vocational content can be organised around quite specifically defined occupations from the beginning of students' programme of study, as in Austria's school-based vocational programmes. In other cases, as in Sweden's 14 national vocational programmes and as in newly developed vocational education programmes in Hungary, the content is organised around quite broad occupational or industry groupings at the point of entry, with specialisation being delayed until the later years of the programme. In Finland 25 study lines at the point of entry are followed by 250 fields of specialisation.

– *Apprenticeship-type vocational pathways*. Almost without exception these have as their objective the provision of an occupational qualification. Young people in apprenticeship-type pathways normally spend the majority of their time in the workplace, undertaking both productive work and learning, and a minority of their time in schools. The content of the courses undertaken within schools is normally closely related to the occupation of the apprenticeship.[4] Section 4.2 discusses this pathway in more detail. Among countries participating in the Thematic Review, participation in apprenticeship is greatest in Switzerland, where it accounts for around 60% of all young people, and in Austria and Denmark where it accounts for roughly 40% (Table 2.2).

– and apprenticeship-type pathways.

In nearly all countries there is also a small minority of young people who fall in none of the three main pathways. Some of them face special difficulties in either education, the labour market or both. All countries provide some form of safety net services for such young people at risk.[5] The proportion of young people who fall outside of the three main upper secondary education pathways immediately after the end of compulsory education varies widely. It can be estimated to range from around two per cent in the Czech Republic to around ten per cent in Portugal (OECD, 1998*i*) and also ten per cent in the United Kingdom.

All three of the major types of pathways are provided in nearly all of the countries participating in the Thematic Review, but young people's distribution across them varies strongly: Table 2.2 shows the estimated distribution of upper secondary students by the main upper secondary education and training pathways. In some countries – such as the Czech Republic, Switzerland and the United States – one pathway, whether general education, school-based vocational or apprenticeship dominates. Other countries – such as

---

4. However roughly 30% of the two years that form the first half of the Norwegian apprenticeship pathway is taken up by general education subjects.
5. Impressive examples of such provision in the Nordic countries are described in Section 4.3 below.

Austria, Denmark, Norway and the United Kingdom – have a far more even distribution of young people across the three principal pathways.

The design and organisation of pathways varies across countries.

The design and organisation of pathways, as well as linkages between them, vary across countries. Differences relate to: the points at which educational pathways start to diverge; the smoothness of the transition from compulsory education to upper secondary education and from there to tertiary education; the typical duration of different types of education and training pathways; their curriculum and organisational structure; the typical exit points associated with each pathway; and the nature of qualification systems.

Pathways start to diverge at different stages in different countries.

The points at which educational pathways start to diverge and the mechanisms by which young people are channelled into different pathways differ significantly between countries participating in the Thematic Review. In most countries education and training pathways start to diverge formally at the beginning of the upper secondary stage. In some countries, however, such as Australia and Canada, almost all young people participate in general upper secondary education, with vocational programmes at the upper secondary level often being taken largely by young people with lower levels of academic achievement, and having quite low prestige.[6] In these countries preparation for specific occupational qualifications has normally started at the post-secondary or tertiary level in community colleges, CEGEPs (collèges d'enseignement général et professionnel), TAFE institutions, or universities. In Quebec the opening up of a route from secondary level vocational education to the CEGEP aims to make vocational education more attractive.

In Austria and Switzerland, on the contrary, pathways begin to diverge at a much earlier age, and participation in one or the other upper secondary pathway is strongly influenced by the type of lower secondary (compulsory) education programme that has been taken, with these programmes being sharply differentiated by the extent to which they are academically demanding. In Austria, for instance, 65% of young people coming from the more academic lower secondary schools entered the general (academically oriented) upper secondary pathway in 1995 compared to less than seven per cent among those coming from the generally less demanding *Hauptschule*. About 28% of both groups moved on to the highly valued Technical and Vocational Colleges, but drop-out rates there are high (36%) and most of the drop-outs come from the *Hauptschule* rather than from the academic lower secondary school.[7] Early pathway differentiation is often assumed to be typical of apprenticeship countries. However in Denmark a broad apprenticeship pathway coexists with compre-

---

6. However in these countries, as in the United States, it is common for large numbers of those in general education pathways to take at least some vocational subjects. In the United States, for example, 97% of high school graduates in 1992 had completed at least one vocational education course, the most popular being business, and 87% had completed at least one occupationally specific course. At the same time only 24% of all high school graduates could be defined as "vocational concentrators", having earned three or more credits in a single occupational programme.
7. Data for which no reference is provided stem from Country Notes or Background Reports. Many Austrian students choose to complete compulsory education in a TVE college before entering an apprenticeship, because employers prefer them to those coming directly from the Hauptschule. This explains at least partly the high drop-out rates after the first year of TVE college.

hensive education at the lower secondary level. This example show that early pathway differentiation need not be a feature of apprenticeship pathways.

The routes that young people take between the end of compulsory education and the workforce can be quite different from so-called "regular" routes which figure in the presentations of national education systems. Backtracking and sidetracking are common.[8] At times young people appear to be astute at "working the system", swapping between pathways to optimise their outcomes. At other times, young people's progression is slowed down or deviates: because of restrictions in access to the more desirable upper secondary pathways; because of bottlenecks in access to tertiary education; or because of the organisation of programmes in ways which encourage young people to leave without the envisaged qualification. For example:

Young people's routes to work through the available pathways are often circuitous.

- In Denmark around one in five of those who have completed an upper secondary general education programme subsequently take a second and more vocationally oriented upper secondary course. The average delay between completing lower secondary education in Denmark and starting an upper secondary vocational education and training programme is one and a half years: between completing an upper secondary general education programme and starting higher education it varies between one and a half and two and a half years, depending upon the higher education course.

- In some of the countries participating in the Thematic Review, flows between upper secondary and tertiary education have become disjointed as the result of a lack of tertiary education places. The resulting bottlenecks can be one reason for unforeseen routes taken by young people. In Hungary many of the places in labour market programmes are being taken by upper secondary graduates, rather than by early school leavers and those most at risk in the transition. In Sweden bottlenecks at the point of entry to tertiary education have resulted in a direct pathway emerging between upper secondary education and municipal adult education, taken by those wishing to use the adult education system to improve their grades for university entry. In Finland a shortage of places in tertiary education has resulted in many upper secondary graduates from the general education pathway returning to school to complete a vocational education pathway: 12% of graduates from general upper secondary education were "re-dipping" into upper secondary vocational programmes in 1996, compared to 17% who moved on to university and 10% who entered non-university AMK institutions.[9]

- In Australia substantial policy attention has been directed at increasing linkages and upward flows between non-university-level tertiary education and university-level tertiary education. The numbers moving in the

---

8. Such sidetracking and backtracking are among the reasons for the transition in some countries being of extended duration, an issue that is discussed in more detail in Section 3.2.
9. Finland illustrates other consequences for pathways of a difficult labour market situation. The average delay between graduation from upper secondary education and the beginning of additional education is two years. The number of young people entering the labour market from education more than halved from 90 000 in 1988 to 40 000 in 1994. The number of full-time students rose from 308 000 to 470 000 during the same years. At the same time, the relative position of vocational education graduates in the labour market has worsened.

expected directions have increased substantially. However flows in the opposite direction – into vocationally oriented non-university tertiary education by university graduates – have been substantially greater: on a scale of three or four to one (Golding, 1999). A similar trend for university graduates to enrol in vocational or technical courses in community colleges or in the CEGEPs can be observed in Canada (Finnie 1999*a*, 1999*b*).

– A relatively recent phenomenon in countries with highly differentiated upper secondary pathways, such as Austria, Denmark and Switzerland, is the prolongation and increasing variety of transition processes from the lower to the upper secondary stage.

- In Switzerland, growing numbers of young people no longer move on directly to upper secondary education or apprenticeship, but pass through "intermediary solutions" (an orientation year, a tenth year of compulsory school, or pre-apprenticeship). The proportion of young people taking intermediary pathways increased from 13% to 17% of the age group between 1990 and 1996.

- In Austria, many young people try to enter the prestigious upper secondary technical and vocational colleges (BHS) at the end of compulsory school.[10] Most of the dropouts from these schools continue in apprenticeship. This phenomenon is reinforced by employers who prefer to recruit their apprentices among BHS dropouts rather than from the ninth school year or among those finishing compulsory education. Such developments are partly the result of young people's and their families' attempts to keep the doors open into longer and more rewarding pathways, in a context where desirable study places and apprenticeship places are rare. For the least successful students this prolongation is often due to the need to make up for insufficient basic knowledge and skills, in order to make them more attractive as candidates for apprenticeship.

- In Denmark some 60% of compulsory school graduates now take the optional tenth year. The proportion doing so has grown strongly during the 1990s, and the trend appears to be strongly related to peer pressures, and to a desire to delay the transition in order to enjoy a relatively relaxed year of schooling, as well as to a desire to improve grades for upper secondary schooling. As in Austria, the value of this optional tenth year is now a matter of strong debate.

In other countries what appear to be pathway "deviations" can be deliberately encouraged by the structure of educational institutions and by access policies. While participation in tertiary studies has traditionally been relatively high in Canada and the United States, the transition from upper secondary education to community colleges and universities is often an indirect one. Many young adults return to tertiary studies after several years in the labour market. In these countries this is not considered as atypical. In Sweden also it is considered quite normal for entry to tertiary study to be delayed for some

---

10. Young people who have finished lower secondary education in Austria without repeating a year are normally only 14 year-olds, but compulsory schooling lasts till the age of 15. The less successful students are at this point oriented towards the Polytechnische Schule, the value of which is being debated. More successful students not moving on to general upper secondary education will attempt to continue in Technical and Vocational Colleges (BHS).

years after leaving upper secondary school. Responding to insufficient enrolment in upper secondary education the United Kingdom was the first country to develop a system of pathways which explicitly transmits the responsibility for individual routes to young people themselves. This system is organised according to modularised qualifications rather than complete programmes. Taken to the extreme, this could mean that the notion of "non completion" no longer applies, since young people can drop out without losing the modules they have passed (provided that they achieve the full qualification for which they had been training within a limited time period).

At times individually constructed routes are young people's way of negotiating their place in a world where work patterns and skill demands are changing (Dwyer *et al.*, 1999; Roberts, 1998). It seems, for example, that the opportunity for young people to acquire both a high level of general education and an occupational qualification, either at upper secondary level, at tertiary level or both, is increasingly valued by employers. Similarly young people often combine their studies with part-time work because they recognise that this combination is valued by employers, even if their educational programmes give them few opportunities to combine the two. The ability of young people to construct routes to work that provide them with such combinations of skills and qualifications, and of work and study, is in part a function of the degree of flexibility and responsiveness that has been built into national pathway frameworks. In Austria, Hungary and Switzerland for example, young people are able to take upper secondary "double qualifying" pathways that provide them both with a qualification for work and with a qualification for tertiary entry. In Denmark, where such pathways are not available, young people wishing to gain this type of combination must double dip, taking more than one upper secondary programme. It is also significant that, with the exception of Denmark, the proportion of teenaged students who combine their studies with part-time work is high in many countries where structured combinations of education and work such as apprenticeship are fewest. It tends to be low in countries in which such combinations are most widely available (see Figure 4.1).

Enrolment patterns and individual choices by young people depend strongly upon national cultures and traditions, including the labour market prospects perceived to be associated with different pathways. They also depend strongly upon the nature of the pathways that countries provide after the end of compulsory education. Figure 3.1 shows that there is a strong association between the scale of tertiary education participation by youth and the size of the upper secondary general education pathway.

Rates of participation in tertiary education are strongly influenced by the nature of upper secondary pathways...

Where, as in Canada, the United States and Australia, a high proportion of upper secondary students are found in general education pathways, rates of participation by young people in tertiary study are high. Where, as in Austria, Switzerland and Hungary, relatively few young people take part in general education pathways in upper secondary education, rates of participation in tertiary education by young people are low.[11] It would seem that providing a large upper secondary general education pathway will drive up young people's

---

11. The multiple correlation, using data for 22 countries, between the proportion of upper secondary students in general education pathways and the total tertiary education participation rate by young people at the first age at which tertiary participation is at a maximum is quite high at .37.

From Initial Education to Working Life

Figure 3.1. **Tertiary participation rates at the first age at which tertiary participation is at a maximum and participation in upper secondary general education pathways, 1996**

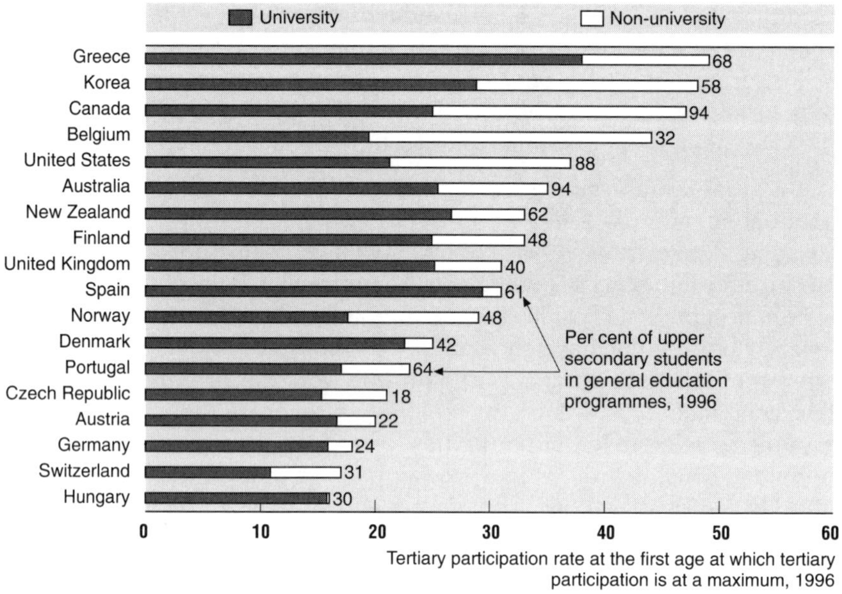

■ University   □ Non-university

Country	University	Total
Greece		68
Korea		58
Canada		94
Belgium		32
United States		88
Australia		94
New Zealand		62
Finland		48
United Kingdom		40
Spain		61
Norway		48
Denmark		42
Portugal		64
Czech Republic		18
Austria		22
Germany		24
Switzerland		31
Hungary		30

Per cent of upper secondary students in general education programmes, 1996

Tertiary participation rate at the first age at which tertiary participation is at a maximum, 1996

Source: See Table 3.1.

aspirations for tertiary study. Where upper secondary pathways are dominated by preparation for work, rather than by preparation for tertiary study, the pathway between upper secondary education and tertiary study is correspondingly smaller.

...as well as by the availability of non-university tertiary programmes.

A further factor influencing the width of the pathway between upper secondary education and tertiary study is the scale of the opportunities that are provided for young people to take part in non-university tertiary study. Figure 3.1 shows that where these are few, as in Hungary, Austria, Switzerland and Denmark, total tertiary participation by young people tends to be substantially lower than in countries such as Australia, Canada, and the United States. In the latter countries Community Colleges, CEGEPs and TAFE colleges provide ample opportunities for non-university-level study after the end of upper secondary education. The scale of the opportunities for young people to study at the non-university tertiary level is likely to be both a cause of relatively high total tertiary participation by young people, and an effect of the aspirations for tertiary study that are a result of large upper secondary general education pathways. It is, in any case, one of the consequences of delaying occupational specialisation to the tertiary stage.

In many of the countries participating in the Thematic Review the major focus of recent initiatives to increase participation in tertiary education has been at the non-university level. Hungary is creating accredited higher vocational education programmes; Austria, Finland and Switzerland have introduced or upgraded non-university tertiary institutions during the 1990s; Sweden has created pilot programmes for qualified vocational education courses at the tertiary level. In each case the decision to concentrate tertiary

© OECD 2000

growth at this level has been taken in response to economic demands for skilled labour not satisfied by universities, and in order to increase educational opportunities for young people.

During the 1990s patterns of participation have shifted between the different types of pathways in quite different ways among the countries participating in the Thematic Review.

- On the one hand there have been countries such as Canada, Finland, Japan and Switzerland where little change has been observed in the balance of participation across pathways. In Switzerland participation in the dominant apprenticeship pathway has remained high; in Canada and Japan there appears to have been little change in the proportion of young people taking the dominant general education pathway;[12] in Finland the proportions in the two main pathways – general education and school-based vocational have remained fairly stable.[13] In Denmark there has been only a small decline in participation in upper secondary vocational education, but this has been the focus of strong policy concerns.

- In another group of countries significant falls have been experienced in the size of upper secondary vocational education pathways, with associated rises in participation in general education pathways. Included in this group of countries are Australia,[14] Sweden,[15] and the United States[16] In Portugal there has been a very sharp increase in total participation at the upper secondary level, with most of this growth being concentrated in general education courses.

- In Austria, the Czech Republic and Hungary participation has fallen in upper secondary vocational courses that do not qualify young people for tertiary study, and risen in both the vocational and the general education pathways that do. In the Czech Republic and Hungary the fall in lower level vocational programmes has been very sharp indeed as the result of the collapse of the system of large training facilities in state-owned enterprises that supported them. In Austria the decline in participation in apprenticeships and lower level vocational courses has been more modest, as has the corresponding rise in participation in pathways that can qualify young people for tertiary study.

Patterns of participation in the different pathways have been changing in different ways among countries participating in the Thematic Review.

---

12. However the proportion in general education programmes in Japan did rise during the 1980s from close to 60% to the present level of around 74%, with an associated fall in participation in school-based vocational education.
13. However Finland proposes a substantial expansion in the size of the apprenticeship pathway in the near future.
14. However a fall in the participation of teenagers in the apprenticeship-type pathway has been accompanied by a rise in the participation of young adults. More recently participation has begun to rise in vocational education courses in upper secondary schools, although many of these are single subjects rather than coherent pathways.
15. Comparing the data in Table 2.2 to early editions of the OECD publication *Education at a Glance*, it would seem that participation in the general education pathway has risen from around one in four of the cohort in the early 1990s to around 40% in the late 1990s. It should be noted that all upper secondary education programmes in Sweden, both general and vocational, can qualify students for university entry.
16. The fall in participation in high school vocational education programmes in the United States has been associated with a rising participation both in those general education tracks that prepare students for college and in those that do not.

– Norway and the United Kingdom have seen rising participation in vocational education at the upper secondary level, and falling participation in general education. In Norway the proportion of students commencing upper secondary education in the vocational pathways (both apprenticeship and school-based) has risen by some ten percentage points since the early 1990s, and participation in the general education pathway has fallen by the same amount.[17] In the United Kingdom participation in vocational education pathways appears to have risen from around one in six of the upper secondary age group in the late 1980s (OECD, 1992, Table P12) to a current level of slightly more than one in two.

While there are many exceptions, a common trend across the countries participating in the Thematic Review has been for participation to fall in upper secondary vocational education pathways, particularly those not leading to tertiary study, and for participation in general education pathways to rise. Both these shifts, and the tendency for young people to use pathways in unexpected sequences and combinations, are related to changing (both higher and qualitatively different) skill demands. They are also related to changing youth attitudes and expectations, and to the changing relative value of qualifications in the labour market.[18] Concern at declining participation in traditional vocational pathways at times takes insufficient account of changing employment patterns and skill demands: a growing concentration of employment in the service sector, and an associated rise in the demand for different patterns of qualifications (Carnevale and Rose, 1998; Ilg, 1996). And the focus upon specific occupational competence at times pays too little attention to employers' expectations that young people will possess generic employability skills (Industry in Education, 1996).

There are strong arguments in favour of allowing young people to qualify at the one time for work and for tertiary study.

Where the choice between the general education pathway and vocational pathways equates with the choice between obtaining a qualification that leads to work and a qualification that leads to tertiary study, participation in vocational pathways can often be less attractive to young people. On the other hand, where vocational pathways generate qualifications that lead to either destination, the attractiveness of vocational education can rise. There is a strong argument from the perspective of lifelong learning for enabling young people to obtain such combinations of qualifications. They can encourage students to see the world of work and the world of study as intertwined from an early age, and to minimise the boundaries between academic and vocational studies. The eventual combination of an upper secondary vocational qualification and a higher education qualification that is made possible by such combined pathways can be seen as a highly desirable form of preparation for an uncertain economy. Yet the most appropriate way of achieving this combination is strongly debated. Such combinations, in whatever form, are highly demanding upon the efforts and abilities of students. This means that they are in effect selective: they invariably leave behind an increasingly stigmatised group of vocational students and apprentices who are perceived to be low-achievers.

---

17. This has been accompanied by the introduction of a new route from upper secondary vocational education pathways to tertiary study at the university level.
18. For example in the United States the gap between the earnings of those with and without college degrees has widened substantially over the last 20 years.

The pathways from vocational education to work, and the linkages between these and the general education pathway, are a central policy concern in most countries. The effectiveness of the general education pathway in preparing young people for work has generally received less attention. Yet, as we have seen, in some countries the direct flows from general upper secondary education to work are sizeable, with perhaps half of all final year secondary students in the general pathway not proceeding directly to tertiary study. In many countries the group who completes an upper secondary general education but does not qualify for tertiary study is of substantial policy concern. This concern arises both in countries where labour markets are relatively occupationally regulated such as Denmark and Norway, and in countries such as Japan where they are not, but where this group has particular difficulties on the labour market.

The pathway from general education to work is receiving increasing attention in some countries.

A group of similar concern, although its size is difficult to assess accurately, is those who drop out of tertiary education without a qualification. In countries with open and flexible non-university tertiary systems, such as Australia, Canada and the United States, many of this group subsequently gain work-related skills and qualifications through Community Colleges, CEGEPs or TAFE colleges. However concern for this group has been one of the reasons for placing an increased emphasis upon introducing more work related content into the upper secondary general education pathway.

3.2. The length of the transition

The length of the transition is a significant policy concern in a number of countries. It is closely linked to concerns about drop out rates, particularly from tertiary study, about the costs of extended study, about the social and personal costs of youth unemployment and of delay in settling into the labour market on leaving education, and about ensuring adequate supplies of qualified young labour market entrants at a time when populations are ageing. These concerns need to be set against the benefits, often insufficiently understood, of what is widely perceived to be a lengthening transition period.

The length of the transition is of significant policy concern.

The present analysis sheds some initial light upon the issue through systematically defining the starting and end points of the transition[19] in order better to describe and analyse differences between countries in the duration and nature of the transition, and change in the status of entire cohorts over time.

In looking at the length of the transition both the perspective of individual young people's routes through education and work pathways, and outcomes for complete cohorts of youth are important. From an individual young person's perspective the initial transition to work could be seen as starting at one of several points: when a pathway leading to a defined destination has been entered and the doorway on others closed; at the point of leaving initial education; or when paid work is first undertaken. Here we use cohort indicators as the basis of discussion. From the perspective of entire cohorts, the starting point of the initial transition to work can be defined in several ways:

The beginning and end of the transition can be defined in various ways.

- The first age at which fewer than 75% of the population are in education but not working. This definition was adopted in OECD (1996d);
- The average age at which young people leave education (full- or part-time). This definition has been adopted by Eurostat for

---
19. This, of course, does not shed light on what happens between these two points.

use in supplementary Labour Force Surveys that examine the transition from school to work;

– The first age at which education is not compulsory. This is the point at which young people can choose between staying in education or taking their chances on the labour market. In most countries it is the point at which those who stay in education must make a choice between the principal education and training pathways leading to work or to tertiary study: to orient themselves primarily to tertiary study, to work, or to both; to take a general education pathway or a vocational education programme; and if the latter, which one.[20] It is a point that is of key concern to policy makers, and has been adopted as the working definition of the initial transition's starting point for purposes of the Thematic Review. It has the advantage of being known for all countries. In contrast the first two definitions require special data collections, and are not readily able to be specified for some countries.

For purposes of the Thematic Review the end point of the transition is defined as the first year of age in which 50% of the population are not in education and are working.[21] This defines the point at which the cohort begins to be primarily composed of workers rather than students.

The transition consists of two separate periods.

The transition to working life can be described in terms of two periods:

– The period spent in the post-compulsory education system. This is defined as the difference between the compulsory school leaving age and the age at which 50% of the cohort are not in education, and can be calculated fairly easily from standard OECD education statistics. This definition does not preclude young people also combining their initial education with work. However it focuses attention upon the period when they are primarily students.

– The period taken to settle into work after leaving education. This is defined as the difference between the age at which 50% of the cohort are not in education and the age at which 50% of the cohort are not in education and are employed. This can be calculated using *Labour Force Survey* data in conjunction with OECD education statistics, but is not available for all countries. As defined the period can encompass a range of activities. During it some young people will be in full- or part-time study, some in full- or part-time work but not in study, some will be combining work and study, some will be unemployed, some will be involved in labour market programmes, and some will be in a range of other activities, neither in education nor in the labour market. It focuses attention upon the period when the youth cohort is neither primarily studying nor primarily working.

---

20. However there are some significant exceptions. In countries such as Austria and Switzerland the choice of the type of compulsory school attended significantly influences the types of post-compulsory pathways that will be available to the young person. In Denmark over half of all young people delay the choice of a post-compulsory pathway and undertake an optional additional year in the compulsory school after the minimum school leaving age.
21. It would be preferable in some ways to adopt a tighter definition: the point at which 50% of the population are not in education and are in full-time or permanent work. However this would severely limit the number of countries for which data could be obtained. Even the definition that has been adopted results in data not being available for all countries participating in the Thematic Review.

Table 3.2 shows, for those countries for which relevant data is available, the total duration of the transition and the length of its two components in 1996.

The length of the transition averages 7.4 years for the 18 countries for which it can be calculated, but varies widely: it ranges from 5.0 years in the case of the United Kingdom and the United States to more than twice this (11.3 years) in the case of Italy. Among the Thematic Review participants it is longest in Denmark, Norway and Portugal, at around 8.5 years.

The length of the transition varies widely between countries.

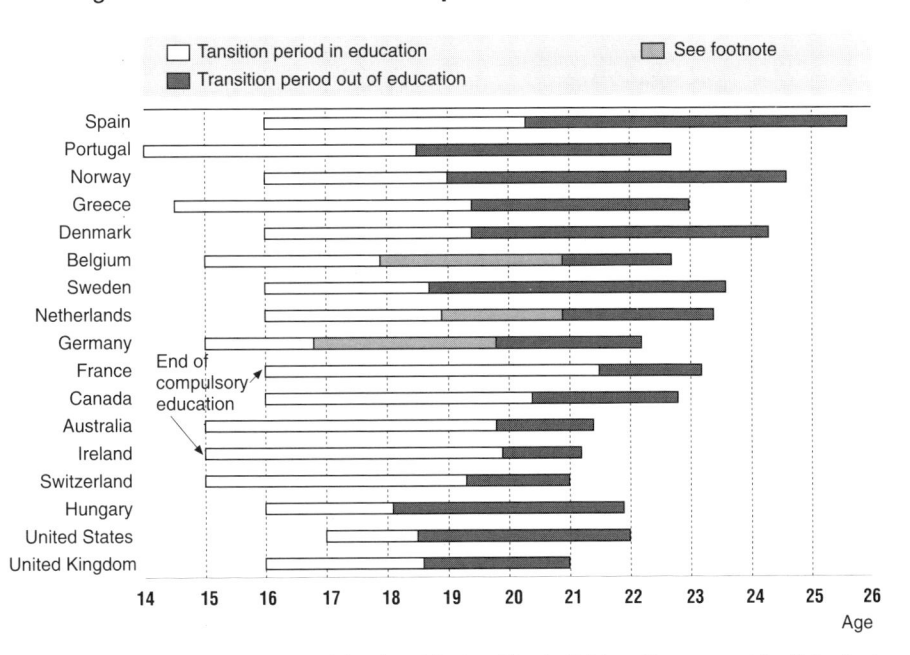

There are wide differences between countries in the composition of the transition period, as well as in its length (Figure 3.2), although the underlying reasons for these differences are not always immediately apparent. For example the United Kingdom and the United States have the same, and short, transition periods. However in the United States the period taken to settle into work occupies 70% of the total, compared to slightly less than a half in the United Kingdom. Norway and Portugal have similar and quite long average transition periods. In Norway the period within education represents only a third of the total, and the transition is extended because of the comparatively long time taken to settle into work after leaving education. In contrast the transition is a long one in Portugal because of a comparatively long time spent in post-compulsory education.[22] Among Thematic Review participants the time taken to settle into work after leaving education ranges from a quarter of the

Figure 3.2. **Duration and composition of the transition, 1996**

Note: Countries are ranked by the total duration of the transition. In Belgium, Germany and the Netherlands compulsory education ends at the age of 18. However young people may leave full-time education at the age of 15 in Germany and Belgium and at 16 in the Netherlands and continue with some form of part-time education, normally while in the labour force.
Source: See Table 3.2.

---

22. And partly because compulsory education finishes at the early age of 14 rather than the later age of 16 as in Norway.

From Initial Education to Working Life

total period in Australia and close to this in Switzerland to 70% of the total in the United States.

And it is commonly taking longer.

During the 1990s the duration of young people's initial transition to working life has grown by an average of nearly two years: from roughly five and a half years in 1990 to roughly seven and a half years in 1996 (Table 3.3). The extent of the growth has varied widely. The average duration of the transition rose by only seven months in the United States over the period, but by nearly five years in Sweden, and by close to three and a half years in Denmark, Portugal and Italy.

Countries differ widely in the factors unerlying this longer transtion from initial education to work (Figure 3.3). In the case of Sweden, Denmark and Switzerland most of the increase is the result of longer periods taken to settle into work after leaving initial education. In the case of Australia and the United States an extended period of initial education accounts for 80% or more of the increased duration, and increased periods taken to settle into work account for very little of it. In the case of Canada and the United Kingdom the two factors account for roughly equal proportions of the growth.

Figure 3.3. **Change in the duration and composition of the transition, 1990-96**

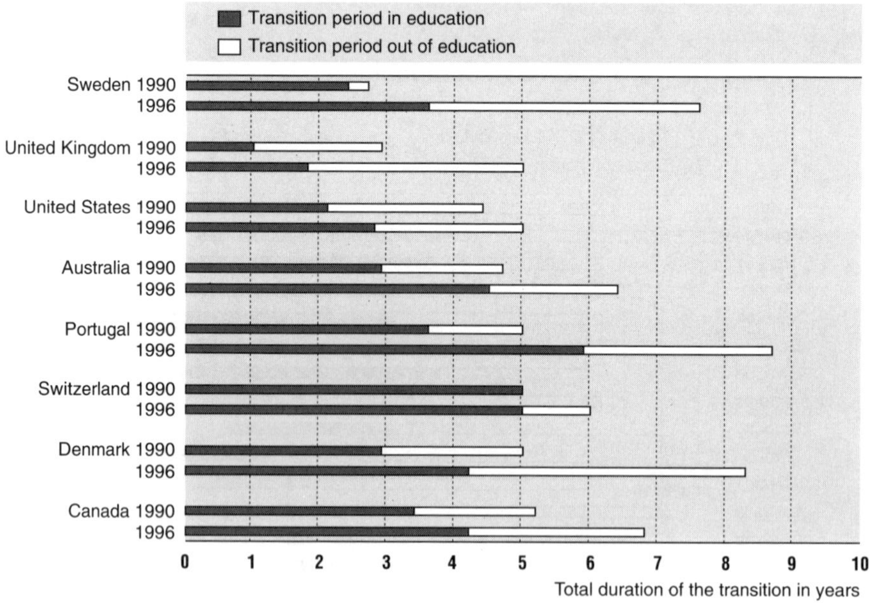

[Bar chart showing Transition period in education and Transition period out of education for Sweden, United Kingdom, United States, Australia, Portugal, Switzerland, Denmark, and Canada in 1990 and 1996. X-axis: Total duration of the transition in years, 0 to 10.]

Countries are ranked in order of the total duration of the transition in 1990.
Source: See Table 3.3.

The transition is starting both later and earlier.

The fact that the age at which 50% of the cohort are not in education rose by a year between 1990 and 1996 (Table 3.3) indicates that in one sense the initial transition to work is beginning later in many OECD countries, as well as taking longer (OECD, 1996d). But alongside this delay in the onset of the transition through an extension of the period of initial education there sits, in many OECD countries, an earlier engagement by young people with work. This is the

© OECD 2000

result of increasing proportions of young people combining their education with part-time or summer jobs (OECD, 1999b, Table 7).

The factors that underlie national differences in the duration of the transition, and its increasing duration, are complex.

Explanations are complex.

Differences between countries and over time in the rates at which young people participate in the different levels of education are one important factor. Among countries participating in the Thematic Review educational participation at the age of 16 ranged from 83% in the United Kingdom to 98% in Japan in 1996. At age 18 it ranged from 52% in Hungary to 94% in Sweden. At the age of 22 it ranged from 16% in Hungary to 46% in Finland (Table 1.1).

Some relate to educational participation levels...

National Background Reports make it clear that nearly all Thematic Review participants have seen increased participation in and completion of upper secondary education during the 1990s. For example in the six Thematic Review countries for which common data is available, total educational participation among 17 year-olds rose by an average of eight per cent between 1990 and 1996 (Figure 3.4). This increased educational participation has been associated with falling levels of low educational attainment. Across 12 OECD countries for which data is available the proportion of 20-24 year-olds with less than an upper secondary level of education fell by an average of nine per cent between 1989 and 1995 (OECD, 1998h).

Increased rates of participation in tertiary education have also been the common experience. Total growth in tertiary education enrolments between 1990 and 1996 ranged from six per cent in the United States to 144% in Portugal among countries participating in the Thematic Review, and averaged 53%. Part of this growth, and hence part of the extension of the length of the initial transition period, is fuelled by rising demand from young people for tertiary education. Part of it is the result of rising demand for qualifications and skill in the labour force.

Figure 3.4. **Total educational participation among 17 year-olds, 1990 and 1996**

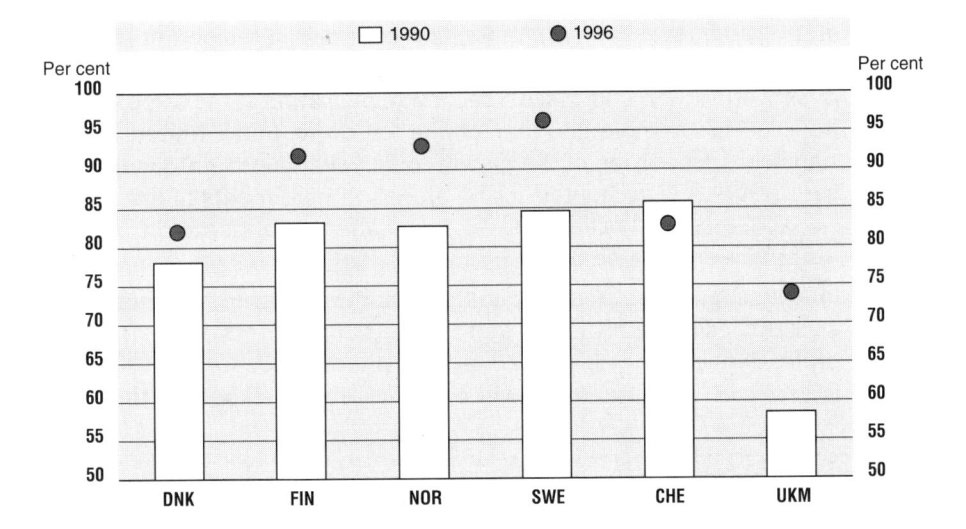

Source: OECD education database.

... and some to the amount of time that is spent in any given level of education.

Countries vary widely in the amount of time that young people typically spend in education at any one level, and this in turn can change over time:

- The formal time required to complete a qualification at a given level can vary. The typical duration of upper secondary schooling is two years in Australia but three years in the United States. In Austria, upper secondary general education programmes last for four years, and those wishing to qualify both for tertiary study and for technician level jobs must commit themselves to a programme lasting five years. In Switzerland, most apprenticeships last three or four years. Two year programmes are planned to be eliminated in the new law on vocational education and training. During the 1990s Norway, Sweden and Finland each standardised the length of their upper secondary programmes to three years, eliminating the two-year programmes in which many young people previously participated, and this resulted in the average transition duration rising. Hungary has extended compulsory general education from the age of 14 to the age of 16, delaying the age at which vocational programmes can be commenced.

- The balance of enrolments between long and short programmes can change over time. The Czech Republic, for example, has found that the average period of study within upper secondary education has risen because a higher proportion of students now take the four-year Maturita programme that leads to tertiary study, and smaller proportions are found in two- and three-year programmes that do not lead to the Maturita.

- In Denmark the introduction of three-year bachelors programmes in tertiary education has done little to reduce the average length of tertiary study, with students and employers continuing to prefer the longer five-year masters programmes. In Switzerland the average age at which a first university diploma (licence) is obtained is 27. Completion rates can also vary. Survival rates in first university-degree programmes range from an estimated 81% in Hungary to an estimated 49% in Portugal (OECD, 1998a).[23]

Part of the explanation lies in "double dipping" at the one level of education.

- The proportion of young people who obtain more than one qualification at the same level can vary. In Finland over one in ten and in Denmark some one in five of those who have completed an upper secondary qualification then undertake a second qualification at the same level. In the OECD as a whole less than one in ten do so. In the United States a significant proportion of the growth in university-level enrolments during the 1990s is accounted for by growth in enrolments in first professional degrees at bachelors level, taken after initial bachelors degrees. A similar trend can be observed in Canada (Finnie, 1999a).

- In Switzerland, the double qualifying pathway providing access to an apprenticeship certificate as well as to tertiary level education (maturité professionnelle) has increased rapidly since its creation in 1994, and it is expected that this trend will continue. This is expected to lead to

---

23. The impact of differing and longer periods of tertiary study upon the average duration of the transition for the entire cohort will be a function of the proportion of the cohort entering tertiary study. Where this is relatively small, as in Switzerland, the impact will be less than where it is relatively large, as in Canada and the United States.

considerable enrolment growth in tertiary level education, especially in the Universities of Applied Sciences (*Fachhochschulen*). Box 4.1 provides further details.

In many European countries these several factors have coincided to lengthen that part of the transition period that is spent in education: falls in the proportion leaving secondary education with no qualifications; switches in the proportions taking long rather than short post-compulsory programmes; and an increase in the proportion taking more than one course at the same level (Green, Wolf and Leney, 1999).

Countries differ widely in the amount of time that young people take to move from one level of education to another.

- Where unmet demand for places in tertiary education is high, as in Hungary, Finland and Sweden bottlenecks are created.[24] These result in many young people who have completed an upper secondary programme returning to upper secondary education to improve their marks, or undertaking vocational training to gain employment skills before trying again, or working for a period before trying again to get a place.

- In some of the Nordic countries it is common for a period of work, travel abroad, study abroad or military or community service to come between completing one level of education and commencing another. The impact of this upon young peoples' activity status is striking in the case of Sweden: the proportion of youth neither in education nor in the labour market jumps sharply from under two per cent at the age of 18 to 15% at the age of 19, the typical age at which upper secondary education is completed, drops to ten per cent at the age of 20, then remains at around four per cent from the ages of 21 to 29.

A simple index of the varying time that it takes young people to move through upper secondary education to tertiary education is provided by the difference between the first age at which education is not compulsory and the age at which tertiary participation first reaches its maximum level. This varies from only two years in the USA to seven years in Denmark and Switzerland among Thematic Review participants (Table 3.4 and Figure 3.5).[25]

The time that it takes to move from one level of education to another can vary.

---

24. In 1996 75% of Finnish upper secondary graduates applied for a tertiary education place. Of these only 27% were offered a place and 12% returned to secondary education. The average delay between graduation from upper secondary school and beginning tertiary education in Finland was two years in 1996. In Hungary only some 40% of annual tertiary applicants gained a place during the 1990s, and as a result many attempt tertiary entrance examinations on more than one occasion.
25. This index is influenced by the varying ages at which education ceases to be compulsory. Where this is relatively early, as in Switzerland and Austria, the period will appear longer. It is also influenced by the nature of countries' tertiary education systems. For example it is shortest in those countries (Australia, Canada, the United Kingdom and the United States) whose tertiary education systems include very flexible non-university sectors (Community Colleges, TAFE Colleges, Further Education Colleges) that offer multiple second chance programmes for both adults and school leavers as well as a wide range of non-university-level occupational programmes.

Figure 3.5. **Length of the transition between upper-secondary education and tertiary education**

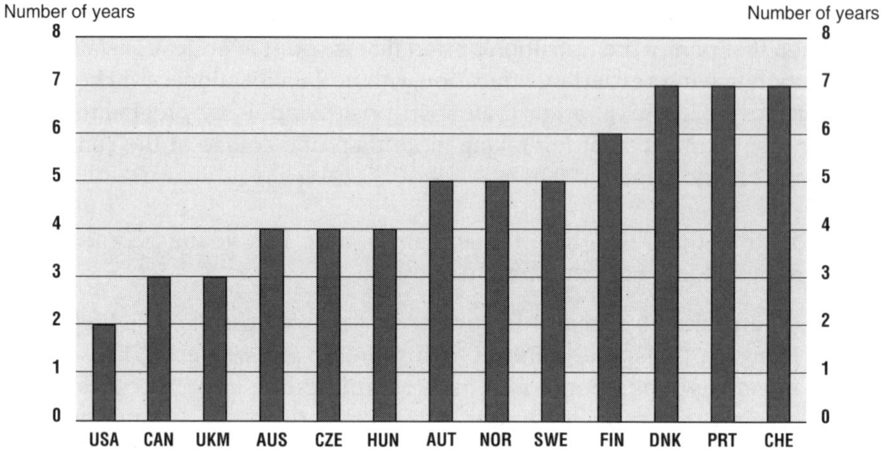

Country	Number of years
USA	2
CAN	3
UKM	3
AUS	4
CZE	4
HUN	4
AUT	5
NOR	5
SWE	5
FIN	6
DNK	7
PRT	7
CHE	7

The chart shows the difference between the first age at which education is not compulsory and the first age at which tertiary participation reaches its maximum.
Source: OECD education database.

The time that it takes to settle into work after education varies for several reason, not all to do with difficult labour market circumstances.

Countries differ widely in the amount of time that it takes young people to settle into work after leaving initial education, and again this can change over time. The reasons for the variation are complex. Difficult labour market circumstances are clearly central in the extended period taken to settle into work in some of the countries participating in the Thematic Review: Finland, Hungary and Sweden are examples.[26] In such countries periods spent in work after leaving initial education are now more likely to be interspersed with periods of unemployment or with spells in labour market programmes, making the transition into permanent work longer and more difficult. This is much less a factor in Norway, where the period taken to settle into work is also lengthy, but where deliberate decisions by young people to delay settling into work are more likely to be significant, and a healthy economy and labour market make this possible.

Young peoples' attitudes and values are also important.

The attitudes and values of young people, as well as cultural values and traditions should not be discounted in seeking to understand why the length of the transition varies. There are, for example, marked national differences in expectations about the age at which young people will assume independence. The extended period taken to settle into work in many Mediterranean countries is not only a function of labour market circumstances, but also of cultures which accept it is normal for many young people to remain in the family home for extended periods, and for some to choose this option rather than enter the labour market (Hannan and Werquin, 1999; Planas, 1999; Ryan, 1999).

---

26. In each three countries total employment fell by over ten per cent between 1990 and 1997. The impact of these changes upon youth is illustrated by the case of Sweden, where total employment fell by nearly 12% between 1990 and 1997, but by 56% among 15-19 year-olds and by 38% among 20-24 year-olds.

In some cases labour market entry, as well as progression from one level of study to another, is deliberately postponed for travel or study abroad. This form of delay is made easier in countries such as Norway and Denmark where GDP per capita is high and national currencies are strong. It is more difficult in countries with lower levels of GDP per capita such as Hungary, and is not a major part of the transition experience in all countries with a high GDP: for example Switzerland. In countries in which large areas of the labour market are not tightly occupationally organised, such as Australia and the United States, it is commonly accepted for many young people to test out a number of jobs, perhaps returning to study for periods in between – but not always completed periods of study – before settling into permanent work (Dwyer and Wyn, 1998; Klerman and Karoly, 1995; Gardecki and Neumark, 1997).

Swedish research shows that despite the deterioration of the labour market between the early and mid 1990s, over the same period young people attached growing importance to doing interesting work, and the importance attached to job security fell (Hagström and Gamberale, 1995). Japanese research[27] shows significant national variation in the extent to which work is seen as a social duty, rather than as a form of self-realisation. The former value is higher in Japan and the latter higher in Sweden, with the United Kingdom and the United States falling between the two. Japanese research also shows that young people's attitudes towards job security have been changing in that country during the 1990s. The proportion willing to tolerate unsatisfactory work has fallen, and the proportion indicating a willingness to change jobs in order to more fully use their abilities and aptitudes has risen.

The duration of the transition period, and its lengthening, are strongly influenced by public policies, as well as by the attitudes, values and preferences of young people. For example where upper secondary pathways are not flexible enough to allow young people to combine general and vocational education within the one qualification, significant numbers of young people can be observed taking both general and vocational qualifications at the same level, one after the other: as in Denmark and Finland. Where pathways allow vocational and tertiary entry qualifications to be obtained through a single programme of study, as in Austria, there is no need for such double dipping. A related trend can be observed at the tertiary level in some countries – Australia and Canada are examples – for young people to undertake a non-university level programme after completing one at university-level (Golding, 1999; Finnie, 1999b). This back-tracking or topping-up is often undertaken in order to gain practical work-related skills not provided by the first qualification, and hence to obtain more interesting jobs.

Public policies have a significant impact.

The availability of second-chance general or vocational pathways for those young people without completed upper secondary qualifications will also influence the length of the transition, making it longer, but more secure, where such mechanisms exist. Second chance pathways can take various forms: the Danish Production Schools (Moeller and Ljung, 1999), the Swedish and Norwegian municipal follow-up responsibility for early leavers, Australia's Technical and Further Education colleges and the United States' Test of General Educational Development or GED (Rumberger and Lamb, 1998) are examples.

---

27. Summarised in the Japanese Background Report, pp. 48-56.

Student income support policies are important.

There are important, but insufficiently understood, interactions between student income support policies, student access to part-time work and the earnings limits attached to this, and the taxation system which influence tertiary students' incentives to complete their courses quickly or slowly. Policy concerns relate to possible impacts upon drop out rates, to changes in the balance of enrolments between sectors of education, and to ways in which young people may be encouraged to prolong their studies. For example:

- In the United States there has been a substantial rise in the tuition costs of tertiary study, yet relatively constant levels of student financial aid. This has had a negative impact upon enrolment rates among low income students, and has been associated with an increasing concentration of lower income students in two-year Community Colleges rather than four-year institutions (McPherson and Schapiro, 1998). Rising costs help to fuel an increasing tendency to combine work with study, with concerns that this may have an impact upon quality and drop out rates.

- In Denmark 20 year-old tertiary students living by themselves can receive close to 70% of a final year apprentice's wages if receiving the basic student grant plus a loan. In addition to this, maximum earnings from part-time work can reach 85% of the maximum grant plus loan before a penalty is applied. In total the loans, grants and income from wages can exceed the wages of a skilled worker. This has lead to concerns that the incentives for students to finish their degrees in minimum time are insufficient.

- In Sweden income support in tertiary education is also relatively generous, and is available for a maximum of six years regardless of whether the formal length of the course is two, three or four years, and is independent of parental income. Students can provide evidence of progress in their studies by passing courses unconnected to their principal degree of enrolment. This also is associated with concerns that completion rates are not high enough and that students have an incentive to prolong their studies, particularly at a period of high youth unemployment (OECD, 1998g).[28]

While illustrating concerns within particular countries, these examples help to underscore how little is known about the real impact of interactions between student income support policies, student access to part-time work and the earnings limits attached to this, and the taxation system upon young people's transition through education to work.

Is a longer transition desirable?

The longer transitions that can be observed in most OECD countries carry both costs and benefits. Some of these can be readily understood. A more highly educated population both responds to demands for higher levels of knowledge and skill, and equips a country to innovate and better cope with change and uncertainty. These higher levels of education and qualification require longer periods to be spent in education by bigger proportions of the population, and cannot be achieved without this occurring. And to the extent that increased educational participation reduces labour supply when demand is weak, it contributes to higher proportions of those who are not in education

---

28. In 1995 Denmark spent 1.39% of GDP upon financial aid to students and Sweden 1.20%, the highest levels in the OECD. These levels compared to an OECD average of 0.33%.

being employed, and reduces the proportion of those who are neither in education nor in work. On the other hand extended periods spent looking for work, in labour market programmes, or in non-constructive activities outside of both education and work are indicators of poor future labour market success, particularly if they occur in the immediate post-school period.

Other indicators of a longer transition period are less easy to interpret. Travel abroad interspersed with education is a case in point. While it takes young people out of education and work for a period, it broadens their horizons in a globalising world and can increase their language skills. Extended periods of part-time work and tertiary study might prolong the transition, but also increase the prospects of employment upon graduation, but on the other hand if too extensive reduce academic performance. Such periods might build the habit of combining work and learning, and form the first step on career paths, particularly in growing industries such as tourism, hospitality and entertainment. Light (1998) shows that ignoring work while studying over-estimates rates of return to education, with a proportion of the returns able to be ascribed to the benefits of working whilst studying.

The short transitions which result from high rates of early school leaving carry substantial costs – for individuals as well as for governments – that are by now fairly well understood: poorer labour market prospects; lower earnings and productivity; higher social transfer payments; and foregone taxation receipts are among these (Conference Board of Canada, 1992*a*; King, 1999; OECD, 1998*c*). A clearer understanding of the costs – and benefits – of longer transitions is now needed to complement those public policies that are directed at reducing the costs associated with early school leaving.

3.3. A more uncertain transition?

The transition to work is only one of the transitions that young people make on the way to adulthood. During this period of their lives they are also faced with a need to establish economic independence, to establish an independent household, and to begin family formation. There are indications that, on several key dimensions, these transitions have become more uncertain for young people during the 1990s. Across 14 OECD countries the proportion of young adults (those aged 20-24) living with their parents rose slightly for men between the mid 1980s and the mid 1990s, but more sharply for women. Across the five countries participating in the Thematic Review for which data is available[29] the proportion of men of this age living with their parents rose from 57% in 1985 to 59% in 1997, but among women it rose from 40% to 45%. When asked why young people leave home later, European surveys show that the most common response from 15-24 year-olds is that they cannot afford to move out (OECD, 1999*b*). We have already seen (Section 2.4) that there has been a general trend across the OECD for young workers' earnings to fall relative to those of older workers during the 1990s, and this has occurred despite rising levels of education among youth. In some countries – for example Australia, the United Kingdom and the United States – an increased concentration of young people in low paid jobs is a matter of concern (Wooden, 1998; Wooden, 1999; Hannan and Werquin, 1999; Schrammel, 1998).

Greater uncertainty in the transition to adulthood can be observed on some dimensions.

---

29. Australia, Canada, Portugal, the United Kingdom and the United States.

For many the transition is both more "blurred" and longer.

Whether or not it is more uncertain, the transition is certainly becoming more "blurred" in many countries. Young people are now more likely to combine their studies with work for a period before entering the full-time labour market, either, as Section 4.2 illustrates, through formal arrangements such as apprenticeship, or through part-time and summer jobs. As a result it is likely that the transition from being a student to being a worker is now less sharp than it once was. When young people do leave initial education, for many who find work the jobs that they find are part-time or temporary. In 1996, across 15 OECD countries, one half of the jobs held by 16-24 year-old leavers from initial education were temporary, while some 30% were part-time (OECD, 1998*b*).[30] As we have seen in Section 3.2, the transition is also becoming longer. The types of unexpected pathway combinations that are intended to maximise outcomes that we observed in Section 3.1 are part of the reason for this longer transition. In many instances this is also the result of the longer periods that it now takes young people to settle into work after leaving initial education.

In some countries periods of "swirling" are common before young people settle into permanent work.

Extended and unstable transitions in some countries can also be the result of "milling and churning" or "swirling" during the transition phase. Australian evidence (Landt and Scott, 1998) shows that some 30% of 15-19 year-olds change their main activity at least once in any six months period, with significant movements occurring in and out of the labour force and between unemployment and other activities. In the United States, where the debate on this issue is most highly developed, "milling and churning" or "swirling" can refer to a period during which young people move from job to job, with each job lasting for relatively short periods, before settling into permanent work. In a wider sense it can refer to a period in which young people move frequently between a diverse set of activities, only one of which is work, before settling into permanent work: unemployment; labour market programmes; out of the labour force; back into education for short spells; part-time jobs; brief full-time jobs. Those who leave upper secondary education in the United States spend significantly lower proportions of the subsequent five years in work than do upper secondary graduates in Germany (OECD, 1998*h*). Table 3.2 and Figure 3.2 show that whilst the overall duration of the transition is relatively short in the United States, a higher proportion of the total duration is represented by the time taken to settle into work after leaving initial education than in any of the 16 countries for which the calculation can be made. Over the 16 countries an average of 44% of the total transition occurs after leaving initial education. In the United States it is 70%.

Early career instability can be seen in two lights.

"Milling and churning" or "swirling" in the period after leaving initial education can be regarded in two ways. On the one hand it can be argued that early career instability represents costly and unproductive floundering. The "chaotic" nature of the transition for many young people in the United States has often been used as an argument in favour of a more structured approach to the transition in that country (Stern *et al.*, 1994). On the other hand it can be argued that young people receive positive returns from "job shopping", and that funnelling them too quickly into long-term jobs could be counter-productive if it prevents them from finding a better match between their skills and interests and a job than otherwise they might have. For example Ryan (1999) has recently argued that too rapid a matching between the young person and long-

---

30. The two categories are not mutually exclusive.

term employment is a problem with Japan's otherwise efficient recruitment system for school leavers. Which of these two views is adopted depends upon the extent to which the period of swirling occurs largely within employment rather than out of it, and upon the nature of the early career instability. There is a difference between early career instability that involves young people testing out a series of short-term jobs, and early career instability that consists of movements between a series of low paid insecure jobs, unemployment, labour market programmes and out of the labour market. Questions of costs and benefits will in part turn upon whether the narrower or the wider view of swirling is adopted.

Gardecki and Neumark (1997) examine the relationship between young people's early labour market job stability (months of work experience, longest job tenure) and their labour market outcomes in their late 20s or early to mid-30s. They conclude that it is at best weakly related to adult labour market outcomes in the form of access to full-time work, wages, or employment benefits. Using a somewhat different measure of job tenure (the period taken after leaving education to enter a stable job, rather than the duration of the current job) Klerman and Karoly (1995) conclude that the extent of swirling by American school leavers before achieving stable employment has been exaggerated. However their key finding is that the extent of swirling before settling into stable employment varies widely between groups. It takes high school dropouts substantially longer to achieve stable employment than high school graduates; women take longer to make the transition to stable work than men; differences between high school dropouts and graduates are greater among women than among men; and members of minority ethnic groups lag substantially behind their white and non-Hispanic counterparts in the transition to stable employment. Whilst patterns of transition to stable employment were found to differ little over a 25 year period for high school graduates, they were found to have worsened for high school dropouts.

The concentration among particular groups of career instability in the early years after leaving initial education is a key concern in a number of countries participating in the Thematic Review. Despite a generally favourable labour market both for adults and for youth in that country, Norwegian research suggests that the problem of repeated spells of unemployment is concentrated in young people from working class families with low levels of education, and in those working in retail and construction industries in which employment tends to be highly seasonal (Hammer, 1997). Swedish research (Schröder, 1996) reveals the existence of a significant group of young people who are trapped in a cycle of temporary low paid and low skilled jobs, unemployment, and labour market programmes. Australian research (McClelland, MacDonald and Macdonald, 1998) points to a substantial group of young people – some nine per cent of the population – who, by the age of 19 have not participated in higher education, apprenticeships or training, have been unemployed for more than one third of their time since leaving school, and who are unemployed or in part-time work at the age of 19. Young people in this category are more likely to be early school leavers, to have parents from an unskilled manual background, and to have low levels of mathematics achievement at the age of 14. There is a substantial difference between young people in these circumstances and young people whose swirling during early career consists of a succession of full-time jobs interspersed with periods of full-time study, whether completed or not.

Early career instability can mean different things for different groups, and can be concentrated among particular disadvantaged groups.

The character of national labour markets appears to influence young people's chances of escaping from short-term jobs to more permanent work.

Whether those who begin their working career in short-term and temporary jobs eventually end up in permanent jobs with better prospects is partly, as we have seen, a function of their education and family background. But it is also a function of the type of national labour market that they find themselves in. Contini, Pacelli and Villosio (1999) examine the consequences of periods of short-term employment both for later wages and for the probability of later making the transition to a more secure permanent job. They conclude that in the more flexible and less regulated labour market of the United Kingdom, the incidence of short employment spells is greater, but the negative impact of these upon later wages is substantially less, than in the more regulated German labour market. They find that the probability of making a transition from short-term to longer-term employment is twice as high for young adults in the United Kingdom as it is in Germany, and that higher levels of education have a positive impact upon the probabilities of making this transition in Germany, but not in the United Kingdom.

Broader definitions of those who are at risk in the transition are needed in order to reflect more complex transition patterns.

Those who are at risk in the transition from initial education to work have most commonly been identified, for purposes of access to assistance, in terms of formal measures of unemployment: most typically registered unemployment of a defined duration. In a number of countries the adequacy of this measure is increasingly being questioned when defining both the size of the potential target group for assistance, and individual eligibility for assistance. In Denmark for example those who are targeted by the national safety net measures for early school leavers, described in more detail in Section 4.3, are defined partly by the fact that they have left school without a qualification for either work or further study, and are not taking part either in education or in work. But the requirement to participate in the safety net measures extends not only to those not in work, but also to those who are in part-time, temporary or low skilled work.

Recent research in the United Kingdom (Bentley and Gurumurthy, 1999) shows that for each young person aged 16-24 who is claiming unemployment benefits there is another who is not in education, training or work. Two thirds of this group do not come within the standard definition of unemployment: that they are available for and seeking work. Not all within this group can be assumed to be at risk. Some are studying part-time, some have chosen to be full-time parents. However they have other characteristics that suggest that they are at risk: low levels of qualifications; living in workless households; and limited or no work experience since leaving school. Australian research (McClelland, MacDonald and Macdonald, 1998) suggests a similar relationship, among 15-19 year-olds, between the size of the group that is formally unemployed, as measured by labour force surveys, and the size of a wider group that is neither in education nor in full-time employment. In Hungary, where there were sharp falls in total employment levels after 1989, the number of 15-24 year-olds who were inactive (neither in education nor in the labour market) in 1997 was three times the number counted as unemployed in the Labour Force Survey. There, both unemployment and inactivity are strongly concentrated in particular regions, among those with at best a compulsory level of education, and among ethnic minorities.

Not all of those who are neither in education, in work, or formally unemployed need be regarded as being at risk in the transition. In some of the Nordic countries, as is indicated in Section 3.2, there is a strong tradition of taking time out in the transition for travel, community or voluntary service or other activities not classified as education, employment or unemployment in labour force surveys. Many of these activities make a positive contribution to young people's personal development. Australian data shown in Table A4.5 in Appendix 4 shows that some one in six of the group of 15-19 year-olds not in education and not in the labour force are accounted for by travel, leisure and voluntary activities. Home duties and child care account for a high proportion of young women in this category, and disability, illness or injury account for around one in six of the total group.

There seem to be strong grounds for adopting wider definitions of those who are at risk in the transition than formal unemployment of a fixed duration. Issues of early intervention for those at risk will be raised in Section 4.3

Chapter 4

KEY FEATURES OF EFFECTIVE TRANSITION SYSTEMS

4.1. Well organised pathways

Cross-country differences in pathways structures and participation patterns are partly a result of national education and labour market traditions, partly of deliberate policy choices, and partly of the education and labour market incentives that young people are provided with. The common challenge over the past decade has been to develop education and training pathways that can accommodate the growing diversity of student needs and interests at upper secondary and tertiary education levels, that offer both tight and supple connections between initial education and the labour market, and that are part of coherent systems of lifelong learning.

A common challenge is to develop well organised education and training pathways.

Common elements of pathway reform policies that can be observed across countries during the 1990s include:

- The broadening of vocational programmes and qualifications.
- The creation of linkages between general and vocational education
- The development of combinations of school- and work-based learning.
- The establishment of bridges between secondary vocational education and training and tertiary education; and
- The development of more flexible education and training pathways

In a number of countries we can see a reduction in the number of specific entry points to vocational education and training pathways, and the creation of fewer and more broadly defined entry points concentrating upon occupational or industry areas rather than single occupations. Examples include a broad construction programme instead of separate programmes in areas such as carpentry, painting and bricklaying; and a broad business studies programme instead of separate specific retailing, office work, or travel services programmes. These changes are thought to better prepare young people for a changing labour market, to allow them greater opportunities to make informed career choices and to reduce unproductive backtracking within upper secondary education and training.

Broad vocational pathways prepare young people better for changing labour markets.

Between the mid-1980s and the mid-1990s Finland, Norway and Sweden have reformed their upper-secondary pathways by significantly reducing the number of vocational programmes. Hungary also has introduced reforms of this nature. In Finland, the number of vocational education fields was reduced from 650 occupational programmes to 25 basic study lines in the first year of post-compulsory education, followed by 250 fields of specialisation. In Norway, Reform 1994 reduced the number of foundation level courses from 109 to 13, ten of which are vocational courses. These 13 courses at the foundation level lead to some 90 at the next level, and then some 200 possible courses in the final year of upper secondary education. In Sweden, all upper secondary vocational education has been re-organised within 14 programmes corresponding to broad areas of economic activity (in addition to two general education programmes). As in Norway these allow for specialisation in later years, but with a smaller number of possible choices, reflecting a labour market that is less occupationally organised. In Denmark an even smaller number of initial programmes at the point of entry to vocational education and training has been proposed. Throughout the 1980s and 1990s Austria and Switzerland have gradually reduced the number of training occupations and developed common foundation programmes for neighbouring occupations. Apprentices can then specialise further in the second and third year of apprenticeship. Another way of broadening vocational education and training consists of increasing the theoretical or general education content of vocational education. This has been part of the reforms undertaken in Finland, Norway and Sweden. In Hungary the age of entry to vocational education has been delayed from 14 to 16 in order to ensure that students who enter it have a broad and solid foundation of general education.

But not all employers are ready to provide additional training needed for specific jobs.

The advantage of such developments is that young people are initially prepared for broader fields of activity and that specialisation is postponed to a stage where they are better informed and prepared to choose. Broad foundations of occupational qualifications also enable young people to be more multi-skilled or polyvalent workers, and broad initial foundations prepare them better for further learning. On the other hand, however, broader programmes will prepare young people less thoroughly for specific jobs, and employers will have to invest more in training young workers entering the labour market after they complete an apprenticeship or vocational education programme. This tends to raise problems, especially in small enterprises in traditional economic activities, where young people are appreciated if their skills are closely matched to the specific needs of the enterprise.

General agreement exists, at least in rhetoric, about the need for broad skills, but there is continuous debate, in countries with large vocational education and apprenticeship systems, among large and smaller employers, and among employers in different industry sectors, about the skills which young people should acquire as apprentices or as vocational school students. In order to be successful in labour markets with diverse and changing skill demands young people clearly need both solid generic skills – such as reasoning, problem solving and communication skills – which are needed in all jobs, and solid key qualifications and expertise in broad occupational fields. This means that both school-based vocational education and apprenticeship will increasingly have to equip young people with generic skills and with the foundations for further learning, and that additional job specific introduction will have to take place upon the completion of an apprenticeship or school-based vocational education programme.

Improving the linkages between general and vocational education remains a difficult task.

Efforts to overcome the traditional divide between general and vocational education can be seen in the increased proportion of general education that is now included in vocational education pathways in countries such as Sweden and Norway. It can also be seen in the increased opportunities for general education students to take some vocational education subjects that is evident in Australia. Another approach to reducing the divide is based on the modularisation of both general and vocational courses, accompanied by qualification frameworks which allow students to take modules from both streams. The United Kingdom and Finland are examples of countries where modularisation has been explicitly associated with the objective of integrating general and vocational education. In the United Kingdom two different strategies are being experimented with. In England and Wales, equivalences of qualifications and institutional links are expected to create bridges between the two pathways, which are intended to remain distinct from each other. In Scotland, on the other hand, a unified system is being developed at the post-compulsory stage. In Finland, large scale experimentation in the form of the so-called Upper Secondary Education Experiment has been undertaken in order to enable young people to combine courses from general and vocational programmes and from different schools. Optional participation in vocational courses has also long been open to general education high school students in the United States.

Attempts to combine general and vocational education in which the initiative is left to students can strike many problems. Often schools have only the specialised equipment and resources to allow quite limited choices of subjects or modules across the different pathways. Often neither the expectation of employers nor the entry requirements of universities favour such combinations, and this can discourage students from taking different subject combinations. The most successful students therefore concentrate on general education oriented towards higher education, or, in countries with strong traditional vocational education pathways, on high quality qualifications for the labour market. In Finland, for instance, among the students included in the Upper Secondary Education Experiment 60% did not take any advantage of the choice option; 20% choose a few courses from other schools (mostly language courses); six per cent of the vocational students have taken the university matriculation exam; and only two per cent of general education students have acquired full qualifications for both work and tertiary study. These results suggest that the integration of general and vocational education cannot be left to individual students alone as long as it is contrary to qualification requirements in tertiary education and in the labour market. On the other hand in Australia, where the labour market is less strongly based upon specific occupational qualifications and where vocational education in schools has been weaker, there has been a very strong growth in the number of students who combine their general education with vocational subjects during the 1990s: some 30% of upper secondary school students are now reported to take some vocational education.

More successful attempts to combine general education and demanding theoretical studies with vocational qualifications can be seen in the upper secondary double qualifying pathways that exist in Austria, the Czech Republic and Hungary. These prepare young people for labour market entry with technician level qualifications and, at the same time, for tertiary education. In Austria about 20% of an age cohort complete this pathway and close to 40% in the Czech Republic and Hungary. However, these programmes contain considerably less general education subjects than the general upper secondary education pathway which prepares for university entry. While they provide qualifications for both work and tertiary study, their programmes are often not "integrating" general and vocational education. Rather, highly demanding technical and vocational curricula are expected to equip young people with the generic and academic skills needed as a basis for successful tertiary level

Double qualifying vocational-technical pathways are another solution.

studies, usually in fields of study which are close to the preceding secondary programmes.

Increasingly pathways are combining school- and work-based learning.

Increased combinations of school- and work-based learning are developed either through the introduction or strengthening of apprenticeship pathways – for instance in Norway (where 25% of an age group now commences in the apprenticeship pathway) and Finland (where 20% of all vocational education students are expected to be apprentices in 2001), or through workplace experience organised by schools as part of the regular curriculum. Such programmes have recently been introduced as an obligatory part of all upper secondary vocational programmes in Finland and Sweden. A detailed discussion of different sorts of combinations between learning at school and learning at work is presented in the following section (Section 4.2).

There is an increasing interest in creating bridges to tertiary education from vocational education and apprenticeship.

One successful bridge between upper secondary vocational education and tertiary education is the double qualifying pathway mentioned above. Other approaches that allow apprentices and vocational education students to access tertiary education can be seen in Australia, Austria, Switzerland and Norway. In Australia substantial policy effort has been invested during the last decade in increasing articulation and credit transfer between TAFE (Technical and Further Education) qualifications and university-level tertiary programmes. This has been associated with those admitted on the basis of TAFE studies comprising a small but growing proportion of university admissions (Golding, 1999). In Austria, a new tertiary education entrance examination was created in 1996 for skilled workers. Courses preparing former apprentices for this examination are provided in the framework of adult education. In Norway, apprentices and vocational education students now have the possibility of moving on to tertiary education through an additional general education programme of six months duration taken after completion of the vocational pathway. In Switzerland the *maturité professionnelle* can be prepared for either during apprenticeship by taking additional and more demanding courses, or through an additional one year programme after completing an apprenticeship. This examination can also be taken by graduates from general upper secondary education who have completed one year of training in an enterprise. This allows students who complete the general education pathway to acquire a recognised labour market qualification. Together with the creation of "universities of applied sciences" (Fachhochschulen) the *maturité professionnelle* is part of a major reform which intends to open up a broad pathway from apprenticeship to tertiary education. Box 4.1 describes these initiatives in more detail.

Another way to open the doors from upper secondary vocational education to tertiary education, at the non-university level, is to develop very open types of further education institutions: Further Education colleges in the United Kingdom, TAFE colleges in Australia and Community Colleges in Canada and the United States. In these countries the permeability between the secondary and the tertiary level is assisted by several mechanisms. One is the granting of credit within non-university tertiary level courses to those who have completed upper secondary vocational programmes. Another is the use of these programmes as entry qualifications for the tertiary-level courses. Such models can be seen in the Tech-Prep programmes that have grown rapidly in the United States. In these, studies completed in the last two years of high school are counted as credit towards a two-year associate's degree or two year certificate in a Community College. They can also be seen in Australia, where upper secondary students can

> **Box 4.1. The Swiss *maturité professionnelle*: an apprenticeship certificate combined with access to tertiary studies**
>
> Compared with other countries, the proportion of university students in Switzerland is relatively low. However Switzerland is notable for having a highly developed provision of non-university tertiary education which prepares students for professional management positions in all sectors of the economy. The candidates must in principal have completed an initial vocational training programme and obtained the federal apprenticeship certificate (certificat fédéral de capacité, CFC). In addition, they must, in many cases, pass an entrance examination.
>
> In order to better respond to the challenges of social, economic and technological change, the most demanding among the traditional *écoles supérieures* (post-secondary schools) are currently being transformed into Universities of Applied Sciences (Fachhochschulen or Hautes Écoles spécialisées: HES). Their main objective, apart from research and development, is to provide practically oriented scientific teaching. Their students therefore are recruited mainly from among holders of apprenticeship certificates.
>
> The intellectual and scientific quality of teaching in the HES, as well as the goal of not unduly prolonging the duration of studies, have made it necessary to broaden and deepen theoretical preparation at the upper secondary level. As apprenticeship is to be maintained as the principal means of access to the HES, the challenge has been to add to the dual system a complement of general education without diminishing its occupational content. The goal was to offer a double qualification: both an apprenticeship qualification and an entry qualification for tertiary level education in an HES. The solution adopted is the *maturité professionnelle* (MP). It had to reconcile partly divergent positions: certain enterprises did not appreciate the increase in school-based learning – two days a week instead of one – while the advocates of classical education considered one day per week of general education to be insufficient, given that the other day in school is devoted to technical theory in the field of the training occupation.
>
> Today the results are still provisional (the first generation of MP holders graduated in 1994). Nevertheless, some conclusions do appear to be emerging. First, the practical training results and the productivity of apprentices preparing for the MP are at least as satisfactory as those of traditional apprentices, in spite of longer absence from the work place. Second, their intellectual achievement in mathematics, languages, history and other theoretical disciplines is not that of students following the full-time Gymnasium pathway. However their capacity for abstraction and analysis, and their problem solving abilities – considered to result from an education which mixes practical and theoretical learning – clearly provide them with all the competences needed for successful tertiary level studies.
>
> The MP can be integrated into three year – although more often, four year – apprenticeships. It can also be offered after the end of an apprenticeship. It clearly responds to a social and economic need: while 240 MP certificates were awarded in 1994, there were 5 650 graduates in 1998, representing 12.2% of all holders of an apprenticeship certificate. For gifted and motivated young people the MP has become a valuable alternative to the Gymnasium, and most MP graduates continue into HES studies.
>
> Intending to abolish as far as possible the obstacles to permeability between different pathways, Switzerland is currently searching for ways to establish bridges between the vocational and the general baccalaureate on one hand and between Fachhochschulen and traditional universities on the other.

complete all or part of national vocational qualifications during upper secondary school, and gain credit for these in TAFE courses.

However in the Canadian province of Quebec links between the two levels have been less possible, as selection into post-secondary CEGEP (*collèges d'enseignement général et professionnel*) courses continues to be based upon upper secondary general education performance, and so far takes little account of performance in upper secondary vocational education pathways. Even where links in the form of credit or new admission procedures have been negotiated, students may not take advantage of them. American research has pointed to this as a feature of Tech-Prep programmes (Urquiola *et al.*, 1997).

In addition to formal credit transfer or articulation arrangements between upper secondary education and such tertiary institutions, the openness of pathways into tertiary education is helped by the provision of a wide variety of programmes in these open post-school institutions for those who have not completed upper secondary education. This allows both young people and adults to return to education and to add on further qualifications to those acquired in initial education and training. These re-entry options differ in their nature. In the United States for example it is most common for high school dropouts who return to education to complete high school or its equivalent. In Australia, in contrast, relatively few high school dropouts return to complete it, but many enter TAFE vocational courses, apprenticeships and traineeships that do not require the completion of upper secondary education for entry (Rumberger and Lamb, 1998).

Developing flexible education and training pathways is a common goal of pathways reforms.

A common goal of all pathway reforms in recent years has been to make education and training pathways more responsive to the diverse needs of students and to changing skill requirements in the economy. The strategies adopted to achieve more flexible programmes and pathways have included the modularisation of education and training programmes and qualifications to increase options for students' choices, the creation of a variety of non-university tertiary institutions and programmes, and growing decentralisation of education and training curricula in vocational education to allow local employers greater say in the content.

Modularised courses allow young people to choose between different course options, and can provide some freedom in the sequencing and speed at which the modules required for a qualification can be completed. Within the framework defined for each qualification, young people can compose their own skill profiles rather than complete a fully prescribed set of courses according to a prescribed schedule. They can thus construct their own learning routes according to their interests, including according to opportunities which they see in the labour market. The notion of non-completion tends to lose some of its importance under such conditions. Students can leave the programme at any time, with taking along the modules which have been completed at that time. These partial qualifications are not lost if students return to further education in their initial field of study later on. They can also be completed by qualifications acquired through work experience and demonstrated through competency based assessment.

In countries with varied and flexible pathways at the upper secondary level the development of a large variety of post-secondary and tertiary programmes in the form of further education which is open to young people and adults alike is part of overall strategies to make education and training pathways both more flexible and more coherent. To the extent that such programmes are developed in close contact with local and regional industries their relevance to existing skill demand in the labour market can be improved. In some countries, such as Australia, Denmark, Finland and Sweden, mechanisms have been developed to allow local employers to be more directly involved in adjusting part of the vocational education curriculum to the needs and opportunities of local labour markets. Section 4.2 provides an example of how this is done in Denmark.

The goals of pathway reforms can be contradictory.

Tensions frequently arise between partly competing objectives of pathway reforms. As a result pathways engineering is never simple. Increased flexibility and openness of education and training pathways can sometimes be achieved at the cost of less rigorous quality standards, of less transparency of educational "markets" and qualifications, and of increased, though perhaps less visible, inequality. Similarly, education and training systems promoting highly individualised learning routes and skill profiles may not serve all young people equally well. It seems appropriate for education and training pathways to reflect the diversity and instability of labour demand. However it is not evident that individual young people will be able to choose the most appropriate learning routes and to assemble the most valuable skill profiles unless supported by high quality information on trends in the demand for skills and qualifications and by expert guidance on how to use this information. Not all questions have been answered as to the best ways of preparing young people for labour markets which seem to be less occupationally organised than in the past, or where new occupations and less clearly defined activities are gradually emerging.

Establishing tight connections between pathways and their destinations – whether jobs or tertiary study – remains a continual challenge. In some countries such as Australia and Norway the proportion of those who complete an upper secondary general education programme who do not immediately continue on to tertiary study is relatively large. In some countries, such as Japan, concern exists at the greater difficulty that young people in such a situation have in settling into the labour market. Tighter connections are also harder to establish in labour markets such as Sweden's where occupational regulation is quite limited and few occupations require formal occupational qualifications for entry. Failure to obtain a full upper secondary qualification or its equivalent is another way in which connections between pathways and their destinations can be loose. In the United Kingdom, for instance, while full-time enrolment of 16 year-olds in post-compulsory education and training has increased from less than 50% in the mid 1980s to 70% in 1996-97, only 58% of 17 year-olds and 18% of 18 year-olds are still in full-time education. Many young people leave upper secondary vocational education and training after only one or two years and with less than complete level 3 NVQ or GNVQ qualifications.[1] Table 2.4 shows that the proportion of young people who leave education within a year of the end of compulsory schooling in the United Kingdom is, at 26%, the highest, together with Hungary, of the countries participating in the Thematic Review.

Establishing tight connections between pathways and their destinations remains a continuous challenge.

How to adapt education and training programmes, institutions and qualifications to skill demands in knowledge-intensive and increasingly competitive service economies is an issue which is also being taken very seriously in countries where the apprenticeship pathway is large such as Austria, Denmark and Switzerland. In these countries occupational qualifications continue to both reflect and shape the profiles and structures of jobs in the labour market. Apprentices and vocational school graduates are generally transiting to regular employment with ease. However, concern is expressed about the capacity of industry and of the education system to adapt, in particular apprenticeship programmes and institutions, to the need for higher levels of skills, and to a demand for more abstract skills. How to adapt to these needs while continuing to attract large numbers of young people into apprenticeship is a closely related concern. The Swiss approach to opening up broad pathways from apprenticeship into tertiary education, and thereby potentially redesigning apprenticeship itself, merits attention. It differs fundamentally from policies that attempt to introduce or re-introduce apprenticeship largely as a safety net

---

1. The equivalent of completed upper secondary qualifications in other countries.

for low achievers that can be seen in Sweden and in some North American youth apprenticeship programmes. It remains to be seen to what extent reforms such as those undertaken in Switzerland will be able to overcome problems of inequality between general education students and apprentices or vocational school students, as well as inequalities between young people in different training occupations: for instance in construction and retail on one the hand and banking and insurance, or high-tech occupations, on the other.

Pathways engineering is never simple.

There are other contradictions which policy makers engaged in pathways reforms must face. For example:

– Increasing the share of general education content or, more generally, of theoretical learning and abstract reasoning in upper secondary vocational education and apprenticeship will increase the value of such programmes as a preparation for tertiary education, but it will also make them more selective. Less successful students will tend to be demotivated. Inversely, trying to tailor apprenticeship too exclusively to the needs of less successful students will make it unattractive to successful students. This, in turn, could devalue apprenticeship altogether as a desirable pathway in the eyes of young people and employers.

– Attempts to broaden the entry points to vocational pathways, and to make their content more generic to a number of related occupations or industries, can collide with employer demands for more specialised skills. In addition, such attempts may flounder in the face of physical facilities in schools or enterprises designed to meet the needs of more narrowly defined pathways or because of teachers having the wrong sorts of skills. These factors are often not taken into account sufficiently when reforms are being planned.

– Attempts to broaden the vocational content of general education pathways in countries such as Australia, Canada, the United States and the United Kingdom can suffer from lack of clarity about the purpose of the changes: to provide full occupational qualifications; to provide credit towards such qualifications; to develop generic work skills; or to improve career awareness and decidedness. This confusion is not made easier by the fact that some segments of the labour market in the countries concerned are tightly coupled to occupational qualifications, whereas others are not.

– In countries where skill demands of employers and entry conditions to tertiary education are clearly defined, modular curriculum structures might result in little real change in young people's choices and skill profiles, because young people will adjust their strategies to such skill demands and entry conditions. In countries where qualification requirements are less clear modularisation can encourage young people to leave initial education with only partial skills and qualifications.

Improving the status of vocational education and training is not easy, but the Thematic Review suggests some lessons.

It is not easy to halt or reverse the falling status of upper secondary vocational education. However the Thematic Review does point to some important lessons. These include:

– Avoid making it a residual and dead-end pathway, linked to poor quality jobs and directed at the lowest achievers.

- Provide institutionalised bridges between vocational education and apprenticeship and tertiary education and ensure that significant proportions of students and apprentices do take this pathway.
- Design vocational education and training programmes for less successful young people as part of safety nets rather than as ordinary vocational programmes, and make sure that safety net programmes prepare young people for participation in mainstream vocational education and training; and
- Pay attention to the financial costs and benefits for individuals and firms, for instance by providing support to employers training young people in safety net programmes and by ensuring that participants in vocational education and training programmes are not disadvantaged in terms of income support and rights to welfare programmes.

4.2. Workplace experience combined with education

Work experience during the transition phase can have important consequences for the ways in which young people find their way into the labour market and into regular employment. Education and work can be combined in a variety of ways. Among these are: apprenticeship, based on agreements and training frameworks developed jointly by governments, employer organisations and – in most cases – trade unions; a variety of structured programmes organised by schools; or part-time jobs not connected in an organised way to students' education, motivated largely by young people's desire for income and independence.[2] In most countries several of these can be found at once. The ways in which education and work are combined vary widely from one another in their nature and organisation, as well as in their educational and labour market purposes. Wide variation can also be found within any one model of the combination, such as apprenticeship. This Section describes the characteristics of the principal ways of combining education and workplace experience, reviews some of the changes in them that can be seen in recent years, and discusses their impact.

Education and work can be combined in several ways.

The opportunity to combine education with workplace experience can be important for several reasons:

Workplace experience can be important for several reasons.

- It can allow young people and employers to get to know one another. This can help to make both young people's job search and employers' recruitment more efficient.
- It can facilitate job search, because young people with work experience are believed to have acquired important generic work skills as well as positive attitudes and habits.
- It can improve the efficiency, effectiveness and pleasure of learning by providing opportunities for contextual and applied learning.
- Depending upon its nature it can be essential in developing expert skills which cannot be acquired, or cannot be acquired as well, in the classroom.

---
2. It can also take the form of employment programmes for young people who have difficulty finding work on leaving initial education. These share many of the characteristics of other forms of work and education combinations.

– It can have a positive impact upon the firm as a learning organisation through the additional skills and knowledge gained by young people's in-firm trainers and mentors.

Models of workplace experience

Apprenticeship is the best known model of organised workplace experience.

Apprenticeship-type programmes[3] involve a contractual agreement between an employer and a young person through which the young person acquires the status of an employee. The agreement includes the obligation for the young person to participate in classroom learning during the period of the apprenticeship. Apprenticeship programmes are designed to equip young people with both generic and expert skills, which are certified through widely recognised qualifications. During the time spent in the enterprise the apprentice is expected to participate increasingly in productive work. Apprenticeship wages, usually fixed by industrial agreements, tend to evolve accordingly. Normally the time spent in the workplace represents a majority of the total time spent in the programme, and the time in the classroom a minority. Of the countries participating in the Thematic Review young people are most likely to take part in apprenticeship-type arrangements in Switzerland, as well as in Austria, Denmark and Norway. At least some young people may be found in apprenticeship-type programmes in most of the countries taking part in the Thematic Review, as can be seen from Table 2.2.

Within apprenticeship-type programmes the time in the workplace is used to achieve several purposes: to develop many of the skills which the young person must acquire in order to become a qualified worker; to assist the young person's personal and social development as a worker; and to provide productive labour to the employer.

Apprenticeship is a highly diverse institution, and some of the variations in its key features are illustrated in Box 4.2. All of these variations affect the quality and nature of what is learned during the apprenticeship, as well as the strength of the connection between the young person and the enterprise. At its worst, apprenticeship uses young people as cheap labour in enterprises and sectors of industry which might not be viable without it, and which offer no future to the young person beyond the training period. At its best, apprenticeship produces high quality qualifications that are needed in the economy, ensures a smooth transition into regular employment and provides access to tertiary education and life long learning.

School-organised workplace experience can take many forms and its purposes can vary widely.

School-organised workplace experience encompasses a wide variety of ways in which young people combine education with time in the workplace: the common characteristic is the school's role in organising it. School-organised work experience varies widely with respect to: the age at which young people can participate; its purposes; its duration; the organisational and didactic links between learning in school and what occurs in the workplace; and the extent to which it is part of the regular curriculum or occurs spontaneously. Some of the more common forms of school-organised work experience include: co-operative education; shorter periods of workplace experience, often

---

3. While the term apprenticeship is used in nearly all countries to describe such programmes, there are some examples, such as traineeships in Australia, of other terms being used.

> Box 4.2. **Apprenticeship programmes differ widely both between and within countries**
>
> There is wide variation between countries, as well as within, in matters such as the way in which apprenticeship is entered, the length of the training contract, the balance between on-the-job periods and periods spent in education, and the ways in which these are sequenced (Bertrand, 1999). In Austria and Switzerland access to apprenticeship is provided mainly through the recruitment of young people by employers. In Denmark only 30% of apprentices enter apprenticeship this way, with the majority entering through an initial period of education and training in a vocational college. In Austria and Switzerland apprenticeships can last between two and four years, but most of them last three years. In Denmark their length can range from one to four and a half years but normally they last between three and four years. In Australia traineeships have normally lasted for one year and apprenticeships for four. In Norway with very few exceptions apprenticeship programmes all last for two years, namely the last two years of four-year vocational programmes.
>
> In Austria and Switzerland apprentices normally spend 70% of the total period of the apprenticeship within the firm, attending vocational school for one and a half days each week. In Denmark it is common for apprentices to spend the first year of their apprenticeship in a college, and then in later years to attend college for some weeks at a time, alternating these with time in the firm in a sandwich pattern. Norwegian apprentices spend the first two years of the apprenticeship period in school and the second two years within the enterprise.* Australian apprentices have traditionally spent around 88% of the apprenticeship period within the firm, and trainees 75%. The nature and quality of what apprentices learn is highly influenced by the size and other characteristics of the firm. For example there are wide differences between apprentices' experiences in large, well equipped high-tech firms that have their own training centres, and small artisans' firms. In the latter apprentices may learn a lot about how to run a small firm, but may not be exposed to as wide a variety of tasks and skills in their occupational field as they might be in a larger firm.
>
> * This pattern is associated with some student and employer dissatisfaction with opportunities for practical and theoretical learning to be integrated.

less systematically organised than co-operative education; and very short spells of familiarisation with the world of work.

Co-operative education programmes place students in real jobs with employers as one component of their formal course of studies. The work can be jointly supervised by the employer and a teacher or another co-ordinator from within the school, and it is commonly paid. The co-operative education model has been most highly developed in the United States and Canada. In both countries up to ten per cent of those in the last two years of high school are involved in it. A common attendance pattern involves the student spending half of each day in each setting (Stern *et al.*, 1994; Marquardt, 1998; Munby, Hutchinson and Chin, 1998).

Co-operative education is a well known North American model.

Many post secondary and short-cycle tertiary courses build time in the workplace into formal course requirements. Co-operative education programmes or similar forms of work experience are found within tertiary education in countries as varied as Australia, Austria, Finland, Hungary and the United States.[4] In Sweden the new Qualified Vocational Education courses at this level that were established in 1996 require one third of students' time to be spent in the workplace. Similarly in Canada co-operative education students at tertiary level typically spend one trimester per year in work placements and

---

4. Most commonly this occurs in non-university tertiary education, but is found in all forms of tertiary education.

> Box 4.3. **Co-operative education at Limoilou CEGEP**
>
> At Limoilou College in the city of Quebec 250 students out of a total number of 6 540 were involved in co-operative education at the time of the country visit in 1997. All of them were technical education students. Periods of practical work in enterprises are dispersed throughout the three years of college studies: during the first four semesters students should spend altogether at least 12 weeks in an enterprise, beginning with an initial one week "observation" programme followed by several "training" periods, usually of two weeks duration. In addition, students are expected to pass another 16 weeks within an enterprise during the so-called "integration stage". During the first two types of practical learning periods the students are closely followed and evaluated by their teachers. Student performance during these periods is assessed as part of the study programme. This is not the case for the "integration stage" during which the teacher pays only one visit to the enterprise. Nevertheless, four weeks after the beginning of the "integration stage" students must send a report on their work experience to the school. The evaluation of the student's work and progression at this stage is left to the enterprise which can deliver a letter of recommendation to the student.
>
> Not all students who want to participate can be included because of a lack of enterprise training places. Beyond the availability of training places in different fields of study, participants are selected and can return to further practice periods depending on the success achieved in their theoretical studies. In order to obtain a practice place students must have successfully passed 75% of the preceding courses. If successful students cannot be placed during their studies the college tries to find training places for them at the end of the college programme. The job placement rate of graduates from co-operative education programmes at Limoilou College is 100%. 40% find a job within their training enterprise.
>
> The college's students see several advantages in co-operative education: it provides work place experience which enterprises ask for when hiring employees; it makes learning at school less abstract and motivates students to succeed in their theoretical studies; and students are paid. Salaries and working conditions are determined by the training enterprise. The enterprise receives a tax credit or subsidy of up to 40% of the student's salary.
>
> The college supports co-operative education because it leads to effective learning, helps students get jobs when they graduate, and increases teachers' contacts with enterprises. At the same time there is concern about a lack of training places in enterprises, and about insufficient resources for the organisation and follow-up of practical work periods. In Limoilou College three staff and two secretaries are occupied with student placement in enterprises, while the follow-up of students is assumed by the teaching staff. Like other institutions, Limoilou College is obliged to use resources from other budget items to finance the placement service.

two in formal studies. An example of co-operative education at tertiary level in the province of Quebec is presented in Box 4.3.

Shorter periods of workplace experience take many forms and serve many purposes.

In addition to co-operative education, many examples exist of shorter periods of generally unpaid structured work placement, perhaps ranging up to one day a week at a maximum. These are a required component of school-based vocational education in Finland and Sweden, where they represent around 15% of the student's total time.[5] Many programmes of this type exist in North America. Evaluation of the types of workplace experience that have developed in the United States as a result of the 1994 School to Work Opportunities Act show that there the greatest growth has occurred in very brief

---

5. Sweden requires all students in vocational programmes to spend 15% of their total time in work placements (APU) over three years, and in 1997 Finland set a target of all students in school-based vocational programmes spending six months in the workplace over three years by the year 2001. In Sweden close to 80% of vocational students undertake APU: however the amount of APU undertaken by 37% of vocational students is less than the required 15% of their total time. Some eight per cent of students in general education programmes also undertake APU.

placements that make the fewest demands upon students, schools or employers. (Silverberg, Haimson and Hershey, 1998). In Australia around 12% of upper secondary students undertook some form of work placement in 1996, although most commonly in programmes requiring at most ten days work placement over the course of a year (Ainley and Fleming, 1997). In Austria, most students in full-time vocational schools are required to work during the summer holidays in an enterprise which agrees to employ them as trainees. Usually students are paid, depending on the employer's interest in employing trainees. In rare cases students may even be obliged to pay the employer for the opportunity to gain experience. Students must usually prepare a report on their work experience. Sometimes they return to the enterprise towards the end of their studies in order to do "real life" project work which helps to solve particular problems identified by the enterprise.

The purposes of the workplace component of these forms of school-organised workplace experience can vary widely. They include: acquiring knowledge and skill needed in particular occupations; allowing skills acquired in the school to be practised at work; allowing projects that require work experience to be completed; assisting career exploration and planning; developing the personal and social competence needed at work; and increasing students' motivation and academic achievement.

There are several important differences between co-operative education and other forms of school-organised workplace experience on the one hand, and apprenticeship on the other. These include the lack of a contractual relationship between the young person and the employer,[6] a weaker connection between the student's school-based learning and what occurs within the firm (Stern et al., 1994), a lack of organised involvement in the design and management of the programmes by employer associations and trade unions, and the absence of recognised occupational certification. Unlike apprenticeship, where the basic design and quality control rests with industry bodies, co-operative education and similar programmes are generally initiated by the educational institution and implemented through partnerships with individual enterprises.

Finally, short periods of job shadowing and work experience are found in nearly all countries as part of career education programmes, including at the compulsory level as, for instance, in the United Kingdom. Their main purpose is to help students' career exploration and choice by widening their understanding both of the general nature and requirements of work, and of differences between particular occupations, industries or firms. These objectives can be achieved either by placing the same student briefly in different jobs, by exploiting the experience of different students in different jobs through subsequent group work at school, or both.

In addition to the several organised ways in which students can combine education and workplace experience, part-time and holiday jobs let students combine the two in a way that is not formally organised, either by industry or by educational institutions. In most cases these jobs have no connection to students' educational programme. The most common reason that students undertake part-time work is to earn money, with other important motivations including a desire for independence, the enjoyment of the work itself, and to

Students' part-time and holiday jobs also allow work and education to be combined, but in a non-organised way.

---

6. However in Finland's school-organised workplace experience programmes standard contracts must be signed between the school and the employer.

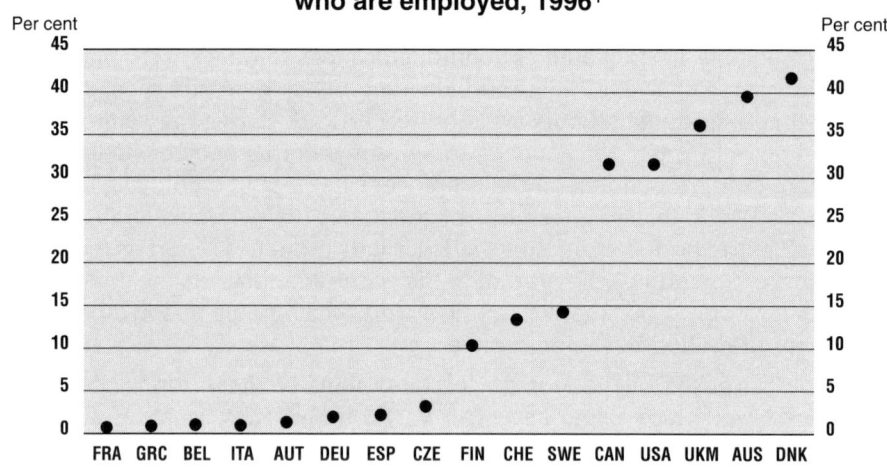

Figure 4.1. **Percentage of 15-19 year-old students who are employed, 1996[1]**

[Chart showing percentages for countries: FRA, GRC, BEL, ITA, AUT, DEU, ESP, CZE, FIN, CHE, SWE, CAN, USA, UKM, AUS, DNK]

1. Excluding those in apprenticeship-type programmes.
Source: Table 4.1.

improve the chances of getting a job after leaving education. Some students work to contribute to their family's income. For many students, and in particular tertiary students, part-time work is essential for them to finance their studies, but this is a less important motivation for upper secondary students (Robinson, 1999).

The incidence of part-time work by students[7] varies widely. Among countries participating in the Thematic Review it is most common in Denmark, Australia, the United Kingdom, the United States and Canada. In these countries *Labour Force Survey* data indicate that between 30% and 40% of teenage students mix their study with work. It is least common in Austria and the Czech Republic among Thematic Review participants, but also in Belgium, France, Greece, Italy, Spain and Germany (Figure 4.1).[8] The proportion of students who work increases with age, with close to half of all 25-29 year-old students working in 1996 among the 16 countries for which data is available (Table 4.1).

Student participation in the labour market is influenced by a number of factors. These include:

– The organisation of work and the nature of employment arrangements in key industries such as retail, tourism and hospitality. Important factors include the existence of extended opening hours, the degree to which consumer demand fluctuates over the day, week or year, and the extent to which part-time or temporary employment by youth is encouraged or permitted.

---

7. Excluding apprentices.
8. Based upon Labour Force Survey first quarter data. Estimates of the proportion of students who work that are based upon participation over the course of a year or of a programme of study generally lead to higher estimates. For example Swedish school leaver surveys (Statistics Sweden, 1997) show that 57% of school leavers had combined their upper secondary education with work, with work during school holidays being the most common form. This is substantially higher than the figure of 15% for Sweden indicated in Figure 4.1 and Table 4.1.

- The level of student grants and the costs of education.
- The overall availability of employment within the economy; and
- THE extent to which national values encourage students to work as opposed to concentrate upon their studies.

The various forms of workplace experience vary widely in the extent to which they are associated with or require learning. This is partly a function of their length. Only minimal learning is possible from a short one-day work shadowing experience where the principal emphasis is upon observing others at work rather than carrying out work as such. Very substantial learning is possible within the framework of a three-year apprenticeship combining organised learning at work and complementary and closely related learning in the classroom, with both theoretical and practical learning being encompassed within the total package.[9] Between these two extremes the amount of systematic learning, as opposed to experience not embedded in a structured learning process, will largely be a function of how well the programme is organised. For example recent case studies by Stasz and Kaganoff (1997) of high school programmes in the United States that involve work-based learning show that these can vary widely in the amount of real student learning that takes place. This variation is largely influenced by the quantity and nature of the targeted training provided within the firm, which in turn is a function of the way that programmes are organised. Ways in which the quality of the learning that occurs within school-organised workplace experience can be raised will be discussed below.

Not all forms of workplace experience are as learning – intensive as others…

The different forms of workplace experience vary widely in the demands that they make upon the firm and in the distribution of costs and benefits between the firm and the young person. At one extreme are programmes that give the firm little or no choice over which young person will spend time with it, which involve quite short periods being spent in the workplace, and which focus more upon generic employability skills. At the other extreme are programmes such as apprenticeships in which the young person is carefully recruited by the firm, in which the young person spends an extended period in the firm, and in which the skills taught expand beyond general employability to encompass those that are specific to the occupation, the industry and the firm itself. In the first instance the capacity of the firm to capture any benefits from the programme will be minimal, and altruism and a sense of community responsibility are more likely to be the major reasons for participation (Bailey, Hughes and Barr, 1999). As pro-

… and they vary widely in the demands that they make upon the firm.

---

9. However within apprenticeship the amount and quality of the learning that occurs in the workplace can also vary widely. Among other factors it is influenced by the extent to which skills acquired at work are formally assessed as part of the requirements for gaining a qualification, and by the level of apprenticeship wages. Where, as in Switzerland, these are regarded principally as pocket money and set at a low proportion of the adult wage, the employer has an incentive to use the apprentice's time for learning. Where these are close to those of qualified workers the incentive for the employer to use the apprentice's time in the workplace for productive work rather than learning will be increased. For example in Australia, where apprentices' wages are high, compared to other countries, as a proportion of those of qualified workers, employer expenditure on apprenticeship training is lower than on many other forms of training, and very little of this training occurs within the firm (Sweet, 1995). On the other hand, Swiss apprenticeship wages are low in comparison to qualified workers' wages - they are called "pocket money" for apprentices - and Swiss firms invest intensely into apprenticeship training.

grammes move along the scale towards the second extreme, the capacity of the firm to capture benefits will increase. As these benefits increase, employer participation is more likely to be a function of the amount of productivity contributed by the young person in relation to training costs, and the benefits to the firm of being able to recruit the young person after the programme has been completed.

Recent trends

The proportion of young people who combine work and education has been growing.

In recent years there has been substantial growth in many of these ways of combining education and work among OECD countries. One indication of the overall extent of this growth comes from a comparison of the proportion of 18 and 22 year-olds who were in education and in employment in 1984 and in 1997 in a group of 17 OECD countries[10] (Table 4.2). Over the period the proportion combining both activities rose from 13.9% to 18.4% among 18 year-olds, and from 6.6% to 11.1% among 22 year-olds. However the extent to which each of the different ways of combining education and work have contributed to this growth is not clear.

However the reasons for this growth vary widely.

Trends in young people's participation in apprenticeship-type programmes, summarised in Box 4.4, have been quite variable among countries participating in the Thematic Review. In the Czech Republic and Hungary traditional models of apprenticeship collapsed after 1989 and have had to be replaced or rebuilt. Substantial declines in the number of teenagers but not of young adults taking part in apprenticeship-type programmes can be observed in Australia, where such programmes have traditionally played a minor role. In Austria where apprenticeships have traditionally been strong a decline in apprenticeship participation is also evident. Little change has occurred in participation either in Denmark[11] or Switzerland, two countries in which apprenticeship has traditionally been strong. Attempts to revive apprenticeship for youth can be seen in a number of countries, with some success in Norway but little in Canada or the United States.

Only a few countries gather systematic data on rates of student participation in co-operative education and other forms of school-organised workplace experience, and where it is gathered surveys are often too recent to allow trends over time to be estimated. However experience gained during the Thematic Review indicates that during the 1990s substantial policy effort has been invested in introducing, extending or improving the quality of such programmes in Australia, Canada, Finland, Sweden, the United Kingdom and the Unite States.

Comparative time series data on student participation in the labour force through part-time jobs is not readily available. However one indication of the extent of its growth during the 1990s is change in the proportion of teenagers' jobs that are part-time rather than full-time.[12] This data is readily available and is shown in Table 4.3 for 1990 and 1998. The table suggests that during the

---

10. Australia, Austria, Belgium, Canada, Denmark, Finland, France, Germany, Greece, Ireland, Italy, Luxembourg, Netherlands, Portugal, Spain, the United Kingdom and the United States.
11. Nevertheless the very small decline that can be observed in Denmark is a significant policy concern within that country.
12. In most countries the great majority of teenagers who work part-time are students. However in some, such as Australia, there has also been growth in the numbers of teenagers not in education but in part-time jobs during the 1990s (McClelland, MacDonald and Macdonald, 1998), suggesting the need for caution in interpreting the indicator.

Box 4.4. Trends in apprenticeship participation by youth have varied widely during the 1990s

Australia The number of teenagers taking part in traditional four-year apprenticeships – predominantly in areas such as manufacturing, construction and public utilities – fell by 44% between 1989-90 and 1996. Shorter one-year traineeships largely in service and white collar areas were introduced in 1985, and the annual number of teenagers commencing these had by 1996 grown to around 70% of the numbers commencing the longer apprenticeships. The combined numbers of teenagers entering either form of contractual training fell by around a quarter between 1989-90 and 1996. Offsetting this there has been growth of around 300%, from a small base, in the number of young adults taking part in apprenticeship-type programmes.

Austria The proportion of the cohort who enter apprenticeships has been falling during the 1990s: from 47% in 1990 to 40% in 1995, and there has been further decline since. At the same time participation has risen in school-organised vocational education programmes which involve shorter periods of workplace experience.

Canada Apprenticeship in Canada has traditionally confined to a small number of occupations and has been entered largely by young adults with some work experience rather than by young people. Attempts to revive youth apprenticeships during the 1990s have met with limited success.

Czech Republic The traditional apprenticeship model centred around vocational schools closely linked to large state owned enterprises largely collapsed after 1989, and has largely been replaced by school-based vocational programmes.

Denmark The proportion of young people entering a vocational education programme stayed roughly stable during the 1990s. As a proportion of all upper secondary students those in vocational programmes, of whom some three quarters are apprentices, fell from 56% in 1990-91 to 53% in 1995-96.

Finland During the 1970s and 1980s the number of apprenticeship contracts in Finland was comparatively low, varying between 3 000 and 8 000 apprenticeships per year. With new legislation in 1992 the status of apprenticeship was strengthened and the number of apprentices has risen sharply to 17 900 in 1996 and 25 500 in 1998. The majority of these have so far been adults, whose training is subsidised through the European Social Fund and other public finances. By the year 2000 it is intended that 20% of the yearly intake of young people in upper secondary vocational education and training will be provided with apprenticeship places.

Hungary The traditional apprenticeship model centred around vocational schools closely linked to large state owned enterprises collapsed after 1989, and was largely replaced by school-based vocational programmes. However in recent years Hungary has put in place the framework for a new national apprenticeship system closely modelled on the German dual system, including a strong role for employers' chambers in quality control and requirements for all firms to belong to these chambers. As yet it is too early to assess the impact of these major reforms.

Japan Not applicable. Apprenticeship or its equivalent are not significant institutions within Japan's training or transition frameworks.

Norway Like Canada and the United States apprenticeship in Norway has traditionally been entered by young adults with some work experience rather than by young people. Major reforms in 1994 introduced a new apprenticeship model with a standard attendance pattern in which two years of full-time schooling is followed by two years in the firm. As part of the reforms new broader curricula were introduced, apprentices' wages were reduced from roughly 80% to 50% of a skilled worker's, and employer subsidies were restructured. In the first year of the new arrangements the number new apprenticeship contracts rose by 22% and young people's share of these rose from 21% to 36%. Roughly a quarter of all those who commence upper secondary education enter the apprenticeship track.

Portugal The number of apprentices in Portugal represents five per cent or less of the number of secondary education students. The total number in apprenticeship doubled between 1990 and 1993, but fell between then and 1996 to only around 30% more than the numbers in 1990.

From Initial Education to Working Life

> **Box 4.4. Trends in apprenticeship participation by youth have varied widely during the 1990s** (*cont.*)
>
> **Sweden**
> In 1970 Sweden abolished apprenticeship as the dominant model by which young people received vocational education and training, and replaced it with school-based vocational education programmes. In 1998 a small number of pilot programmes of a "New Modern Apprenticeship System" were introduced. Those who take part in them remain students rather than becoming employees and are unpaid. Substantial control of the programmes remains with the school, and students who take part must meet the same curriculum goals as students taking part in school-based vocational courses in the same occupational or industry area. Unlike students in standard school-based vocational programmes those in the pilot programmes spend 50% rather than 15% of their time in the enterprise over three year with provision for the in-firm training period to be extended for a fourth year.
>
> **Switzerland**
> The proportion of young people entering upper secondary vocational education and training has varied little over the past decade, ranging between 74% and 80%. Of these about 85% are in apprenticeship. However there are significant variations by gender and regions. Apprenticeship is more developed in the German speaking parts of Switzerland and young men participate more frequently and in more programmes that lead to higher level qualifications than young women. In the German speaking parts of Switzerland almost 87% of all young people in upper secondary vocational education and training were apprentices in 1997. The comparable proportion in the French and Italian speaking regions was 75%. The young women's share of apprenticeships has increased from 30% in 1970 to around 42% in the late 1990s, but young women are under-represented in four year apprenticeships – and over-represented in two and one year apprenticeships, the latter existing only in the field of home economics.
>
> **United Kingdom**
> The numbers in apprenticeship-type programmes declined steadily in the United Kingdom between the mid 1960s and the beginning of the 1990s. As an example, the number of apprentices in manufacturing fell from 240 000 in 1964 to 54 000 in 1990 (Gospel, 1994a). Modern Apprenticeships were launched as a national initiative in 1995. They are to provide young people aged 16-25 with training leading to NVQ/SVQ skills at Level 3 or more. In February 1998 there were 117 000 Modern Apprentices in England and Wales. Modern Apprenticeships are regulated by Training Frameworks designed for each sector by employers in conjunction with the relevant National Training Organisation and the Department for Education and Employment.
>
> **United States**
> As in Canada apprenticeship in the United States has traditionally been confined to a small number of occupations and has been entered largely by young adults with some work experience rather than by young people. Attempts during the 1990s in some states to revive youth apprenticeships appear to have been marginal in their impact.

1990s there has, among countries participating in the Thematic Review, been substantial growth in the incidence of part-time work by students in Australia, Denmark, Finland, Sweden and the United Kingdom, and lesser growth in Canada, Norway, Switzerland and the United States where it was already high at the beginning of the 1990s.

The impact of workplace experience on transition outcomes

It is not always easy to assess the impact of workplace experience on transition outcomes.

The ways in which workplace experience and education are combined vary widely: between countries in the dominant models that are adopted; between countries among ostensibly similar models; and within countries in the nature and quality of ostensibly similar models. So it is not surprising that attempts to evaluate the effects of combining work and education upon transition outcomes often do not produce conclusive answers. The variability within models is often too high.

Nevertheless there are a number of ways in which the impact of combining workplace experience with education can be examined. One is to compare, across countries, the proportion of teenagers who participate in the labour market as students, in whatever way, with employment rates among young adults. Figure A4.2 in Appendix 4 shows that in general there is a fairly strong relationship between the two. In countries in which substantial numbers of teenage students participate in the labour market the proportion of young adults who are in work is higher than in countries in which few young people do so. It also shows that several forms of participation in the labour market by teenage students can be associated with strong employment rates by adults. For example Australia, Denmark, Switzerland and the United Kingdom all have both high rates of labour market participation by teenage students and good employment outcomes for young adults. Yet students participate in the labour market in quite different ways in each. In Switzerland apprenticeship is the dominant model; in Australia and the United Kingdom it is part-time jobs held by students, together with a smaller number of apprenticeships and the like (as well as a smaller component of participation in school-organised work placements not measured by this data); and in Denmark it is through a combination of apprenticeships and high rates of participation in part-time work by students.

However in broad terms it is clearly associated with positive outcomes.

In Table 2.1a countries have been classified according to the dominant or characteristic pathways available within upper secondary education. It shows that in general the best transition outcomes in labour market terms even if not always in educational terms – low teenage unemployment, high employment rates among young adults, low rates of long term youth unemployment – are achieved in countries in which either a majority or a substantial proportion of young people enter work through apprenticeships: Austria, Denmark, Germany, Norway and Switzerland. These same countries also exhibit very few poor transition outcomes. However in some of these countries – for example Austria, Denmark and Norway – only a minority of young people take the apprenticeship route, even if a large minority. And so the extent to which the good overall transition outcomes achieved by these countries can be attributed to the combination of education and work through apprenticeship is not immediately apparent. At best the evidence is suggestive.

Apprenticeship is associated with good transition outcomes, even if it is not always clear why this is the case.

The transition systems of all of these countries exhibit a number of important features in addition to widespread opportunities to combine work and learning through apprenticeship. Many of these features are shared with countries that do not have large apprenticeship systems, but that nevertheless achieve solid transition outcomes. Among such features are: strong employment growth; occupationally organised labour markets and valued occupational qualifications; strong employer and trade union involvement in education and training as well as in labour market assistance for the unemployed; high relative expenditure on employment services and labour market programmes; labour markets that are youth friendly in other ways, such as the existence of many opportunities for students to get part-time jobs, and low levels of employment protection; and a high priority and substantial resources devoted to career guidance and information.

A recent review of the economic evidence on the merits of apprenticeship (Ryan, 1998) points out that within-country evaluations of the impact of apprenticeship upon young people's outcomes face the problem of strong selection effects. Young people of characteristically different abilities enter the different pathways to work available within any country; and these pathways are closely tied to sectors of the labour market (occupations, industries) that offer widely different occupational rewards in terms of employment opportunities or income levels. It concludes that apprenticeship is unevenly associated with economic advantages for youth. Its principal advantage is as a source of stable employment for young male adults, and its value for females is low in some countries. Its advantages are more evident when it is compared to labour market programmes than when it is compared to full-time vocational education.

In Switzerland unemployment rates among those who have recently completed a qualification are higher in Latin than in German regions. This is found both for apprenticeship graduates and for tertiary graduates. This has been explained by the greater interactions between young people and the labour market that occur within German-speaking parts of the country – within both general education programmes and apprenticeship programmes. This can take the form of part-time work, periods of full-time work before commencing advanced studies, and greater opportunities for practical work (OECD, 1997c).

Co-operative education appears to have mixed outcomes.

In a detailed analysis of the effects of co-operative education Stern et al. (1997) find that, compared to students' part-time jobs, it creates closer connections between school and work, and between students and employers. However when pre-existing differences between students in co-operative education and other students are taken into account, the effect of co-operative education on subsequent wages does not appear to be significant. Where co-operative education students do appear to be earning higher wages, this is attributed to them being less likely to enter tertiary education than students not participating in co-operative education. The authors point out that to the extent that work-based learning is available only in programmes that direct students towards immediate jobs, rather than towards both jobs and further education, students seeking the benefits of work combined with schooling must sacrifice some of their educational aspirations.

Evaluations in Canada lead to similar conclusions. They suggest that co-operative education students are less likely to go on to post-secondary education, and that such programmes have no discernible impact on the labour market success of those who do not continue to post-secondary education. However it is not clear whether such results are due to the quality of co-operative education programmes or to the types of students who participate in them. Such programmes normally do not provide credits which count for admission to post-secondary education, and students intending to continue to tertiary education will therefore focus on accumulating academic credits. (Marquardt, 1998.)

Swedish evidence indicates that structured work placements can have a positive effect, but that this effect is less than that of students' part-time jobs.

The wide variety of arrangements under which school-organised workplace experience occurs within countries makes evaluation of their impact upon young people's transition difficult. However in Sweden a common national framework exists for structured work placements.[13] Surveys of Swedish school leavers show that most of them enjoy their work placements or APU, would like to have more rather than less of it, and are satisfied with their supervisors, the tasks that they are given to do, and the types of equipment that they are allowed to work with. Australian research comes to a similar

---

13. APU, as it is referred to in Sweden, is to occupy 15% of the total time of students in vocational programmes, takes place within normal school time, and is to be organised so as to achieve agreed learning outcomes that are contained within the curriculum.

conclusion on students' positive reactions to time spent in the workplace (Teese, Davies and Ryan, 1997). As with co-operative education, structured work placements appear to have positive effects while students are participating in them.

However Swedish evidence indicates that it is less clear that this time in the workplace has a major impact upon students' post-school employment chances. Across all Swedish vocational programmes there is only a six per cent difference between the employment rates of those who undertake work placements and those who do not, and in only a small number of vocational programmes is there a clear cut advantage in favour of those who have done APU (Statistics Sweden, 1997). Of course this could be the result both of different labour market circumstances in the occupations or industries connected to different vocational programmes, and of selection effects resulting in the poorer quality students getting reduced access to APU. However the suggestion that the impact of APU upon students' outcomes is positive but only slightly so is given strength by other evidence from the same survey. The impact of students' part-time or summer jobs upon their chances of getting a job after leaving school was substantially greater than the impact of their workplace experience organised by the school. Those who had had APU as well as part-time jobs had better prospects than those who had had only part-time work. But the difference was not great.

Longitudinal studies within both Australia (Robinson, 1999) and the United States (Lucas and Lammont, 1998) show that there is a clear relationship between part-time employment while at school and a lower incidence of unemployment in the post-school years. This is likely to be due to the work skills that students gain in their jobs, to the impact that the experience has upon their personal development, and to the contacts that they make with firms and employers through their part-time work. At the same time this part-time work mostly has no adverse effects upon their chances of completing school or their level of performance at school, although the evidence from both countries indicates that those who work for long hours each week (ten or more) are likely to see their school performance suffer. Swedish evidence from school leaver surveys (Statistics Sweden, 1997) shows that upper secondary school graduates who have had part-time and summer jobs have employment rates in the year after leaving school that are twice as high or more as those who have not combined their studies with work.

Within country evidence shows that combining study with part-time work is normally associated with better transition outcomes.

Countries wishing to improve their transition arrangements have often looked with envy at the outcomes achieved by countries with large apprenticeship systems: many examples can be found of enthusiastic advocacy of the advantages of wider adoption of apprenticeships (see for example Hamilton and Lempert, 1996; Gitter and Scheuer, 1997; and Steedman, Gospel and Ryan, 1998). Enthusiasm for the benefits of apprenticeship as the best way for young people to gain experience in real workplaces, or in a wider sense for them to make the transition to work, should be tempered with some caution when drawing policy conclusions. Apprenticeship takes widely different forms in different countries. All of the observed variants on its key features can affect its outcomes, requiring considerable clarity and precision about which of its features are to be emulated if its benefits are to be achieved.

Apprenticeship is not the only answer, even in countries where it is a major pathway.

- Many countries that do not rely heavily upon apprenticeship achieve excellent transition outcomes for their young people. Japan is one example of a country which relies neither upon apprenticeship nor upon other forms of workplace experience as part of its transition arrangements. Yet it achieves many excellent transition outcomes for its youth. Some of the key features of Japan's transition arrangements are set out in Box 4.6.

- The so called "apprenticeship countries" often exhibit a number of features of successful transition systems that are shared with countries that do not have large apprenticeship systems.

- Within countries where apprenticeship accounts for a significant but not the dominant proportion of the youth cohort, those who take the apprenticeship pathway do not always achieve the best outcomes.[14] And where only aggregate national outcomes are used in comparative studies involving such countries, it is not easy to say which pathway has made what contribution to the overall outcomes.

- Apprenticeship is difficult to organise institutionally, and only a few countries that have attempted to re-establish or revive it have been willing to take key steps such as the reform of wage structures and incentives to firms, requiring compulsory membership of employer associations, and the fostering of intermediary bodies at the regional level.[15] Experience in the former East Germany shows that without an appropriate institutional base, the introduction of apprenticeship cannot be achieved without heavy government subsidies (Culpepper, 1999).

- Successful apprenticeship-type arrangements depend heavily upon the nature of the in-firm organisation of labour, and the quality and extent of firms' training resources. Failure to pay attention to these, as the case of Korea illustrates (Jeong, 1995), can impede reform efforts, even where institutional arrangements external to the firm are addressed.

- Concern about declining apprenticeship numbers or about declining employer willingness to offer training places is evident in those countries in which apprenticeship has traditionally been strong. Many of these concerns are related to structural changes in the economy, in the labour market and in the organisation of work which the apprenticeship system has had difficulty in adapting to. There is also concern at the adequacy of the base that apprenticeship lays for lifelong learning.

---

14. For example unemployment rates for apprenticeship graduates in Austria are higher than for graduates from school-based vocational programmes. However such evidence is not without its difficulties because of selection effects.
15. Such changes have generally not been made in attempts to introduce youth apprenticeships in Canada and the United States. However among countries participating in the Thematic Review two – Hungary and Norway – have tackled these fundamental structural and institutional issues. Hungary has required all employers to join economic chambers, and has given these substantial control of the quality of apprenticeship training (Lannert, 1999). Norway has restructured apprenticeship wages, reducing them from close to 80% of a qualified worker's wage to 50%. In implementing Modern Apprenticeships the United Kingdom has established a network of national Training Committees to develop training frameworks for some 70 industry sectors.

By itself workplace experience does not ensure that workplace learning will take place (Hamilton and Hamilton, 1997; Stasz and Kaganoff, 1997). If young people and employers are to benefit from many of the newer forms of school-organised workplace experience that have been developed for students in many countries during the 1990s, or to gain greater benefits from those forms such as co-operative education that have existed for some time, substantial effort must be devoted to improving programme quality. The Thematic Review has highlighted a number of important lessons about steps that need to be taken to ensure that workplace learning programmes that are managed by schools result in substantial learning by students. These are summarised in Box 4.5.

Effective school-organised alternatives to apprenticeship require careful attention to quality.

Box 4.5. **Making school-organised workplace experience a success**

High quality workplace learning programmes are characterised by:
- Work placements that are long enough for real learning to take place.
- Systematic analysis of the training capacity of the workplace, to see what it can realistically supply.
- A formal training plan, setting out what has to be taught and learned, and clarifying the work-based and school-based parts of a student's programme.
- Employer involvement in student selection for work placements.
- The presence of a trained programme co-ordinator, able to liaise between the school and the firm and troubleshoot when problems occur.
- The use of qualified, highly competent workers as workplace trainers or mentors.
- Regular face-to-face contact between the co-ordinator and employers and in-firm supervisors.
- Monitoring of students on the job by the programme co-ordinator.
- The evaluation of student performance against the training plan at the end of placements, with the evaluation carried out by the job supervisor and the co-ordinator jointly; and
- Deliberate efforts by schools to relate what has been learned at work to students' school-based learning.

Lack of employer participation is at times cited as a reason for the limited expansion of school-organised workplace experience programmes. American research (Hughes, 1998) indicates that employer participation cannot be addressed in isolation from questions of programme quality and structure, student demand and parental acceptance. Wide-scale employer participation in workplace experience programmes is also easier when it is organised and supported by appropriate employer and educational structures on a national and regional basis. In the case of apprenticeship, for example, employer organisations normally have a formal role in setting the parameters of the system and in its on-going quality control. In Section 4.5 the example is given of formal Danish employer involvement in the management of technical and commercial colleges as well in local curriculum adaptation. Such formal involvement of employers in educational institutions can assist in clarifying the objectives of workplace experience in relation to students' work at school. Short term government grants to employer organisations can be one way to stimulate such organised employer support where it is lacking.

Employer participation depends upon programme quality, but is easier if supported by proper structures.

Barriers to quality improvement exist within schools.

Achieving effective student learning through workplace experience is often impeded by the organisation of the school, by the absence of appropriate central policies to support workplace experience, and by insufficient resources for programme monitoring and quality control. In the United States, for example, much of the workplace experience that has occurred as a result of the 1994 School to Work Opportunities Act has occurred only out of normal school hours (on weekends, during vacation periods, in the evenings after school). It lets students observe and experience work for very short periods, often as little as one day or half a day. Extended and carefully structured contacts with work that allow experience to be translated into learning have been much rarer. The main reasons for this have been the rigidity of high schools' timetables, a fear that students will miss out on "real" (*i.e.* classroom) learning if they are not in school, and resistance by teachers and other key personnel within school such as counsellors. Australian research has demonstrated a strong link between effective workplace learning and the internal organisation of the school (Cumming and Carbines, 1997).

Box 4.6. **The case of Japan: strong transition outcomes yet few opportunities to combine education and workplace experience**

There are many indicators that Japan achieves excellent transition outcomes for its young people. School drop out rates are low; upper secondary graduation rates are high; unemployment to population ratios are low for both teenagers and young adults; and employment rates are high among young adults. Yet very few young Japanese have the opportunity to combine their education with workplace experience. Three quarters of all upper secondary students are in general education courses, and there is a high general education content in vocational courses. While guidelines for vocational courses require substantial time to be devoted to practical work, very rarely does this involve any experience in the workplace (Dore and Sako, 1998).

Nevertheless the connections between schools and firms in Japan are close, and both this and some key features of the Japanese labour market combine to achieve good transition outcomes for Japanese youth. Job opportunities in Japan are highly segmented by educational level, and young people with different levels of education rarely compete for the same jobs. Strong internal labour markets and an emphasis upon internal training result in firms placing heavy emphasis upon general educational achievement, attitudes, and trainablity when selecting school leavers. There is a strong institutional linkage between schools and employers. High schools and firms tend to establish long-term recruiting relationships, with local firms recruiting from a small number of high schools that they have relied upon in the past. These relationships take into account the ranking of high schools by academic achievement level, and take account of the ranking or preselection of students carried out by schools themselves. In effect employers delegate the selection to schools, which act as gatekeepers in the linkage between school and work (Ishida, 1998). This system of semiformal contracts (or *Jisseki Kankei*) is largely a consequence of the Japanese Employment Security Law and arrangements established in the 1960s which permit the Public Employment Service Office to delegate some parts of its duties to schools for the job placement of their students or graduates. Maintaining these contracts is crucial to a school's success in placing its students in jobs, and to employers' success in recruiting suitable graduates on an ongoing basis. Thus schools seek a dependable future demand for their graduates, and firms seek a dependable future supply of new recruits.

These institutional arrangements are complemented by some features of the Japanese youth labour market, referred to in Section 2.2: youth wages are relatively sensitive to economic fluctuations; steep age-wage profiles and relatively low entry level wages are supported by strong internal labour markets and intense on-the-job training for new recruits, and age- and skill-based wage systems (Mitani, 1999).

Together these arrangements result in a highly efficient transition system. Whilst efficient, concern has been raised that this represents a "mass hammering of square pegs into round holes", with reduced qualitative efficiency in the matching of young people to firms (Ryan, 1999). These concerns are reinforced by rising quit rates among young workers.

Expansion and improvement to the quality of school-organised workplace experience programmes, particularly in those countries where the expansion of apprenticeship is not a feasible option, will require educational policy makers and educational administrators to pay greater attention to the framework conditions under which programmes take place. In Sweden and Finland, for example, formal national frameworks support workplace experience. The mandating of fixed amounts of workplace time within the curriculum in these countries both imposes clear obligations upon schools and helps to drive appropriate resource allocation.

These need to be addressed by policy makers.

Among the issues needing to be addressed in order to improve the quality of school-organised workplace experience programmes are: the availability of adequate resources for programme co-ordination; training for programme co-ordinators; the organisation of school timetables; the quality of the learning plans that guide students' time in the workplace; the provision of systematic programmes to support and train employers; mechanisms for allowing systematic employer involvement in programme design and management; and student assessment. Most of these dimensions of programme quality are given serious attention in good apprenticeship programmes. And are important in making them successful.

4.3. Tightly woven safety nets

Inclusive transition systems for youth seek at the one time to keep the numbers who are not in education, training and employment low, and to ensure that the small numbers who do fall through the cracks are closely monitored and rapidly re-inserted into education and training. These dual goals can be achieved through a number of strategies. Education and training systems that encourage high rates of both participation in and completion of upper secondary education are one way of keeping the numbers of young people at risk low, as evident in Finland, Japan, Norway and Sweden. Another way are institutional structures which give favoured treatment to youth, as occurs in apprenticeship countries through occupationally organised training systems and labour markets, and in Japan through its *Jisseki-Kankei* system. In the case of Austria, Denmark and Switzerland the organised involvement of the social partners to create multiple training places for young people within firms plays an important role in giving a wide range of young people, including those at risk, a chance in the labour market.

Inclusive transition systems can be created in a number of ways.

Intensive assistance for those who do fall through the cracks can be more affordable if the number of young people requiring early and intensive assistance is kept low in the first place. Especially at times when overall unemployment is high, the capacity of the school system to absorb large numbers of young people can reduce unemployment in the age group. This requires the attractiveness and quality of upper secondary education to be seen as key elements of strategies designed to reduce the number of young people who are at risk. Denmark, Finland, Norway and Sweden are among the countries which strenuously attempt to keep the incidence of early school leaving low by making the school system as inclusive as possible. Each offers a broad range of general and vocational education programmes within upper secondary education, and around half of all young people are to be found in each type of programme (see Table 2.2). Vocational education programmes are available in a diverse range of occupational or industry areas, and national policies require

Strong efforts to keep the incidence of early school leaving low are an important part of such strategies.

these to be readily accessible to a wide range of students.[16] This helps to ensure that the interests of the full range of adolescents are able to be accommodated by upper secondary education.

The Nordic countries participating in the Thematic Review provide an example.

A priority is given to the needs of the weakest students, who are most at risk of dropping out early and of struggling to find work if they do. For example national policy in Sweden requires the counties to pay particular attention to raising the standards of the weaker students. An individual programme is provided within upper secondary schools, in addition to the 14 national vocational programmes and the two national general education programmes. This is intended for those whose achievement, particularly in core subjects such as Swedish, English and mathematics, is not sufficient to cope with one of the 16 national programmes. Some ten per cent of those commencing upper secondary school enrol in an individual programme. While students can remain in the individual programme for the full three years of upper secondary education, it is intended to be a route back into a national programme, and is designed to bring them up to the required standard so that they can join (or re-join) a national programme and thus complete a full upper secondary programme. Some 60% of those who move from compulsory school directly to an individual programme subsequently transfer to a standard national programme.

In Denmark special provision for the needs of the weaker and less motivated students tends to occur within separate institutions, rather than within separate programmes within the normal high school. For example all municipalities are required to operate a Municipal Youth School for 14 to 18 year-olds. These both supplement and serve as an alternative to the regular school programme. These schools, operated in the afternoon and evening, offer both leisure courses and courses to help students who are falling behind in their required compulsory school courses. They also offer language programmes in Danish for young immigrants. Around 60% of 14-18 year-old Danes attend Youth School activities each year. For those who have dropped out of upper secondary education without obtaining a qualification either for work or for tertiary study, Production Schools[17] provide highly flexible and individualised programmes designed to encourage a quick re-entry to a standard upper secondary programme.

In each of the four countries substantial emphasis is placed upon the availability of guidance and counselling during upper secondary education, so that those at risk of dropping out can be given support and advice at times of difficulty.

The priority given to employment services and labour market programmes varies widely.

Labour market programmes have been a traditional response to the needs of those young people who fall through the cracks and become unemployed. There are wide differences, among countries participating in the Thematic Review, in the priority that is given to public employment services and to labour market assistance to the unemployed. Figure 4.2 illustrates this, showing the per cent of GDP that is spent on such services for each one per cent of total unemployment in 1998 (or the nearest year). At one extreme we

---

16. In Norway and Sweden, where the total number of national programmes is limited to 13 and 16 respectively, each of the principal geographical areas (counties or municipalities) responsible for upper secondary education is required to offer each of the national programmes.
17. Further details are provided in Section 5.2, and in Moeller and Ljung (1999).

Figure 4.2. **Percentage of GDP spent on employment services and labour market programmes for every one per cent of total unemployment, 1998 or nearest year**

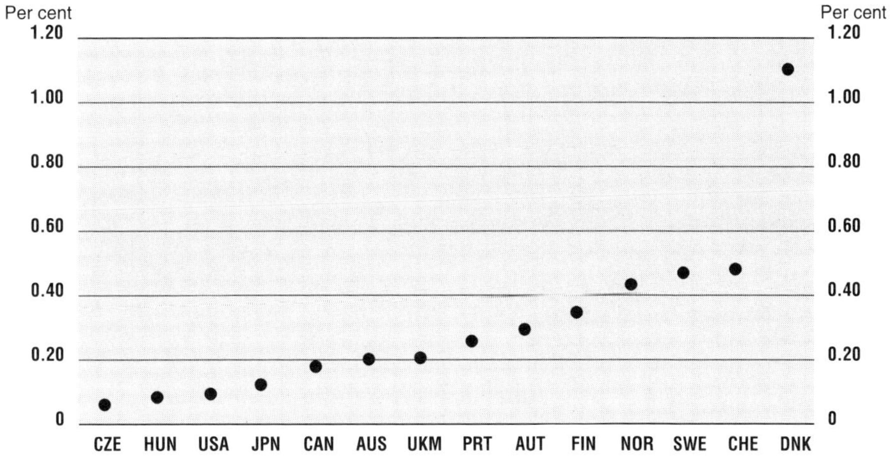

[Chart showing values from low to high: CZE, HUN, USA, JPN, CAN, AUS, UKM, PRT, AUT, FIN, NOR, SWE, CHE, DNK]

Sources: OECD (1999a) Tables B and H, except for the United Kingdom for which the source is OECD (1998b) Tables B and J.

find Denmark, which spends more than one per cent of GDP for every one per cent of total unemployment. At the other extreme are the Czech Republic, Hungary and the United States, where expenditure on such services is less than one tenth the level in Denmark. In general the highest levels of expenditure on employment services and labour market programmes are found in the Nordic countries taking part in the Thematic Review, as well as in Switzerland.

A substantial body of work both within the OECD and elsewhere has been devoted to analysing the effectiveness of labour market programmes – see for example OECD (1996a), Friedlander, Greenberg and Robins (1997) and Lerman (1997). The conclusions from this work have tended to be gloomy, suggesting that their overall impact has been minimal, and that the benefits gained by participants have been small, particularly from programmes that concentrate upon the provision of short-term training. More recently (Martin,1998; OECD, 1999a and b) attention has been focused upon the features of such programmes that are likely to lead to success, as well as upon the question of their overall effectiveness. This has increased understanding of what does and does not work, and in what circumstances. These lessons are summarised in Box 4.7.

Understanding of what makes labour market programmes effective is growing.

During the 1990s tightly knit safety nets targeted at unemployed young people and early school leavers have been developed in some of the Nordic countries. They form part of wider attempts to give concrete meaning to the notion of a youth guarantee, a concept that emerged in the Nordic countries during the 1980s in response to disappointing results achieved by many of the programmes developed when youth unemployment rose in the 1970s (Hummeluhr, 1997). The key concept is that of a guaranteed opportunity for all, through a position in education, training or work (OECD, 1998h). Labour market programmes form but one part of this broader approach.

Labour market programmes are only part of a broader approach.

© OECD 2000

> **Box 4.7. Labour market programmes: what works**
>
> Labour market programmes are more likely to achieve effective outcomes if they:
>
> – *Maintain close contact with the local labour market.* Effective programmes work closely with local employers and try to target jobs with high relative earnings, strong employment growth and opportunities for advancement. They try to understand local employers' hiring practices, and try to link their training to large, stable firms.
> – *Have an appropriate mix and intensity of formal education and work-based learning.* An appropriate integration of remedial or basic education, occupational skills and work-based learning is most likely to help the full range of occupational competencies to be developed. The length of the education and training is important, with short-term (3-12 week) programmes invariably leading to disappointing results.
> – *Pay close attention to what is being taught and learned.* Good programmes pay close attention to the quality of instruction, recognise the teaching challenges that are involved, and pay attention to teacher training.
> – *Provide opportunities for further education and training.* Effective programmes try to provide participants with a pathway to further education and training, rather than an educational dead-end.
> – *Provide a range of support services tailored to individual need.* Services such as child-care, counselling and placement are built into effective programmes, and tailored to the needs of individual participants.
> – *Are rigorously evaluated, and the results are used to improve their quality.* Effective programmes systematically collect information on performance measures and use this to enhance performance.
>
> *Source:* OECD (1999a, pp. 10-11).

Tightly knit safety nets for early leavers and unemployed youth in Denmark, Norway and Sweden are of particular interest.

Highly developed safety nets for early leavers and unemployed youth can be seen in Denmark, Norway and Sweden. These safety nets apply particularly to those under the age of 20, but some of their features may also be observed in the ways that the needs of unemployed young adults are addressed. While differing in their details, each has a number of central features:

– A focus upon prevention as well as remediation.
– An integrated approach to education, labour market and welfare policies.
– Local delivery mechanisms that are able to co-ordinate education, labour market and welfare services on a case by case basis.

Box 4.8 illustrates the ways in which Denmark's safety net operates for those under the age of 20 who have left school early and failed to find a stable slot in work or education.

Integrated education, labour market and welfare policies are required for safety nets to be effective.

Not uncommonly the success of measures taken to assist unemployed and disadvantaged youth is measured in terms of the young person *either* obtaining a job *or* obtaining an education or training place. This entails a degree of ambiguity about their purpose. Is the basic goal to ensure a solid foundation of knowledge, skill and qualification for working life, or is it to obtain work, regardless of its quality and longer term prospects? This uncertainty about the basic purposes of programmes and policies targeted at unemployed youth makes co-ordination between education and employment ministries more difficult, and increases uncertainty about where priorities should be placed in resource allocation.

> Box 4.8. **How the Danish safety net for teenagers works in practice**
>
> In Denmark every effort is made to reach those who have fallen through the cracks and to give them another chance to obtain a qualification, either for work or for tertiary study. They are actively encouraged to return to education through a combination of carrots and sticks. Each municipality is legally obliged to follow up all young people under the age of 20 (and in some areas this is voluntarily extended to those under the age of 25) who drop out of education without obtaining a qualification. Schools are legally obliged to notify the municipal follow up or youth guidance service of such drop outs. Among those who have dropped out the service identifies those who are not in education and who are either unemployed or not in secure work. The latter includes those in jobs such as petrol station attendant that do not require a recognised vocational qualification, those who are in part-time work, and those who are in jobs that they expect to be temporary.
>
> Those identified in this way as being at risk are called in for a personal interview and, in association with an adviser or mentor, are required to develop a personal action plan. This can involve work, education and training, but must be intended to reinsert them into mainstream education as soon as possible so that they can gain a qualification. They must have at least two interviews a year to check their progress in achieving the plan. Young people who are under the age of 18 are not entitled to any form of income support unless they are involved in education and training, and those aged 18 and over will only receive income support if they are actively engaged in attempting to fulfil the plans developed in co-operation with the youth guidance service. If young people refuse the assistance of the youth guidance service, they are reported to the municipality (which also administers the social security system) and their eligibility for income support will be affected.
>
> The youth guidance service can offer the young person a wide range of education and training programmes to choose from, depending upon their circumstances, interests and talents. These could include regular schooling on a part-time basis in association with part-time work, basic education courses, or participation in special schools for a period. If the young person is under the age of 18, the local labour office does not become involved at all, as the sole aim is to reinsert the young person into education.

Safety nets that have been put in place in Denmark, Norway and Sweden, particularly when directed at those under the age of 20, have avoided this dilemma by firmly setting the basic policy goal of ensuring that all young people have the opportunity to obtain a full upper secondary qualification, either for work or for tertiary study. This ensures that educational, labour market and welfare and support measures are not in competition with one another, but are each directed towards the one objective. As an example, this philosophy ensures that the periods of subsidised employment that are commonly part of the repertoire of labour market assistance are used primarily to motivate the young person, and to enable the relevance of education to working life to be more clearly appreciated.[18] They are not perceived as a way to help the young person more quickly obtain a job. This philosophy underpins Denmark's view that those early leavers who are in temporary, part-time and insecure jobs should be regarded as being at risk just as much as those early leavers who are unemployed, and included within the provisions of the safety net. The view is taken that such jobs might be easy for a young early school leaver to find, but they are likely to be easy to lose as well, and unlikely to lay a solid foundation for working life.

In each of the four countries young people of upper secondary age can only receive income support, except in special circumstances, if they are participating in education and training or in programmes that have been organised as

---

18. Norway has found that combinations of subsidised employment and education and training are among the most effective measures in helping early school leavers to quickly re-insert themselves into upper secondary school.

part of the safety net arrangements. The obligation that this imposes upon young people in each case is balanced by rights: the young person has a right to a full upper secondary education, and the state has an obligation to ensure that the young person has an opportunity to exercise this right.

Complex policy co-ordination is involved.

The Nordic safety nets require complex and co-ordinated initiatives in order at the one time to:

- Raise educational participation among those whose motivation and achievement is lowest.
- Increase the incentives for young people to complete a full upper secondary education.
- Provide a broad range of opportunities and services for those who leave education early; and
- Reduce the incentives for young people to make inactivity their preferred option.

Community organisations, employers, and employee representatives need to be involved in their design at the national level if they are to be effective, as well as in their implementation locally.

Integrated and individualised local delivery mechanisms are the key to making them work in practice.

The key to making this integrated set of policies, and of rights and obligations, work in practice is programme co-ordination and delivery that is locally managed. In each country the state imposes an obligation upon the municipalities (or counties in the case of Norway) to put in place a follow-up service that tracks early school leavers, ensures that those at risk do not fall through the cracks, helps them to develop individually constructed action plans, and monitors their progress in implementing these plans.

Local follow-up services are able to be effective for several reasons.

- They are given a clear and explicit responsibility to track and monitor early school leavers. This makes sure that early leavers do not fall through the cracks of education and employment programmes managed by different sectors and levels of government. It means that intervention occurs quickly if early school leavers cannot find work. This is important, as leaving education for unemployment increases the chances of unemployment spells being experienced over the following few years (OECD, 1998*b*).

- They generally have sufficient resources for the task in hand. As an example, the follow-up service in Norway's Akershus county in 1997 had a potential target group of around 800 young people and a full-time equivalent staff of 14 to meet their needs. This was in addition to employees of the school psychological service, the school counselling service and the youth officers of the Public Employment Service with whom they worked closely.

- They have a mandate to work closely with a wide range of community agencies: education, employment, health, welfare and police services are among those whose assistance is able to be drawn upon to meet particular individual needs and to put a particular individual action plan into effect. In each of the three countries these services span more than one layer of government – central government, the county, and the municipality.

- Their services are not standardised, but deal with each young person on a case by case basis, providing a highly individualised service tailored to need through personal action plans. Each young person is dealt with by a counsellor or mentor who is their principal point of contact. Counselling, advice and guidance are an integral part of the service, and personal action plans are reviewed on a regular basis.

- They are normally able to call upon a wide range of education, employment and training programmes, including labour market programmes, to meet young people's needs. These can include basic or remedial education, vocational education and training, recreational courses, periods of subsidised employment, personal development programmes and on-the-job training. Their ability to do so is aided by the high priority given to labour market assistance in these countries.

- They cast the net more widely, in targeting those in need of assistance, than the use of registration by young job seekers at public employment offices. The latter often results in many of those who are most at risk in the transition being under-represented in conventional labour market programmes (Nicaise, 1999).

To recapitulate, the key features of the Nordic safety nets for early school leavers and unemployed youth are: a focus upon prevention as well as remediation; integrated education, labour market and welfare policies; and locally managed delivery mechanisms that track early leavers and are able to co-ordinate services across several portfolios and several levels of government. The success of this approach is suggested by a number of indicators. First it seems to keep the proportion of those who go directly from school to unemployment low: among 14 European countries in 1995 the proportion of unemployed 15-24 year-olds who were seeking their first job was lowest in Denmark and Sweden (Figure 4.3).

Tight safety nets seem reduce the number who are at risk in the transition.

Second, it is associated with a relatively low incidence of long-term unemployment among 15-24 year-olds: among the same group of 14 countries the proportion of unemployed 15-24 year-olds who had been unemployed for 12 months or more in 1995 was the lowest in Denmark and Sweden, together with Austria (Figure 4.3).[19]

Third, in Sweden and Denmark the proportion of 15-19 year-olds who are unemployed and not in education is well below the average level in the 15 countries for whom comparable data is available (Table 4.4), together with, among Thematic Review participants, Austria, Switzerland and the United States.

Among 20-24 year-olds, however, the proportion who are unemployed and not in education is not notably lower in those countries with well developed safety nets. Among countries participating in the Thematic Review this was lowest in Austria, the Czech Republic and the United States in 1996. In Denmark it was only three quarters the average level in the same group of countries, and it is nearly equal to it in Sweden (Table 4.4).[20]

Finally, the incidence of long-term youth unemployment is among the lowest in the OECD in Denmark, Finland and Norway (Table 2.10). Furthermore, Denmark and Norway have seen the incidence of long-term unemployment among teenagers fall during the 1990s. They are the only two OECD countries

---
19. Data for Norway is not available from the same source.
20. Again, Norwegian data is not available for this indicator.

From Initial Education to Working Life

Figure 4.3. **Percentage of unemployed 15-24 year-olds who
i) were seeking their first job and
ii) had been unemployed for 12 months or more, 1995**

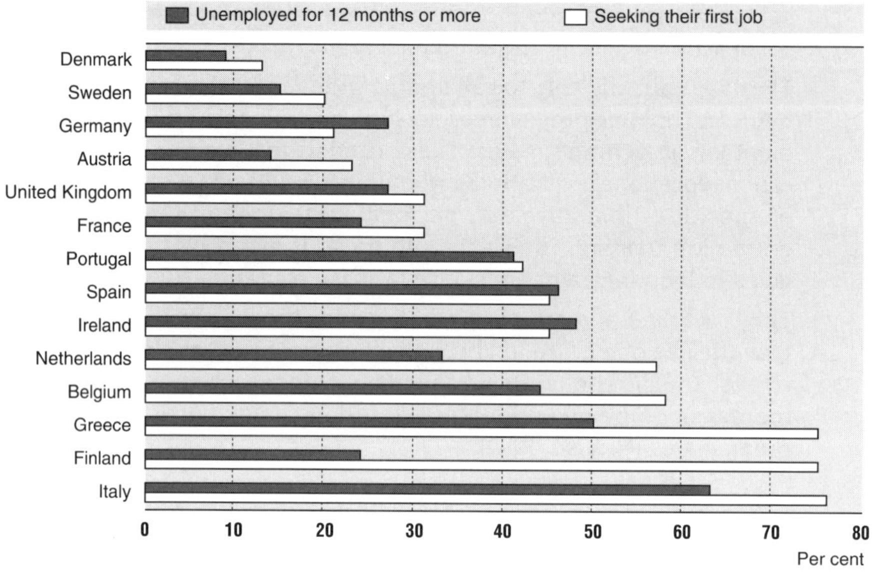

■ Unemployed for 12 months or more   □ Seeking their first job

Denmark
Sweden
Germany
Austria
United Kingdom
France
Portugal
Spain
Ireland
Netherlands
Belgium
Greece
Finland
Italy

0   10   20   30   40   50   60   70   80
Per cent

Source: EUROSTAT (1997)

where this has occurred, and the pattern of the decline in each case closely corresponds to the timing of the policy processes associated with the development of the safety nets. In Denmark the policies and programmes that comprise the safety net have been put into place in an incremental way during the 1990s. This has been associated with a progressive decline in the proportion of unemployed teenagers who have been unemployed for six months or more.[21] Norway introduced its safety net policies and programmes as a package in 1994, in association with major reforms to upper secondary education. This was associated with a sharp and sudden decline in long-term unemployment among teenagers after 1995 (Figure 4.4).

In Sweden the incidence of long-term unemployment among teenagers has not fallen during the 1990s. However it has been consistently below the OECD average, and it has not risen, despite a very sharp deterioration in the Swedish labour market over the period.[22] The Swedish experience contrasts with that of Hungary, for example, where a similar fall in overall employment levels during the 1990s has been associated with the incidence of long-term unemployment among teenagers rising sharply (Table 2.10).

21. Since the introduction in the mid 1990s of requirements for income support for youth to be linked to participation in locally administered individual action plans, flow rates out of youth unemployment and inactivity have risen to around a half compared to around a third in the early 1990s, and retention rates in employment have risen (Barrell and Genre, 1999).
22. However it is important to stress that these outcomes can coincide with many young people experiencing repeated short spells of unemployment, a concern that has been expressed in Swedish research (Schröder, 1996).

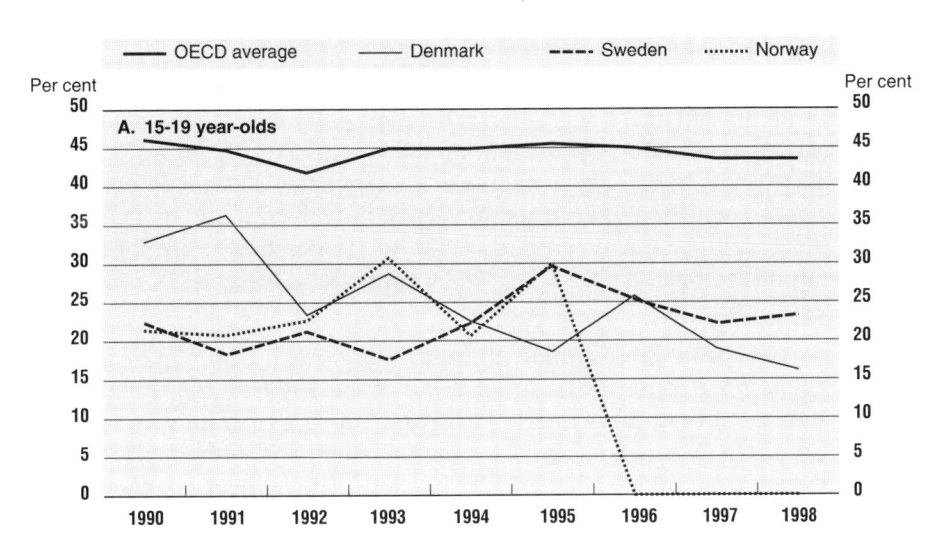

Figure 4.4. **Percentage of youth unemployment lasting six months or more, 1990-1998**

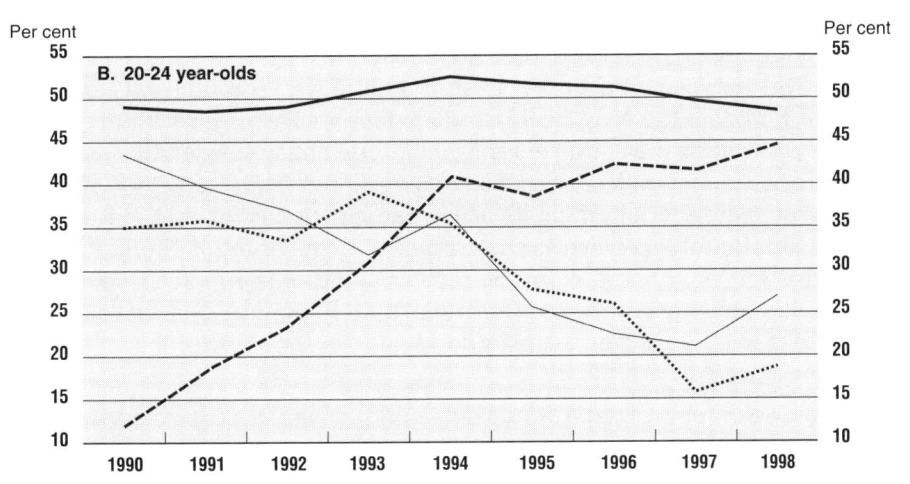

—— OECD average —— Denmark ---- Sweden .... Norway

A. 15-19 year-olds

B. 20-24 year-olds

Source: Table 2.10.

Sweden's experience with long-term unemployment among teenagers during the 1990s also contrasts sharply with the trend in long-term unemployment among young adults over the same period. The proportion of 20-24 year-olds unemployed for six months or more has risen steadily since 1990, from one of the lowest in the OECD to being close to the OECD average. Sweden's safety net policies and programmes have, throughout this period, applied to those under the age of 20 but not to those over 20. It was only in 1998 that some of their elements – such as a requirement for unemployed 20-24 year olds to be provided with earlier assistance, and an enhanced role in case management for the municipalities, rather than the public employment service – were put in place.

The worsening situation of young adults in Sweden over the period thus has been largely a function of the overall state of the labour market. Similarly in Denmark and Norway the progressive fall in the incidence of long-term unemployment among 20-24 year-olds during the 1990s is likely to be closely linked to the overall improvement in the labour market that can be observed in each country since the early 1990s.[23] This supports the conclusion in Chapter 2 that unemployment among young adults is more sensitive to the overall unemployment rate than is unemployment among teenagers.

The safety net measures – both keeping early school leaving low and actively tracking and quickly re-inserting those who do drop out – observed in Denmark, Norway and Sweden are one of the strategies that can be effective in reducing the number of teenagers who are not involved in the mainstream of education, employment or training. However as presently developed their impact upon the overall situation of 20-24 year-olds is lesser.

Elements of these safety nets can be seen in other countries' policies.

The European Employment Strategy (European Communities, 1999b) requires member countries to adopt some of the key features of the Nordic safety nets in tackling youth unemployment: notably, a preventative approach to reduce the numbers flowing into unemployment; and early intervention to assist those young people who are unemployed. The more active approach to keeping the number of young people who are at risk in the transition low can be seen in policy initiatives taken in some of the countries participating in the Thematic Review. In the Czech Republic eligibility for unemployment benefits was tightened in 1992 and their generosity reduced, resulting in weaker incentives for young jobseekers to stay unemployed (Grootings, 1999). In the United Kingdom the New Deal introduced for youth in 1998 with the explicit aim of preventing them from entering long-term unemployment (Layard, 1998; European Communities, 1999b) combines the carrot of an entitlement to assistance with a requirement for active participation in the assistance offered as a condition of receiving income support. A similar requirement for active participation as a condition for the receipt of income support can be seen in Australia's recently introduced Common Youth Allowance, and in many of the welfare to work initiatives in the United States (Bishop, 1998).

What are missing from many of these initiatives, however, are some of the other key elements of the Nordic safety nets: an emphasis upon prevention to complement the focus upon targeted remediation; well integrated education, labour market and welfare policies that put the completion of an upper secondary qualification as a primary goal; and effective local delivery services able to track early school leavers and co-ordinate assistance for them across several sectors and levels of government.

4.4. Good information and guidance

Information and guidance services are becoming more important.

Good information, and efficient and equitable access to it, are important if young people's decisions on jobs and courses of study are to be based on informed choices. In addition to information, young people need personal advice and guidance to clarify their interests and goals and to understand the opportunities and risks that they face in the labour market. Information and guidance are becoming more important as young people face more choices – and more complex choices – among increasingly diverse education, training

---

23. In the case of teenagers it would also have had an impact upon the improvement observed in the incidence of long-term unemployment. As with other factors influencing young people's transition outcomes, effective safety nets for those at risk interact with overall labour market conditions.

and employment options. In particular, information and guidance can play an important role in encouraging those tempted by early school leaving to acquire at least an upper secondary level qualification, and in helping early leavers to find their way back into the system. Recent research indicates the positive effects of very focused guidance and counselling in the development of young people's competency in problem solving, handling interpersonal conflicts and work disciplines and job search skills during the transition phase (Hannan and Werquin, 1999).

As the emphasis shifts from pre-determined pathways and single exit points to modularised and interconnected programmes, young people have to construct more individualised routes through education and training systems. Information and guidance therefore need to respond to more varied needs. And they must support regular personal career planning by all young people over increasingly expanded periods. The trend is away from the matching model – orienting young people towards occupational choices and corresponding pathways and jobs – toward more developmental models – aiming to prepare self-directed individuals who take responsibility for their own choices and progression (OECD/CERI, 1996).

And need to address more varied needs over expanded periods of time.

The focus of information and guidance services differs across countries. In those with strong vocational education systems and occupationally organised labour markets, information and guidance are likely to insist on occupational choice as the basis for educational decisions, even if more individualised guidance methods are applied. Austria and Switzerland are examples.[24] In countries such as Canada, the United States and Japan, where general education pathways dominate and where a smaller proportion of the labour market is occupationally organised, the principle aim of guidance is more likely to be to orient young people towards education and training pathways according to their educational success and inclinations. Finally, in countries where education systems have been modularised, such as Finland and the United Kingdom, the emphasis will shift to more individualised counselling and career development.

The focus of information and guidance differs across countries.

In recent years information and guidance have been part of important educational reforms in most of the countries participating in the Thematic Review. In addition, information and guidance have become an increasingly important aspect of labour market measures for young people, especially for the long-term unemployed and for others at risk of being excluded. In some countries – for example Norway and the United Kingdom – enhanced co-operation can be observed between schools and local enterprises in informing young people about the world of work. A trend toward stronger linkages between guidance services in schools and in employment services can be seen in some countries such as Austria, Finland and the United Kingdom. Often these developments aim to overcome a perceived academic bias in advice

Many examples of innovation and good practice can be found across countries, but much remains to be done.

---

24. In Denmark, vocational education and occupational labour markets are also strongly developed, and substantial national emphasis is placed upon guidance, both within schools and elsewhere. However, interestingly, in that country the major emphasis in school-based guidance appears to be on educational choice and personal development. Information on occupations, as opposed to courses, appears relatively less well provided.

and guidance and to encourage students to consider alternative vocational pathways. However, the spread and depth of innovation vary within and across countries and much remains to be done in order to improve the quality, coherence and accessibility of information and guidance services and to overcome the divide between different providers.

In some countries career education is included in the curriculum.

A significant trend in some countries in recent years has been the development of career education as part of the regular curriculum in all or part of lower secondary education. Examples include Austria, the Czech Republic, the United Kingdom, about half of the Canadian provinces, and many of the states of the United States in many cases as a result of funds provided under the 1994 School to Work Opportunities Act.

Many career education programmes use active learning methods such as project work and short periods of work experience or job shadowing in local enterprises. They frequently involve local employers and managers, not only as providers of work experience but sometimes also as lecturers who come to the school in order to talk to students and answer their questions (Watts, 1994; Dusseldorp Skills Forum and Career Education Association of Victoria, 1997). Many examples exist of attractive and well prepared curriculum material to support these initiatives, often drawing heavily upon multimedia resources and encouraging students to manage their own learning.

Career education most commonly encourages young people to explore their social and economic environment, to identify key features of jobs, and to start thinking about their own interests, strengths, weaknesses, and plans for the future. At the lower secondary stage the aim is mainly to motivate students at a critical age of adolescence and to prepare them to choose among upper secondary pathways. Nevertheless, those young people who move from compulsory education directly to specific occupational programmes or apprenticeships have to make decisive occupational choices at this relatively early stage.

But in many inequalities in access to advice and guidance persist.

A common problem is that less successful students often receive insufficient or inappropriate guidance and support within schools, and that the greatest guidance effort and the most detailed information are concentrated upon tertiary bound students. This was noted in the Danish review, has been noted in Australian research (Byrne and Beavers, 1993), and has been commented upon in research comparing vocational guidance in the United Kingdom and continental Europe in the early 1990s (Jarvis, 1994).

And academically-oriented students are insufficiently informed about working life and alternative pathways.

On the other hand, academically oriented general education students in most countries tend to get little information and guidance about the world of work, with the information and guidance provided for them concentrating heavily upon tertiary education. This is of particular concern in countries where many young people in the general education pathway do not, or do not directly, move on to tertiary education at the end of upper secondary education. For example in Australia, Canada, Finland, Hungary, Norway, Portugal, and Sweden it seems as if between a third and a half of those in the general education pathway fall into this category. Many such young people risk experiencing a lengthy and unproductive transition period between the end of secondary education and settling down in employment, and they are of significant policy concern in some countries. Better information and guidance about the world of work, not only about tertiary study, could help many of these young people to avoid or minimise such problems.

While it is common for schools in many countries to develop informal contacts with employers, and for employers to approach schools informally when they want to hire young people, it is rare to find institutionalised linkages such as those that exist in Japan.[25] Australia's recent Job Pathways Programme, which provides funds to schools to allow them to undertake a job placement function for their graduates, is a significant exception.

Organised job placement and follow-up through educational institutions is increasing – but not rapidly enough.

Job placement and student follow-up appear to be much more developed in tertiary institutions, especially in countries where such institutions – be they public or private – have to compete for students in order to ensure their budgets. Traditionally this has been the case mainly in North America, and an impressive example of well organised and continuous co-operation with employers can be found at Canada's Sherbrooke University in Quebec. In recent years growing numbers of tertiary institutions in European countries are also moving in this direction. The Center for Occupational Planning at the Wirtschaftsuniversität Wien in Austria provides an example of successful counselling and placement services, including the organisation of job fairs with the participation of several thousand firms. In an interesting model, the careers service at the University of Stockholm, which offers students career planning, job search and placement services, is staffed and funded by Sweden's public employment service.

Computerised methods of delivering career information and guidance have been greatly improved in recent years in all the countries visited. They can be located in schools, in mobile facilities that serve several schools, or in employment centres or information centres which serve both school students and those who have left school. They allow for self-directed exploration of occupations, jobs and labour market opportunities, of typical education and training pathways, and of courses offered by educational institutions. The most impressive examples enable young people to establish their personal profiles based on structured self-exploration and self-assessment of preferences, interests and abilities, and to match these against the characteristics of jobs and courses (Holland, 1997). In some cases, information on labour market outcomes for graduates from different pathways is available at national and regional or provincial level. In Finland, at the time of the country review, the intention was to provide information on labour market outcomes for individual schools.

Computerised guidance services have been greatly improved.

Young people seem to enjoy this type of exploration. However for it to be effective, investment in hardware and software needs to be complemented by time and resources being devoted to other elements of career assistance which allow young people to fully exploit the potential of electronic information: careers lessons as a mandatory part of the curriculum; work experience; and qualified face to face counselling for those who need it.

But they need to be part of a coherent strategy.

---

25. For a more detailed presentation of the famous *Jisseki-Kankei* system see Section 4.2.

Expansion and integration of career services can be observed.

Information and guidance services have traditionally been located in schools and employment offices, which have often pursued partly different objectives. School-based services have frequently concentrated on the academic success of students, while the priority in employment offices has been given to job placement. As the borderlines between learning and work have become blurred, increased co-operation between schools and employment offices has been promoted in many countries. This co-operation has sprung

---

Box 4.9. **Two countries with highly developed – yet very different – information and guidance systems**

Austria

In Austria extraordinary importance is attached to information and guidance for youth. This is related both to rapid change in the labour market, and to a highly differentiated education and training system which requires career-related educational choices to be made at an early age. Vocational information and guidance are provided in many forms, both as the result of legal regulations, and spontaneously through the co-operation of a large number of actors. Local or regional employer and trade union organisations run information and guidance centres for young people. These are in addition to services provided in schools and employment offices. In addition, different ministries, the social partners, educational institutions, regions and municipalities work together: for example to organise career fairs which attract large numbers of visitors. The variety of agencies involved allows young people with different needs to be served effectively, even if at times the plethora of information and guidance providers can become confusing. It also encourages those looking for advice to compare information and suggestions coming from different sources and perspectives. Young Austrians' knowledge of working life is also enhanced by widespread opportunities for structured work experience, both for apprentices and for students in full-time vocational schools.

In spite of extensive information and guidance, Austria experiences relatively high drop-out (drop-down) rates from upper secondary and tertiary education. There has been a tendency to hold information and guidance services responsible for these problems. On closer inspection, however, high drop-out rates appear to be related to a number of barriers and inconsistencies in the structure and functioning of educational pathways in Austria, rather than to weaknesses in the guidance system.

Japan

In Japan, counselling and guidance in schools plays an important role in orienting students toward different educational pathways and employment options. At the same time it forms part of the wider *Jisseki-Kankei* system of close and institutionalised linkages between individual firms and individual schools (Dore and Sako, 1998). As 97% of lower secondary students move on to upper secondary education, counselling at this stage concentrates on choosing the right school according to student aptitudes and achievement. In upper secondary education the national curriculum requires ten hours per year to be devoted to career education. Career guidance teachers are appointed from regular teachers and are given a time allocation for tasks which include career guidance classes, employer visits and interviews with school graduates. In addition, normal classroom teachers frequently undertake individual counselling with all of their students. Career guidance differs strongly for students in general and vocational courses. For general education students it focuses on testing, advice and orientation toward universities that are of different levels of prestige. Vocational education students receive more varied information and guidance, including on different options of employment or further education. Students in higher education also profit from different kinds of guidance and job placement support through teachers, and through guidance and placement offices (and, increasingly, from internship during their studies). Japan's Employment Security Law has, for many years, given schools a special role in the job placement of their graduates. It enables the Public Employment Service Office to delegate parts of its functions to secondary schools, allowing them to deal directly with employers (Kariya, 1999; Yoshimoto, 1996).

The integration and intensity of guidance and placement services in educational institutions has contributed decisively to Japan's long-standing positive record of young people's transition to working life. Yet concerns exist about the quality of guidance training for teachers, and about student dissatisfaction with a system which sorts them according to educational success rather than their interests.

both from responsible ministries and from local initiative. The United Kingdom has transformed the career services formerly run by local education authorities into government financed "companies". These are expected to act as intermediaries between schools, colleges, private training providers, enterprises and Training and Enterprise Councils. Careers Service companies provide counselling and placement to young people up to the age of 18. To the extent that education and training providers compete for students in local and regional markets such intermediary institutions can come to play a major role in the functioning of education and training markets.

Within schools, there is need for student counselling to encompass personal, welfare and educational advice, in addition to career information and guidance. Where such comprehensive guidance services are provided they can improve not only the quality of students' educational and occupational decisions, but also their educational performance and the overall climate of the school. A study on a large scale project of this sort in Missouri, USA provides empirical evidence for this argument Lapan et al., 1997).

As labour market measures for unemployed young people and those at risk of exclusion have become more active – often providing young people with formal qualifications rather than short unrecognised training – information and guidance services in community settings and labour offices have come to play an increasingly important role. More active approaches to labour market assistance typically combine unemployment benefits or other financial support with obligatory participation in one of several possible education, training and employment programmes. Information and guidance services must therefore try to reach these young people as early as possible, inform them about alternative programmes and financial conditions and help them to choose solutions in line with their interests and abilities. They must also keep track of programme participants in order to monitor progression and evaluate outcomes after the end of the programme. Section 4.3 outlines the important role that advice and guidance play in the safety nets put in place in some of the Nordic countries in recent years.

Improved guidance and support for young people at risk is important.

In many of the countries participating in the Thematic Review there is a growing recognition that advice and guidance must be an integrated element of the assistance provided to unemployed and at-risk youth (Martin, 1998). The New Deal programme in the United Kingdom is currently among the best-known examples. Personalised support and guidance is an essential element of the tightly woven safety nets that have helped to keep the incidence of long-term unemployment low among youth in some Nordic countries. If they are to be effective, such measures require large numbers of trained and qualified advisors, working in close contact with local schools, employers and social services.

While excellent examples exist in all the countries reviewed, what is commonly lacking is a systematic policy priority being attached to information and guidance, backed by clear objectives and adequate resources so that good examples can spread more widely. The dispersion of responsibility across different levels of government, administrations, and private institutions and competition or insufficient co-operation between different providers are among the reasons for less than satisfactory results.

Excellent initiatives and examples sit alongside a lack of policy coherence, insufficient commitment and insufficient resources in most countries.

There is wide variation between countries participating in the Thematic Review in a number of key dimensions of information and guidance. However an even greater concern is the wide variation that can be observed within many countries in these dimensions: whether or not career education is a mandatory part of the curriculum; the location of principal responsibility for organising information and guidance (the school or other agencies); the ways in which services are provided; the financial and human resources available; and the training and qualifications of those who provide the services. All of these point to a lack of clear policy objectives and priorities for information and guidance.

A climate of financial restraint and devolution of responsibility for funding to individual schools or regions has, in many countries, resulted in the real resources available for information and guidance declining. This has coincided with education reforms that would have required additional guidance capacity in order to enhance their effectiveness and efficiency. Such problems have been observed in Canada, in Finland, and in Sweden, but these are by no means the only countries experiencing similar difficulties.

Within schools, information and guidance are often marginal and poorly resourced activities rather than functions that are central to and clearly integrated with the wider educational purposes of the school. Particular difficulties relate to the guidance qualifications of teachers and specialised counsellors in schools, including their knowledge and understanding of the world of work outside of schools. Another frequently mentioned problem is the lack of time set aside for individual counselling of students.

Some countries have at least one academically qualified and specialised counsellor per school who is not in charge of other teaching or administrative tasks (often a psychologist with additional training in vocational guidance). But most countries provide only in-service career education and guidance training of varying length and depth for teachers in charge of other subjects. The location of in-depth career counselling either in schools or in employment offices or special centres remains a matter of debate. However this does not justify insufficient attention and resources being attached to the qualifications of guidance workers, or insufficient time being allocated to different guidance functions – wherever they are located.

The key question: how to provide universal access to high quality information and guidance in affordable ways?

All young people have a right to help in forging their careers, in the broader sense of a lifelong progression through learning and work. In this process a number of their needs must be met. These include needs for: self knowledge and awareness; educational and occupational information and exploration; skills in decision making and career planning; and the skills to implement plans and decisions (Conger, 1994; Maddy-Bernstein and Cunanan, 1995). If these needs are to be met, universal access to high quality information and guidance is required. The key question for national transition policies is how this can be done in both an affordable and an effective way.

Traditionally such services have been based upon two models: an educational model centred upon teaching in classrooms; and a counselling model, based upon one-to-one interaction between the young person and an adviser. Both have major weaknesses as the basis for universal and affordable high quality careers services. The classroom-based model carries the risk of the teacher lacking expertise in all areas of young people's career preferences, and of the teacher working from an increasingly out of date knowledge base as the world of work changes. It carries a risk of being too focused upon young people's future educational choices, and not sufficiently focused upon job choice. The counsellor-based model can also carry these risks. In addition it is a very expensive option if access to services is to be universal and if the full range of young people's needs is to be met. Both models rely heavily upon the qualifications of vocational guidance and career education specialists, and upon the amount of time allocated to their work. With greatly increased numbers of young people requiring information and guidance, both models imply an increase in guidance personnel to a level which would hardly be affordable in any country.

These traditional models have therefore been contrasted with a more open and comprehensive approach, in which the role of counsellors and teachers is complemented and supported by a coherent set of strategies: career education is more strongly embedded in the curriculum; computers and other media are used extensively; and less formal guidance sources such as alumni, parents, employers and community members are encouraged and enabled to provide careers assistance (Watts, 1994; Dusseldorp Skills Forum and Career Education Association of Victoria, 1997; Chiousse and Werquin, 1999). Such a comprehensive approach requires the role of the careers specialist to be broadened from that of a teacher or counsellor to one which combines teaching or counselling with extensive co-ordinating tasks.

For many young people, particularly those at risk in the transition, face to face counselling and guidance will clearly remain an essential element of the advice and guidance that they need at one or the other stage of education and training. If this is to be effective counsellors and guidance staff need qualifications at a high standard and adequate support through their working conditions.

High quality and affordable information and guidance services for all should be built around the following key elements, rather than being developed exclusively around either the counselling or the classroom based models:

- The production by specialist organisations of high quality information on jobs and working life in several formats.
- The use by students of self-directed techniques (multimedia, paper, group process) of personal assessment and job and course exploration.
- The inclusion of mandatory career education and orientation in the school curriculum.
- Opportunities for all students to undertake periods of experience in real work settings; and
- Systematic and organised involvement by community members such as employers, alumni and parents.

Such a comprehensive policy approach to information and guidance needs to be embedded in wider strategies linking educational, labour market and social welfare services for young people in a client oriented way.

4.5. Effective institutions and processes

Comparative studies of the transition to work (for example Hannan, Raffe and Smyth, 1996; Stern and Wagner, 1999; Shavit and Müller, 1998) have a long tradition of focusing upon the role of national institutional arrangements (pathways, curriculum frameworks, qualification systems, training regulations, labour market structures and the like) in shaping transition outcomes. Clearly these are important. Table 2.1a shows that, of the countries participating in the Thematic Review, Japan, Switzerland, Austria and Norway are the most likely to achieve successful transition outcomes. They are also the least likely to fall

Effective transition outcomes depend upon effective transition institutions.

within the bottom quartile of the OECD on the indicators used in the table to assess transition outcomes. In each of these countries strong institutional arrangements exist to manage young people's transitions, and these arrangements have been developed over a long period. However the nature of effective transition institutions can vary widely from country to country.

In the case of Japan major problems in the transition from school to work in the 1950s and 1960s were the stimulus for the development of national institutions (the *Jisseki Kankei* system described in Section 4.2) that result in strong and close relationships being developed between schools and firms, and in smooth and effective recruitment of school leavers. These support and reinforce clear understanding on the part of schools, young people and employers of the criteria used in recruiting youth. They support and reinforce trust by employers in the capacity of schools to develop the aptitudes that they are seeking, and trust in the assessments that teachers make of young people. Japan has been able to achieve good transition outcomes for its youth despite few opportunities for young people to gain workplace experience as students, despite little that resembles the tightly organised pathways of the apprenticeship countries, and despite relatively underdeveloped safety nets for those who fail to obtain a secure place in education or employment.

In both Switzerland and Austria strong apprenticeship and vocational education systems are supported by system-wide quality assurance through laws, agreements or regulations. These are based not just on token consultation, but on shared ownership of the key institutions that manage the system by key stakeholders (employers, trade unions, regional and state governments). Many of the reforms of the past decade, concerning the re-definition of training occupations and the innovation of training curricula have indeed been initiated and actively promoted by the social partners Norway also has a strong tradition of involving employers, trade unions and other key stakeholders in the on-going management and quality assurance of its vocational education and training system in order to develop shared ownership, and a tradition of building these around negotiated consensus. Such approaches which are based on social partnership, strong institutional frameworks and strong traditions of co-operation between all the actors involved also tend to ensure a good balance between innovation and continuity. While the incremental responsiveness of such training systems to economic change is high, they are usually less than other systems submitted to a continuous series of major reforms.

In other cases, in countries where transition outcomes are not as strong, greater difficulty has been experienced in building effective institutional frameworks to support young people's transition to work. The reasons for this are varied. Since 1989 Hungary has had to build much of the necessary institutional framework from scratch (Lannert, 1999). With little tradition of civil society for some decades, it has had to put in place not only a completely new set of laws and regulations to guide education and training, but also the institutions needed to support them: a modern trade union movement, a network of employer organisations, economic chambers, vocational education and training advisory structures. These efforts have coincided with very difficult labour market circumstances. In the United Kingdom a complex framework has evolved over time to set the standards for, ensure the quality of and finance education and training. Much of this framework has been developed centrally, within government agencies. The complexity of the framework has made it relatively non-transparent to many of those whose commitment is needed for its implementation. In Canada major regional differences and wide ethnic and cultural diversity have made coherent framework development and institution building more difficult. In addition a reliance upon immigration as a significant source of skilled labour has, over a long period, helped to lessen the pressures for organised involvement by employer associations in education and training.

In Austria, Norway and Switzerland the institutional involvement of key stakeholders underpins the on-going management of the vocational education and training systems through which a majority of youth pass. It is also central to the development of new policy initiatives: pathway structures, curriculum frameworks, qualification systems, training regulations, and wage arrangements that support young people's transition to working life. Among the elements that are important in the successful implementation of new transition policy initiatives are an appropriate balance between national, regional and local level actors, and a balance between bottom-up and top-down approaches. Too heavy a reliance upon local initiative, especially if not combined with adequate resources, can lead to problems with quality assurance and regional inequalities. Too heavy a reliance upon centralised decision making will prevent responsiveness to varied and changing skill requirements. Denmark provides a good example of the combination of decentralisation and devolution of responsibility within a negotiated system-wide regulatory framework. It is described in Box 4.10.

Effective policy processes must complement effective institutions.

Box 4.10. **Combining central regulation with local flexibility: the Danish apprenticeship system**

Denmark's technical and commercial colleges are central to the country's vocational education and training system. Each college's board of directors must by law consist of a majority made up of representatives of management and labour from local enterprises.

The local training committee for each programme, also made up of representatives of management and labour, takes responsibility for reviewing the applications of firms to offer apprenticeship training, to see whether that firm is capable of offering a programme to the student that will enable the student to reach the standards in the training regulation. It will either deny the authority to the firm to offer a programme if it finds deficiencies, or require the employer to make arrangements with another employer to offer those parts of the required programme that they cannot themselves offer. The local training committee can also terminate the authority of a firm to offer an apprenticeship programme if it believes that the firm can no longer provide the training and experience that will allow its apprentices to achieve the required standards.

When the student has completed the programme, he or she is examined by a team typically consisting of a teacher, one representative of management, and one representative of labour. All of the reviewers are required to be experts in their field and to use the national regulations for that trade as the basis of their assessments of the candidate's competence.

Local training boards and their representatives on the colleges' occupational programme committees are given quite a lot of latitude in interpreting the national skill standards, as described in the regulations. Nevertheless, it not infrequently happens that a local committee will find that the regulations have not kept up with changes in the state of the art. Because competitiveness increasingly depends on operating at the cutting edge of such changes, Danish law provides that the local committee can go the rector of the local college with a request for exemption from the training regulations or a request that the national boards change the regulations. The rector must forward such requests to the government and the government must act on them promptly.

National and local, bottom-up and top-down approaches need to be balanced.

Although the nature of social dialogue can be quite different between countries, within the so-called apprenticeship countries employer and trade union involvement in education and training occurs not only within peak national bodies, but also intensively at the local and regional level. And it occurs in areas that extend beyond apprenticeship training: career advice; labour market programmes; and full-time vocational schooling are among the more important of these. For example in Austria local employers' chambers and local trade union bodies are heavily involved in the provision of advice, information and guidance to young people to assist in their choice of an apprenticeship, as they are in the assessment of apprentices within a nationally regulated training framework. Local employers' chambers play an important additional role in quality control by assessing the capacity of enterprises to provide the breadth and quality of training required before an apprentice can be hired. In Norway, where, unlike in Austria and Switzerland, employers are not compelled to belong to an employer organisation, the creation of sufficient apprenticeship places to meet demand, as envisaged by reforms introduced in 1994, was more difficult than many in the national employer and trade union organisations had expected. This resulted in substantial effort to communicate the reforms to members at the local level and to persuade them of the importance of creating increased apprenticeship opportunities for youth.

Monitoring and evaluation help policy makers to learn.

Building learning – from successes and from mistakes – into the policy process is an important element in effective policy implementation. This has been one of the reasons for countries participating in the Thematic Review: they were interested in critical views as well as support for current transition initiatives. Learning as part of policy implementation can take several forms. One is the deliberate use of monitoring and evaluation as part of policy development. Box 4.11 provides an example of the deliberate integration of monitoring and evaluation into a major reform of transition pathways.

Box 4.11. **Building monitoring and evaluation into policy implementation**

In 1994 Norway initiated major reforms to upper secondary education. They have led to reduced drop out rates, more rapid re-insertion of drop outs, improved flows through the school system, increased participation in vocational education and training, and increased access to apprenticeships by youth. Reform 94 involved a sharing of responsibilities between the national and county levels of government and individual schools, and an enhanced role for employers. This made it even more important – but also more difficult – to gain an overview of what was happening in upper secondary education and of the outcomes for school leavers. On-going evaluation in order to improve the information base on Norwegian education and training is a notable feature of the implementation of Reform 94. Seven research institutes were commissioned to monitor and evaluate various aspects of the changes brought about by the reform. Topics studied included: the initial cohort's flow through the various levels of courses; the division of responsibilities among education authorities at different levels, and the ways that they interact with each other; the organisation and content of vocational education programmes; the impact of the reform on young people with special needs; and the effectiveness of follow-up services for early leavers.

An important aspect of the evaluations is that they were required to provide information and insights while the studies were in progress. This enabled quick decisions to be taken on adjustments to the reform process. The use of independent research institutes to conduct the evaluations increased the credibility of the evaluation process, compared to the government conducting them itself. The number and range of research institutes involved has broadened the range of perspectives brought to bear on the process, and also deepened the pool of expertise available for future evaluations.

Another way to build learning into the policy development process is to use pilot projects to test the feasibility of new approaches and to monitor the performance of new institutions. Finland has done this with the upper secondary experiments mentioned in Chapter 5, and with the introduction of new non-university tertiary institutions. Sweden has done the same both with the major reforms to upper secondary education introduced during the 1990s, and with more recent experiments with the re-introduction of apprenticeships. Yet another way for countries to learn in implementing transition policies is a readiness to accept successful local initiatives as the basis for wider policies and programmes. Lessons learned from successful local initiatives were important in shaping the nature of the reforms that flowed from the 1994 School to Work Opportunities Act in the United States. Successful local initiatives were an important basis for the 1994 decision by the Australian government to stimulate local school-industry partnerships through establishing the national Australian Student Traineeship Foundation.

Pilot projects and successful local initiatives can also provide lessons for wider policy initiatives.

Many countries participating in the Thematic Review have undertaken reforms during the 1990s to education, employment and social and welfare policies in order to improve young people's transition to work. Some of these reforms have been incremental, some have been of the "big bang" variety. Some have been comprehensive, others have focused upon only single aspects of the transition. Norway and Finland have implemented a comprehensive reform to their upper secondary pathways encompassing several policy domains; Hungary has put in place a comprehensive set of structural reforms to build a new institutional foundation for education and training.

Co-ordinated and comprehensive reforms are to be preferred.

Lack of co-ordination and coherence can impede good policy development and implementation. Where policy co-ordination is less than optimal policies can work at cross purposes; gaps in provision can emerge, and some young people's needs may not be assessed adequately; and good practice, innovation and new ideas may not be disseminated effectively. Policy coherence has both horizontal and vertical aspects: between different national policy portfolios, and at times within the one portfolio; between national and regional levels of government; and between governments and other key stakeholders.

Isolated or partial reforms at best result in partial success. As in other areas of social policy the most successful reforms are comprehensive (Agell, 1999; Werner, 1999). They consider education, employment and social and welfare issues. And within any one of these domains they are comprehensive. For example within education they consider the curriculum, qualifications, advice and guidance, teacher training, and evaluation and monitoring. Within the employment domain they consider wages, employer incentives, and labour market assistance for those at risk. Within the social and welfare domain they consider income support, the impact of income support upon incentives to participate in education and employment, and the young person's needs for support and guidance. An additional key element is a strong will to reform, and persistence in seeking to implement reforms over an extended period (Gill *et al.*, 1999).

Sound transition outcomes require effective personal relationships between the key parties involved, in addition to successful institutional structures and effective implementation processes (Abrahart and Tzannatos, 1999). These key parties include individual young people, their teachers, employers, parents and community members, not simply representative organisations.

Effective relationships improve the transition.

The success of Japanese school to work transition structures has been ascribed to their ability to build and reinforce linkages between these key parties (Rosenbaum, 1999). In Japan the semi-formalised recruitment contracts with specific firms that exist at the school level are replaced at the tertiary level by the deliberate use, by firms as well as by universities, of alumni networks. These networks are used to convey information about jobs and firms to current students, as well as to convey information about potential recruits to firms (Kariya, 1999). Effective co-operation between the key parties in the transition process, based upon shared expectations, is important for several reasons: it can improve the quality of information sharing, help build mutual obligations, and promote trust and sharing. All of these help to reduce the chances of young people falling through the cracks of different programmes run by different sectors and levels of government. The tracking mechanisms that are typical of the safety net measures described in Section 4.3 and their associated local delivery mechanisms are important ways of creating and reinforcing the individual relationships and linkages that assist young people's transitions.

Many countries are trying to encourage local partnerships as a way of improving the transition.

Both in countries with and without strong institutionalised connections between employers and initial education and training, there is growing interest in education-industry partnerships as a way of sharing responsibility for young peoples' transitions (OECD/CERI, 1992). Such partnerships are most relevant – and perhaps most needed – in societies that do not have strong traditions of close collaboration between government, employers, trade unions and community organisations. In some instances the development of local partnerships and intermediary bodies has been stimulated by government policy. In other cases such developments have occurred because employers and others have perceived serious deficiencies in public policy on transition.

Of particular interest are partnerships at the local or regional level between enterprises (or chambers of enterprises), educational institutions, labour market services and community organisations to assist in programme delivery and in the tailoring of programmes to local circumstances. Growth in local partnerships between schools, employers and communities can be seen in countries as diverse as Australia, Austria, Canada, Norway and the United States. In some of these cases local partnerships are seen as a way to help build close collaboration between government, employers, trade unions and community organisations from the ground up. In other cases they are seen as a way to supplement existing institutional co-operation between these parties at the national level. For example they are an element of Austrian programmes for hard-to-place apprenticeship candidates, in which training is shared over mixed settings: enterprises (sometimes several firms), intermediate training workshops and vocational schools.

Local partnerships can serve a wide variety of purposes.

Local partnerships can serve a wide variety of purposes. At their most basic level they are a way to marshal local employer support for a school or a group of schools. This involvement often carries few immediate benefits to employers other than enhancement of their community reputation. At this basic level employer support can involve providing equipment and materials, providing speakers for schools' career education programmes, providing short work experience placements to help students' career choices, and providing short periods of teacher placement to update teachers' understanding of developments in the workplace. Local partnerships can also be a way to organise employers and community members as mentors and advisers for students at risk, and of gaining community input into curriculum development. Often such local partnerships are staffed and managed on a part-time and voluntary basis by school staff and community members. They require few formal resources, but can also have a limited lifespan, being hard to sustain without solid benefits for both schools and employers (OECD/CERI, 1992).

Where schools have extensive workplace learning and workplace experience programmes, local partnerships can often be the vehicle through which employer support is organised and sufficient work placements are provided, through which programmes are managed, and through which quality assurance takes place. Such partnerships require more extensive resources: often a full-time co-ordinator or programme manager; office facilities; support for travel and employer visits; and access to employer training programmes and on-the-job assessment tools. Sometimes these resources are provided on a shared basis by schools and communities, but most typically they are provided by schools alone. If such programmes are provided within a single school their resourcing remains a matter for the school. However where they are adopted as a matter of policy as a system-wide approach to providing workplace experience, the resources that are required to make them operate effectively become a matter for central policy makers.

Building and maintaining partnerships is often not easy where there is not a strong institutional framework, such as well organised employer associations, to support them. The Australian experience shows that employer participation is often quite passive, with most of the responsibility for managing and operating partnerships being taken by the school, despite the existence of clear recruitment benefits for firms (Malley, Frigo and Robinson, 1999). Experience in countries that have been active in developing and promoting partnerships between schools and firms to assist young peoples' transitions, as well as research conducted in the United States (Stern *et al.*, 1994; Villeneuve and Grubb, 1996; Bassi *et al.*, 1997) point to some common elements that help to make local partnerships work to the benefit of students. These are set out in Box 4.12: they have much in common with lessons learned in other OECD work on the features that help local employment development partnerships to work (OECD, 1999c). There are strong parallels between the features that make local partnerships work effectively and the features that support effective national transition institutions: genuine ownership by all parties rather than token consultation; shared common expectations; and mutual benefits. Where such features are absent, and trust, information sharing and mutual obligations are absent, local partnerships can easily founder (Taylor, 1999).

Local partnerships are not easy to develop and sustain, but can be successful if some basic ground rules are followed.

A related response to the problem of weak formal institutional structures to support the transition has been for governments to create or encourage new types of organisations to provide an intermediary or bridging role. Intermediary bodies, acting as brokers between the young person, schools, employers and training organisations, are, in a number of countries, a special case of the way in which local initiatives can assist young people's transition from initial education to work. In many of the countries participating in the Thematic Review the creation of local partnerships and intermediary bodies to improve the transition to work has been a deliberate element of government policy. In the United States a major result of the 1994 School to Work Opportunities Act has been the provision of funds for the creation of local partnerships between schools and business to improve young people's transition to work or further

In many countries governments are creating or encouraging intermediary bodies or brokers in order to improve the transition.

> **Box 4.12. Making local partnerships between schools and firms a success**
>
> Local partnerships between schools and firms seem to work best if:
> – Genuine ownership by employers and community members is fostered, so that they have real rather than token responsibility in matters such as programme management, the operation and delivery of programmes, and student selection.
> – They are resourced properly, so that teachers and other facilitators are provided with sufficient time to visit firms, place students appropriately, assist firms with assessment where this is an element of programmes, and resolve problems that may arise between the student and the firm.
> – There is appropriate support, resource materials and training for employers and employees who have the direct responsibility for supervising and training students while they are in the workplace, or who play a direct role within the school by giving talks or in other ways.
> – There are close ongoing personal relationships between the teachers, employers and employees involved; and
> – Benefits flow both to the student and to the firm: for example such as improved skills and employment prospects for students and more efficient recruitment of school leavers, improved training skills for employees, and an improved community image for the firm.

study. The Australian Student Traineeship Foundation, created in 1994 to encourage workplace learning partnerships as part of upper secondary education, is another example. In addition to seed funding to help create partnerships, it helps to promote change through fostering networking, through research, through public information and through advocacy. Another option to encourage employer involvement, which can be observed in Canada, is for employers to be compensated through wage subsidies or tax credits for the costs incurred in providing school students with structured experience in work.

Intermediary organisations, frequently operating on a not-for-profit basis, can deliver significant benefits both to young people and to firms. They can spread training over a number of different firms where individual firms cannot provide exposure to a wide range of skills, or do not have the resources to provide a full package of training by themselves. This expands the capacity of smaller and medium sized enterprises to take part in formal training arrangements and ensures that young people's training retains breadth and coherence. Intermediary bodies can assist firms through the experience that they develop in selecting and recruiting apprentices and trainees. For the young person intermediary bodies can both help to expand their training opportunities and reduce the time and cost involved in finding an apprenticeship. Australia's Group Training Schemes, illustrated in Box 4.13, perform such a function.

The United Kingdom is probably the country which has invested most effort in systematically "engineering" not only new pathways, but also a complex set of institutions to implement educational reforms and new policies to improve young people's transition to employment. At the local level, 100 Training and Enterprise Councils[26] (TECs) were established to act as brokers between training providers, employers and young people (as well as adult learners). TECs and LECs are formally private companies, exercising a public mission and financed mainly out of public budgets. They are led by a board whose chairperson and a majority of members must be representatives of private enterprise. The other board members represent the public sector, trade

---
26. In Scotland referred to as Local Enterprise Councils or LECs.

> **Box 4.13. Group training schemes: sharing young people's training among many employers**
>
> Group training schemes developed in Australia in the 1980s as an alternative to apprentices entering into an indentured contract with a single employer. The schemes, which are normally organised by employer associations or regional development bodies, perform the role of an intermediary between the apprentice and employers. Where firms are too small to take on a full-time apprentice, or where the firm's work is too specialised to provide an apprentice with broad experience, the group training company takes on the employment of the apprentice and organises their workplace experience by leasing them on a rotating basis among several different firms. The individual firm is spared the risk and cost of taking on a full-time apprentice, and the young person has more varied work experience than would otherwise have been the case.
>
> Group training schemes have broadened their role to provide a range of employment, training and advisory services for young people. Most group training schemes are organised on a not-for-profit basis. Enterprises receiving apprentices pay the group training scheme a fee based on wage costs, and the group training scheme as the primary employer receives various forms of government financial support and subsidies.
>
> Group training schemes have played an important role in periods of economic downturn by employing "out of trade" apprentices discarded by their original employer. The schemes appeared to have played a major role in encouraging girls to take up apprenticeships in traditionally male domains, and in encouraging structured training in emerging areas such as tourism and retailing.

unions, and voluntary organisations. The main mission of TECs and LECs is to promote local partnerships in support of local economic development, and to implement public training policies and programmes. TECs intervene as mediators and facilitators for large public programmes such as Modern Apprenticeships, National Traineeships, the New Deal and New Start. An example of TEC and LEC intervention is the Compact programme, which involves employers in young people's preparation for working life in the later stages of compulsory education (ages 14-16). Box 4.14 illustrates such an initiative undertaken by one TEC.

In Norway Training Offices assist small firms in a similar way. Organised and approved by county vocational committees, they are commonly located within the regional and sectoral offices of employer groups. Through the pooling by firms of a proportion of their government subsidy payments for apprenticeship training, specialist staff are hired to assist firms with apprenticeship recruitment and assessment, with the development of training plans, and with the rotation of apprentices through several firms in order to ensure training breadth. Inter-enterprise training centres in Austria and Switzerland, in which several firms share common training facilities, are another example of intermediary bodies that help to share the training of apprentices among several enterprises.

Intermediary bodies can assist the transition of young people in other ways. The Austrian Centre of Training Firms assists vocational schools and colleges in the operation of training firms, through which students are able to develop skills in a simulated commercial environment, and it acts as a national co-ordinator of and resource centre for such training firms. In the Czech Republic there are now some 400 simulated enterprises in vocational schools; an annual trade fair of simulated enterprises is held, and links have been established with simulated enterprises and national resource centres in Austria. Australia's Jobs Pathway programme, through which local community organisations act as employment brokers and job placement assistance agencies for school

> **Box 4.14. Gwent Compact**
>
> The Gwent Compact was launched by Gwent TEC. It is a partnership between local schools, colleges and businesses, designed to increase motivation, raise aspirations and improve the achievement records of young people as they prepare for their future careers.
>
> Students, with the help of their tutors, set a number of realistic targets for improvement. Their conduct and achievements are assessed and recorded just as they would be at work. Local employers may also be involved as mentors to students, offering group advice sessions and one to one interviews, mock interview experience, work experience briefing and debriefing sessions, and workplace visits. Students are set targets for attendance, punctuality and attitude to work. If they make substantial improvement they receive certificates and other incentives.
>
> Gwent Compact tries to involve employers by persuading them of the benefits that they will receive through participating. These potential benefits include:
> - Being able to influence the qualities and skills of their future workforce by helping young people to be better motivated, educated and trained for employment.
> - Providing young people with a better understanding of workplace.
> - Helping to ease skill shortages by ensuring that there are sufficiently adequately skilled future employees.
> - Making a positive contribution to the local community by helping young people.
> - Developing the skills of their staff through mentoring students.

leavers, is intended to improve young people's access to local labour market knowledge.

Young people under the age of 25 constitute a significant proportion of the employees of temporary hire agencies in the United States. Such agencies can act as intermediary bodies, assisting the transition to stable employment by job rotation that provides wider experience and a greater network of employer contacts, and through skills assessment and training programmes (Seavey and Kazis, 1994). Australia's La Trobe University has struck a strategic alliance with a major personnel and recruitment firm to help its graduates find work. In return for preferred labour supplier status to the university, the firm will offer students part-time work, career placement on graduation, access to job seeker skills programmes and access to its international network of job and industry information (Healy, 1999).

It is important not to over-complicate the creation of intermediary bodies, as well as to be clear about their purposes.

In the United Kingdom the creation of a wide variety of intermediary bodies between education and business has been a key element of government moves to reform transition arrangements for 16-19 year-olds. In addition to TECs and LECs, other agencies involved in organising, financing and evaluating education and training in preparation of working life include: local Education Business Partnerships, Careers Services, Voluntary Service Councils, the Employment Service, City Councils, Local Education Authorities, National Training Organisations, and numerous bodies that award education and training qualifications Some of these bodies operate at the national level, others at local or sub-regional level.

The creation of all these and other public, private or quasi non governmental organisations was initially motivated by a government objective to establish an education and training market. Public money was to be channelled to education and training providers on a case by case basis, according to the "output" of each provider. In recent years, questions have been raised about the costs and effectiveness of so many intermediaries, and about steering mechanisms which were found to encourage competition for public resources rather than complementarity among training providers – frequently to the detriment of quality and equity. Conflict of interest can also be apparent with the one body at times being both a provider or an awarder of qualifications and a quality controller. At the time of the Thematic Review it was intended to establish Regional Development Agencies which could provide a more coherent organisational framework for education and training provision to young people and adults.

The case of the United Kingdom is of particular interest as an example of government-led system engineering. It illustrates the positive results which can be achieved through strategic planning and active intervention by governments. At the same time, however, it reveals the type of problems which can arise from reforms that are designed at the desks of central administrations and implemented by intermediary bodies which owe their existence to the same offices. It remains to be seen whether employers, trade unions and communities will gradually be able and willing to adopt more active roles as stakeholders and negotiators in the organisation of transition processes.

Whatever the stimulus for the development of local partnerships, governments have an important role to play in monitoring their impact to ensure that quality outcomes are achieved. Governments also have a key role to play in evaluating such initiatives so that that successful strategies are more widely adopted, and mistakes are not repeated. But it is important not to complicate and over-bureaucratise such initiatives, as well as to be clear about their purposes.

4.6. Putting the jigsaw together

The transition from initial education to working life is a complex and multi-faceted policy development and implementation jigsaw. Like a jigsaw, things do not work in isolation, but in combination with one another. Solving it is a matter both of getting the correct pieces on the board and of putting them together correctly. But the number of pieces, their shape and how they fit together will vary from country to country. National cultures, traditions and institutional arrangements influence which pieces can easily be borrowed from other countries, and how easy they are to trim so that they will fit national circumstances. Consequently there can be no single answer to the question of what is effective, nor to questions about what countries should do when the jigsaw is not working properly and needs to be improved. The key ingredients of effective transition frameworks that have been outlined above will work in different ways and in different combinations in different national circumstances.

There is no single answer to effective transition...

Countries can achieve good transition outcomes for many of their young people with quite different combinations of the key pieces of the transition jigsaw. For example: Denmark despite few connections between vocational pathways and tertiary study; Japan with little in the way of safety nets for those at risk and few opportunities for workplace experience; Norway despite relatively high levels of employment protection and high youth to adult unemployment ratios; Sweden for teenagers despite difficult labour market conditions; and the United States despite few well organised pathways for those not bound for tertiary study. Good transition outcomes can be found in countries with quite different institutional arrangements: they can be found in countries in which apprenticeship is the dominant pathway; in countries where the majority of young people take part in school-based vocational education programmes; in countries where general education dominates; and in countries where there is an even mix of all three. Good outcomes can be achieved for teenagers, but not for young adults. They can be better for females than for males, or *vice versa*. Labour market outcomes can be good, but educational outcomes poor, and *vice versa*. Those with higher levels of education generally achieve better outcomes, but not always, and the extent to which they achieve better outcomes varies widely among countries.

... nor is there a single problem

The policy challenges that countries need to face in improving transition outcomes for young people will vary widely according to national circumstances. As an example, differences between countries in the relative levels of unemployment among teenagers and young adults draw attention to the need for different policy priorities in countries such as the United States where it is highest among teenagers compared to countries such as Sweden where it is highest among young adults. In the first group, policy attention is drawn to ways of preventing early school leaving, and to ways of encouraging and supporting early leavers to return to education to gain a full upper secondary qualification. In the second group of countries attention is drawn to the importance of transition policies laying the basis for longer term labour force participation, not just immediate labour market entry, to issues of the transition from tertiary education to the labour market, not just the transition from secondary education to work, and to labour and employment policies that assist young adults to enter work quickly after leaving education, or to re-enter it quickly if unemployed.

Countries with large apprenticeship systems face distinct challenges...

Countries that have large apprenticeship systems face challenges that countries without them do not. They must deal with the problem of what appears to be young people's growing reluctance to embark upon quite specific occupational preparation at an early age, while still retaining the real benefits that apprenticeship has conferred: for example by creating broader entry points to apprenticeship that allow young people better opportunities to sample and experiment before being selected into a particular apprenticeship. Countries in which apprenticeship is large also face the challenge of building better connections between it and tertiary study: through increasing the general education content of vocational programmes; through raising the theoretical level of the vocational content; through creating special bridging programmes; or through creating special tertiary courses and institutions. They also face the challenge of the more inequitable outcomes that are associated with early streaming and a high level of differentiation within transition systems.

... as do countries with large general education systems.

A fundamental problem for countries with large general education systems is how to motivate those whose achievement levels are low or who are simply not interested in or motivated by the prospects of entering tertiary education after the upper secondary level. At the heart of all solutions is the need to establish connections between general education and work in addition to connections between general education and tertiary study. In a sense this is the flip side of the problem facing countries with large vocational education pathways: how to convince students in such programmes that these are not an educational dead end by building links between them and tertiary study.

A number of different solutions can be seen to the problem of building links between general education and work: to date the most successful of these, although not without its own particular problems, is Japan's carefully managed use of school grades and teacher assessments as the key basis for the recruitment of school leavers by employers. This motivates students to work hard at school because they know that how well they perform will have a major impact upon the type of job that they get. Other countries have tried to address the problem by inserting vocational education content into general education programmes. Such attempts have suffered from two sorts of problems. The first is a failure or inability at the same time to build those institutional arrangements which, in addition to curriculum content, help to make vocational education pathways effective: occupationally organised labour markets which require vocational qualifications; well organised employer bodies; and close involvement of organised industry associations in the ongoing operation of vocational education. The second is uncertainty about the purposes of the vocational content: to provide generic employment competencies and to improve career orientation; to motivate students in their general education subjects; to provide partial credit towards a vocational qualification; or to provide a complete vocational qualification at the upper secondary level. An associated problem is students' and parents' fears, in countries in which vocational education has low prestige and tertiary entry is a common objective, that taking too many vocational courses will reduce their chances of entering tertiary education. If the one programme is to meet the two objectives – preparing students both for work and for tertiary study – the solution, as countries such as Austria and Norway have found within their vocational pathways, may inevitably involve an extension of the total length of students' programme of study.

In some countries with large general education systems the thrust of policy initiatives has been to strengthen vocational pathways and vocational qualifications within upper secondary systems that traditionally have not placed a strong emphasis upon preparing young people for working life. In others rebuilding vocational pathways has been seen as a less attractive option. In such cases closer links between schooling and working life can be built in other ways:

- Increasing students' opportunities for contextual learning in community and workplace settings.
- Improving connections between schools and local employers in order to increase students' understanding of the criteria that employers use when selecting school leavers, and employers' understanding of what schools' assessments mean about work-related competencies.
- Improving career information and guidance; and
- Improving the ways that schools both develop and signal generic work related competencies: for example through the use of portfolios and other reporting systems that are based upon wider assessments of student attributes than traditional examinations and grades (Bishop, 1996). In the United States, for example, although high school grades are not widely used by employers when recruiting school leavers, there is evidence that they do in fact predict longer term earnings (Miller, 1998). This argues for better ways to report young peoples' real work-related competences to potential employers.

During the 1990s the integration of school-organised workplace experience into upper secondary programmes has been common both in countries in which general education pathways predominate, and in those that have substantial school-based vocational education pathways. Improving the quality of and outcomes from these programmes should be a key goal everywhere. Building closer connections at the local level between schools and employers is important in doing this. So is improving the management of the local partnerships and intermediary bodies that are often the ways in which workplace experience is organised. Improving the ways in which the organisation of the school helps to support these programmes – in particular through the structure of the school timetable – is also important. Over and above steps that are needed at the local level there is, in some countries, a pressing need to develop the types of national policy and institutional frameworks, within both education and among the industry partners, that are needed to support local initiatives. These frameworks need to address issues such as: the nature and quality of the learning plans that guide students' time in the workplace; the resources that are allocated to programme co-ordination; quality guidelines for employer participation; support and training for employers; and assessment and recognition of the knowledge and skills acquired in the workplace.

Basic labour market institutions can be a barrier to some key features of effective transition systems crossing national borders.

Major barriers to the transplanting across national borders of some of the key features of effective transition systems exist because of differences in the ways in which national labour market institutions work. Where transition outcomes depend upon occupationally organised labour markets and well organised employer associations and trade unions, transplanting part but not all of particular key features is unlikely to be successful. Where outcomes depend upon relatively open and unregulated labour markets, they are unlikely to survive transplanting into countries where labour markets are otherwise organised. This has been one of the principal barriers preventing apprenticeship moving successfully across national borders. Where labour markets are not occupationally organised and occupational qualifications are not a requirement for occupational entry, and where employers are not required to be members of economic chambers, it is difficult to capture many of the key features that make it a successful pathway to work in some countries.

However some key features of effective transition systems are less dependent upon changes to key labour market institutions.

However at least some of the key features of effective transition systems do not appear to be closely dependent upon the basic characteristics of national labour markets, or at the least do not appear to require change to fundamental labour market institutions in order to be effective. Safety net arrangements for early leavers who are at risk in the transition are a prime example. In Nordic countries safety nets that are based upon early intervention to support and assist those at risk appear to be able to operate and be effective in quite different types of labour markets: for example in Sweden where occupational regulation is quite low; and in Denmark where it is quite high. Particularly in those countries where teenage unemployment and inactivity are relatively high, there are a number of valuable lessons to be learned from recent Nordic experience. Policy shifts in favour of earlier intervention and mutual obligations as a basis for assistance can be seen in a number of countries. These are steps in the right direction. The development of local tracking and individualised programme delivery mechanisms to support closer national policy integration across education, employment and welfare is an important next step.

Another example of a key feature of effective transition arrangements that does not appear to hinge upon changes to key labour market institutions is career information and guidance, which almost everywhere needs to be given a clearer priority within national transition arrangements. Here the key priority in many countries must be to develop systematic policy frameworks that can ensure universal access to high quality information and guidance services.

Chapter 5

HOW CAN THE TRANSITION PHASE PROMOTE LEARNING THROUGHOUT LIFE?

The concept of lifelong learning embraces a wide set of aims and strategies, central to which is the notion that learning opportunities should be available over the life-span, and accessible on a wide basis. Many of the strategies needed to give effect to the notion must be implemented in the transition phase. For example OECD Education Ministers have agreed (OECD, 1996c) to foster lifelong learning through promoting coherent links between learning and work, through creating pathways and bridges between the two so that transitions between them can be smooth, and through better mechanisms for recognising skills and competences.

The transition phase must be central to the implementation of lifelong learning strategies.

During the 1990s, many of the countries participating in the Thematic Review have undertaken reforms based upon an assumption that the goals associated with the transition phase should extend beyond getting a first full-time job after leaving initial education and training. These goals include preparing young people for lives in which the boundaries between work and learning are breaking down. The notion of lifelong learning appears to have been a powerful influence upon national reforms to the transition phase in countries as diverse as Denmark, Finland, Sweden, Switzerland and the United Kingdom. The inclusion of initial education and training so prominently within efforts to develop favourable conditions for lifelong learning is a relatively recent development: the concept of lifelong learning has commonly been regarded as relevant primarily for adults (OECD/CERI, 1999).

Lifelong learning has been a powerful notion in the reform of transition policies during the 1990s.

If the goals of the transition phase are limited to the first job, the impact of policies can be evaluated within fairly short time frames. However, it will be another generation before the impact of today's transition policies and programmes upon lifelong learning becomes fully apparent. Only then will it be possible to judge whether the reforms put into place during the 1990s will help the students of today to be successful as the lifelong learners of tomorrow. Lessons based upon today's adults, educated in the schools of a previous generation, provide at best minimal guidance. We know that more initial education encourages and allows greater participation in formal and informal learning by adults, and that less education in the initial phase results in less participation in education and training later on (OECD, 1999a). But we do not know enough about what kind of initial education makes the greatest difference. Nor do we know which institutional frameworks are best suited to make lifelong learning a reality. Different countries have been experimenting with partly similar and partly different strategies, but all are still at the stage of trial and error.

Many of the reforms to the transition phase introduced during the past ten or fifteen years have been designed to meet a number of goals which were initially not seen to relate primarily to promoting lifelong learning: better motivated and more interested students; fewer drop outs; enhanced employability; and more flexible and efficient transition systems are among these. Today, attention is increasingly being paid to the ways in which they may support the development of lifelong learning. For example, policies that encourage young people to combine their education with work have often been put into place mainly to improve the matching of young people's skills to labour demand and to facilitate their transition into a first job. However the opportunity to combine learning and work during the transition period can also send important signals to young people that it is normal for them to organise their lives in this way.

Two kinds of approaches to promoting lifelong learning can be distinguished.

The steps that countries have taken to improve the way in which the transition phase promotes lifelong learning can be seen to fall into two broad categories: structural approaches, focusing on the institutional frameworks of education and training systems; and learner-centred approaches, concentrating on teaching and learning processes. While differences in existing education and training systems may have favoured one or the other kind of approach in the past, it is becoming increasingly evident that the two approaches need to be seen as complementary, and should be developed in tandem.

5.1. Structural approaches to promoting lifelong learning

Structural approaches emphasise the openness and continuity of pathways in initial and further education.

Structural approaches to promoting lifelong learning through reforms affecting the transition stage are aiming to provide institutional alternatives to traditional front-end models of initial education and training. They intend to gradually replace rigid one-way routes from initial education and training to employment with more individualised two-way routes back and forth between learning and work. The ultimate consequence of such approaches could – potentially – be the disappearance of all institutional distinctions between post-compulsory education for young people and formalised adult learning. Underlying this approach is the hope that the transition phase might become less dominated by young people's desire to attain the highest possible tertiary qualifications before leaving initial education, that the early stages of the transition phase (roughly below the age of 20) might place greater emphasis upon learning to learn, and that inequalities produced or reinforced during the transition phase might be reduced.

The following examples briefly illustrate some of the ways in which different countries have tried to ensure the continuity of learning pathways, and how reforms to adult learning can interact with the transition from initial education to working life. In the case of the United Kingdom an attempt is described to make a paradigm shift from a traditional front-end model of transition to an open and flexible model of lifelong learning: in educational institutions, at work, and elsewhere. In this instance reforms to the transition phase are an essential component of efforts to develop a genuine system of lifelong learning.

Better access to tertiary education for adults is one strategy.

Opening up tertiary education to adults is one way in which countries have attempted to increase the continuity of pathways beyond compulsory education, and to reduce the "once-and-for-all effects" of selective upper secondary and tertiary education. Over the past two decades tertiary institutions in many countries have started to provide comparatively accessible and relevant programmes for those adult learners who have either acquired the necessary formal qualifications needed for entry, or who have otherwise been assessed as having the knowledge and learning skills required for admission. Australia through its Technical and Further Education (TAFE) colleges, Canada and the United States both through their Community Colleges, the CEGEPs and through a range of adult and further education courses in university level tertiary education, the United Kingdom through its Open University, and Sweden through it university admissions policies for adults are examples. Australia's TAFE colleges, the North American community colleges and the United Kingdom's Further Education colleges are all examples of highly flexible institutions that allow adults to return to learning at frequent intervals, at times and under circumstances of their own choosing.

The case of Sweden illustrates the effects that system-wide reforms of this sort can have, not only upon adult learning but also on the choices of young people in the transition phase. Since the early 1970s, Swedish universities have been able to admit adults on a different basis from the university entrance qualifications required of school leavers. Those aged 25 or over who have been employed for at least four years and who can demonstrate a knowledge of Swedish and English equivalent to the standard of an upper secondary programme are eligible for admission. This reform has been accompanied by the creation of a right to educational leave. At the time, these arrangements were less designed to establish a system of lifelong learning, than to provide Swedish workers with a broad set of second chance opportunities for achieving tertiary level qualifications. They were meant to make up for inequitable outcomes of initial secondary education. And they were accompanied by reforms aiming to provide all young people of the following generations with school-based upper secondary education.

However during the 1990s the supply of tertiary places in Sweden has not kept pace with the level of community demand – less than half of all applicants were being admitted each year in the late 1990s. As a result bottlenecks have arisen, and many young people have been moving from upper secondary education to municipal adult education (komvux) to try to improve their grades. Others have decided that their chances of gaining entry will be greater if they wait until they are 25, and then apply on the basis of the adult admission rules rather than on the basis of their upper secondary grades. Thus they have an incentive to prolong the transition stage from initial education.

Learning opportunities for adults that lead to highly valued occupational qualifications have long been part of the education and training systems of apprenticeship countries such as Austria and Switzerland. Examples include the Meister and Techniker qualifications in manufacturing industries and comparable expert qualifications in banking and insurance. These opportunities are normally open to people who have upper secondary vocational qualifications in the same occupational field, and who in addition have several years of work experience. These programmes are highly demanding in terms of time, difficulty and – sometimes – cost. They could be described as "elite pathways" for the most hard-working and successful qualified workers. Their existence adds value to apprenticeship training or to equivalent school-based vocational education, which are a pre-condition for entry into such programmes. They can encourage ambitious young people to work hard in initial vocational education and apprenticeship and to maintain their interest in learning during their first years as qualified workers. In Switzerland the new *Fachhochschulen* are intended

Highly respected post-initial qualifications in the apprenticeship countries is another.

to attract mainly former apprentices with a double qualification for both work and tertiary study.

Yet much adult learning remains outside of these qualifications.

During the 1990s countries such as Austria and Switzerland seem to have experienced less pressure to build large scale institutional frameworks for further education and training than have countries with less highly developed initial vocational education and training systems. In both countries a multitude of short programmes of varying quality are provided for adult learners by enterprises, employer and trade union organisations and others. However, as in other countries, many low-skilled workers are excluded from such further education and training. And, most importantly perhaps, there are so far no common frameworks to allow all adults to systematically gain credit for the skills acquired through many of these short programmes, or to receive credit for skills gained through experience at work. In countries where occupational qualifications are of such importance in the labour market, this could be particularly problematic (Lutz, 1994).

And there is concern that the pathways from apprenticeship need to be strengthened even further.

This situation runs the risk of producing worrying negative consequences in the transition phase. The concern is that it might encourage young people to abandon apprenticeship or other high-quality vocational education pathways in favour of general upper secondary pathways leading to university-level tertiary education. The creation of non-university tertiary institutions in the 1990s, and efforts to pave the way from apprenticeship and school-based vocational education to tertiary education, indicate that this risk is taken very seriously in both countries.

Another crucial question in these countries is how to open up qualifying further education and training (or further education and training that leads to a recognised occupational qualification) to people at all ages and levels of qualifications, without sacrificing the quality of existing qualifications. Answers to this question might be inspired by looking at recent developments in countries with very different education and training systems – notwithstanding the problems which these countries may face in implementing new structural approaches to lifelong learning.

The United Kingdom has developed a new paradigm: from providing further education and training to developing a genuine system of lifelong learning.

Starting in the late 1980s, and against a background of comparatively low levels of qualification among young people entering the labour market, the United Kingdom has undertaken a series of wide-ranging reforms that explicitly aim to establish a genuine system of lifelong learning. The intention has been to develop an open and unified system of initial and further education and training, a system in which learning at work, demonstrated through competency-based assessment, is an integral part. The goal has not just been to open up higher or tertiary education to the largest possible number of young people.

The cornerstone of this approach is a national qualifications framework[1] in which academic and occupational qualifications are formally equivalent. The introduction of National Vocational Qualifications (NVQs) in 1988 – initially intended for adults – marked the beginning of the implementation of this approach. It was followed in 1992 by a first set of broader General National Vocational Qualifications (GNVQs), designed for young people and connected through equivalence arrangements to both NVQs and academic qualifications.

---

1. With differences in detail, although not in overall approach, between England, Wales and Northern Ireland on the one hand and Scotland on the other.

Reforms to institutions and programmes – for example the inclusion of polytechnics within tertiary education and the modularisation of courses and qualifications in post-compulsory education – are supporting the goals of the new qualifications framework.

The main elements of the United Kingdom's approach to establishing a lifelong learning system are:

- Formal recognition of learning acquired in settings other than the classroom.
- Modular curriculum and qualification structures.
- Unified qualification systems that create an equivalence between the qualifications awarded by initial and further education.
- Provision of learning opportunities simultaneously to young people and adults through a wide range of public and private institutions; and
- Public financing according to clear targets and measured outcomes.

Notwithstanding the conceptual coherence of the United Kingdom's approach to developing a system of lifelong learning and taking into account the newness of many of its features, its design and implementation raise a number of questions about the solidity of young people's foundations for further learning. For instance, the notion of "completion of upper secondary education" has less of a concrete meaning in a system of modularised qualifications, as young people can leave initial education at any stage, taking with them those modules which they have completed. In such a system what counts is the level of the qualifications achieved, either in initial or further education, or at work. While the increase in the number of young people with Level 2 and Level 3 qualifications over the last decade is impressive,[2] Level 2 qualifications are below the level of complete upper secondary qualifications in other countries. The take-up rate of the new qualifications has been criticised as being too low, with too high a proportion of those that have been awarded being at the lower Levels 1 and 2. The new modularised, competency-based qualifications continue alongside the previous system of qualifications, the take-up rate for which has not diminished as a result of the new system.

Other questions arise about the quality standards of courses and qualifications within the very complex system of accreditation, certification and financing by outcomes. Systems of payment by results have at times encouraged providers to focus upon maximising the number of lower level qualifications awarded. The involvement of numerous publicly financed private organisations (QANGOs or Quasi Non-Government Organisations) in the co-ordination, provision and certification of further education can involve conflicts of interest when the one body performs more than one of the roles of accreditor, assessor, certifier and standard setter. Procedures for assessment, particularly of learning in the workplace, are complex and costly for employers, and difficult for many smaller employers to participate in. Only the future will show to what extent the modularised system, as implemented in the United Kingdom, will equip young people with Level 3 qualifications (comparable to complete upper secondary qualifications elsewhere) and – most importantly – to what extent those leaving initial education at lower levels of achievement will actually engage in learning and acquire further qualifications later on.

---

2. In 1997, 71% of 19 year-olds had achieved Level 2 qualifications. 49% of 21 year olds had achieved Level 3 qualifications.

Elements of the United Kingdom's approach can be seen in Australia...

Elements of the United Kingdom's approach to developing a lifelong learning system have also been introduced in Australia where, since the mid 1980s, there has been a concentrated effort to put in place policies and programmes to expand and strengthen the vocational education and training system. Some key principles have shaped these reforms:

- The development of a national system, rather than a system in which significant differences exist between the several Australian states and territories. To assist this, the Australian National Training Authority has been created to provide strategic direction and advice to the states and territories, and an Australian Qualifications Framework has been adopted to provide a consistent pattern of qualifications across the states and territories.
- The award of qualifications on the basis of competency, rather than of time spent in education and training. This requires course design, curriculum development and assessment, including the assessment of prior learning, to be based upon industry-developed skill standards.
- A system driven by demand. To this end a major policy thrust has been to promote more choice and competition between education and training providers, and to stimulate the creation of a private training market.
- Multiple pathways and flexible delivery. One consequence of this principle has been the creation of new vocational education programmes within an upper secondary school system that had previously focused largely upon general education, with almost no provision of recognised vocational education. These new pathways allow young people to gain occupational skills and qualifications alongside more traditional vocational education routes within apprenticeships and TAFE colleges.

As with the reforms in the United Kingdom, this approach has been associated with mixed outcomes. There have been very substantial increases in adult participation in vocational education and training during the 1990s, and young people's participation in vocational education programmes in upper secondary schools has grown rapidly from a small base. There has been very sharp growth in young adults' participation in apprenticeship-type programmes (Ball, 1999) but this has been accompanied by falling participation among teenagers, and by little growth in teenagers' participation in vocational education pathways outside of the upper secondary school system such as apprenticeships and TAFE. This suggests that the approach has been associated with some substantial changes to the nature of the pathways between initial education and working life.

... and in Finland.

Elements of the United Kingdom's approach to developing a lifelong learning system can also be seen in Finland. Since the mid 1990s Finland has started to set up a competency-based qualifications system, and to modularise all upper secondary programmes. As in the United Kingdom, initially this system was mainly directed at adult learners, but the intention is to make it available to young people in apprenticeship training as well. However, qualifications acquired in school-based vocational education are so far not part of the competency-based qualifications framework and upper secondary school certificates are based on the completion of a required number of modules over three years of study (including six months of evaluated work experience in the case of vocational education). An interesting additional aspect of the Finnish reforms are experiments taking place within upper secondary education which allow students to combine courses from general and vocational programmes and from different schools. These experiments are designed to develop young people's initiative and responsibility in constructing their own transition routes from initial education to work, and in so doing to prepare them for lifelong learning.

It is also interesting to note that in many countries young people are increasingly tending to participate in labour market programmes, and other programmes traditionally reserved for adults, immediately after initial education and training. In Sweden for example 13% of school leavers are to be found in labour market programmes one year after leaving school, and roughly another five per cent are found in municipal adult education. In Hungary, many young people who are awaiting entry to tertiary education enter labour market programmes in order to gain the information technology and business skills required in a restructuring economy. This is another and more spontaneous way in which the borderlines between initial and further education and training are becoming less clear-cut.

Initial and further education: complements or substitutes?

A central policy issue is whether the nature and scale of further education and training depends upon the nature and scale of initial pathways to work and *vice versa*. In other words, to what extent are initial and further education complements or substitutes? Can extensive and well-designed provision of further education and training substitute for upper secondary or tertiary education, and if so, how would it have to be organised and certified? Could the development of stronger initial vocational pathways, which is currently being attempted in several countries, reduce the need for lifelong learning by adults? For example does the strength of initial vocational education in apprenticeship countries reduce the need for adult education and training, or does it complement it? Similarly, could the participation of rising numbers of young people in tertiary education reduce the need for or the attractiveness of certain forms of lifelong learning? Or, alternatively, how would initial and adult education and training need to be designed and organised in order to be genuinely and effectively complementary?

5.2. Learner-centred approaches to promoting lifelong learning

The second set of approaches to promoting lifelong learning within the transition phase focuses upon changes to the teaching and learning process. In the countries reviewed such approaches are at times embedded in structural reforms. For example the 1997 report of Finland's Lifelong Learning Committee (Ministry of Education, 1997) recommends both necessary structural reforms, and reforms such as the development of motivation to learn and learning skills within the school system, and the creation of new opportunities for young people to learn at work. However at times they sit separately from structural reforms. Fostering a love of learning and the skills of learning to learn among young people are the major aims common to these learner-centred approaches, based upon improved and enriched teaching and learning processes.

Learner-centred approaches emphasise the teaching and learning process.

Key elements include the development of generic or core skills and the attempt to introduce more active methods of learning. These are intended to help young people to develop initiative and responsibility for their own learning, and habits of co-operative learning, in addition to a solid foundation of knowledge and skills. Initiatives taken to achieve such aims include increasing the amount of choice that students are able to make within the curriculum, and the use of teaching and learning methods that pay particular attention to contextual and applied learning. These typically include problem-centred learning; project-based learning; team-based learning; and structured work-based learning (Stern and Huber, 1997; Raizen, 1994). Many excellent examples of the use of such pedagogy within individual schools or tertiary institutions were revealed in the course of the Thematic Review. The challenge which all countries are facing is how to take such approaches further, from experimentation to mainstream practice.

Denmark provides examples both of good practice developed by individual institutions and of pedagogical innovation embedded in a solid institutional framework across the country. An example of institutional good practice, illustrated by Aalborg University, is presented in Box 5.1. An example of more system-wide innovative pedagogical practice are Denmark's 108 Production Schools. These are flexible open-entry, open-exit institutions designed to motivate those under the age of 25 who lack a basic upper secondary qualification, and to encourage them to return to school in order to gain one (Moeller and Ljung, 1999). All of students' learning takes place through projects that are worked out between the students and a counsellor. Students can work individually but mostly work in teams. Students' learning is organised individually rather than fitted into a standard timetable. Projects are always practical and designed to contribute to the community or to the running of the school. Student-teacher ratios are low. The schools are open for 48 weeks a year. They employ staff from a variety of backgrounds, including many who are not qualified as teachers, but all staff are on a common salary scale. This has all been made possible through the negotiation of an industrial agreement for Production School staff which differs in significant ways from that which applies in Denmark's standard upper secondary schools.

Core skills are being emphasised as foundations for lifelong learning.

A growing interest in core, key, generic or essential employability skills and competencies stems from the belief that the types of skills that are needed in the workplace are changing, and that all workers will in future have to adapt and upgrade their knowledge and skills continuously throughout their working lives. This assumption has exerted a powerful influence upon educational policy development in many countries (Grubb, 1999). It is believed that the development of core skills will enable learners more easily to transfer their knowledge and methodological skills to different subject areas and learning situations, and thus to lay a solid basis for lifelong learning.

At times they are defined systematically in frameworks...

In some countries these skills and competencies have been defined in systematic frameworks as an aid to both curriculum development and teaching. Examples include the United States' SCANS competencies (Secretary's Commission on Achieving Necessary Skills, 1991), the Australian key competencies (Mayer, 1992), and the Conference Board of Canada's employability skills profile (Conference Board of Canada, 1992b). Box 5.2 illustrates the SCANS skills. Competencies such as initiative and planning, communication, problem solving and teamwork are normally common elements in such frameworks.

... and at times embedded in the curriculum.

In other countries such skills and competencies are explicitly embedded in national core curricula. In the United Kingdom key or core skills typically comprise communication skills, application of number, information technology,

> Box 5.1. **Denmark's Aalborg University**
>
> Aalborg University has 11 000 students and was established in 1974. It has three faculties which span the humanities, the social sciences, public and business administration, social work, the natural sciences and engineering. Since it was founded it has used project based and problem centred learning for all students and at all levels as the heart of its education. In their first year all students enrol in one of three broadly defined knowledge areas. For example all natural science and engineering students are in a common course and only specialise later. This allows them to develop their interests and change their minds. From the start of each course students are formed into teams, which they remain in for the semester. Each semester they do one project, chosen jointly by the students and their supervisor.
>
> Projects are either used to develop knowledge and skills, or are problem-oriented and designed to teach students to ask questions such as "Why is it so...?", and "What is the meaning of...?". Examples include designing a sturdy low weight bicycle frame, or modelling how blood pressure varies during pregnancy. Most projects are carried out in association with industry or the community. Firms often benefit from these projects. One benefit has been the development of very close relationships between the university and the surrounding community and industry. Access to the latest knowledge and research has been important in attracting high-tech firms to invest in the Aalborg area, creating high skilled employment for the community.
>
> About a quarter of students' time at Aalborg is spent in lectures on foundation subjects, and this is examined in the normal way. The rest of it is centred on their projects, mostly through group work, but also lectures. Projects are examined through written reports and group presentations. Normally external examiners are involved, representing the professional world or industry, as well as other academic institutions. Assessment emphasises the value of the project to industry or the community.
>
> In the early stages of their course students work on problems that have known solutions. Later they move to problems for which solutions are not apparent. In all cases the goal is student learning, not finding solutions to problems. The learning is multidisciplinary, and by doing. Students are helped to moved from understanding common knowledge to generating new knowledge, from describing and analysing to synthesising and assessing. The aim is to develop lifelong learners, not just degree holders.
>
> This makes the teaching very demanding for the staff. They cannot keep using the same material year after year. They have to learn alongside their students – constantly. They have to guide students as they explore problems, not present them with solutions. They have to know when and how to bring in someone who has specialised skills or knowledge that students need. Research and teaching become much more closely linked. Joint student-staff publications are common.
>
> Surveys show that student satisfaction is high, even though the courses are demanding. Compared to graduates from conventional universities, final examiners judge Aalborg graduates to have better communication and problem solving skills as well as better general technical knowledge, even if their specialist knowledge is judged not as strong. They find themselves well prepared for their professions, and report that their project work is the major source of the knowledge and experience that they actually use in their work. Aalborg students have lower drop out rates and graduate about a year sooner than students from conventional universities.
>
> *Source:* Kjersdam and Enemark (1994).

working with others, problem solving and improving one's own learning and performance. The latter of these, in particular, is directly related to preparation for lifelong learning. Core skills are developed throughout the education and training system, and are part of the compulsory curriculum in compulsory education. In post-compulsory education and training they are, or will be, provided either as separate skill units (in England and Wales) or embedded in the regular curriculum (in the Scottish Higher Still courses). The extension of core skills to higher education, explicitly formulated as intended learning outcomes, is recommended by the Dearing Report (Dearing, 1996).

There are strong similarities between the content of the clearly expressed goals of education embedded in national core curriculum documents and the content of the skill frameworks previously referred to. Hungary's national core

> **Box 5.2. The SCANS competencies**
>
> SCANS involves five competencies and a three-part foundation of skills and personal qualities that are needed for solid job performance. These are:
>
> **Workplace Competencies:** effective workers can productively use:
>
> - **Resources** – they know how to allocate time, money, materials, space, and staff.
> - **Interpersonal skills** – they can work on teams, teach others, serve customers, lead, negotiate, and work well with people from culturally diverse backgrounds.
> - **Information** – they can acquire and evaluate data, organise and maintain files, interpret and communicate, and use computers to process information.
> - **Systems** – they understand social, organisational, and technological systems; they can monitor and correct performance; and they can design or improve systems.
> - **Technology** – they can select equipment and tools, apply technology to specific tasks, and maintain and troubleshoot equipment.
>
> **Foundation Skills:** competent workers in the high-performance workplace need:
>
> - **Basic skills** – reading, writing, arithmetic and mathematics, speaking and listening.
> - **Thinking skills** – the ability to learn, to reason, to think creatively, to make decisions, and to solve problems.
> - **Personal qualities** – individual responsibility, self-esteem and self-management, sociability, and integrity.
>
> *Source:* Secretary's Commission on Achieving Necessary Skills (1991).

curriculum for compulsory education (Ministry of Culture and Education Hungary, 1996) for example places considerable emphasis upon the development of written and oral communication skills and social skills at all ages, and upon the development of problem solving skills by adolescents. Norway's core curriculum for primary, secondary and adult education (Royal Ministry of Education, Research and Church Affairs, 1997) emphasises the role of the school in developing skills in teamwork, decision making, communication, problem solving, creativity, and using technology. Sweden's curriculum for compulsory schools (Swedish Ministry of Education and Science, 1994) emphasises the importance of students developing skills in acquiring and using knowledge, co-operation with others, and written and oral communication.

Active teaching and learning strategies promote learning in the workplace...

Active teaching and learning methods are seen as another way of developing the habit of lifelong learning during the transition stage. An emphasis upon increasing and reinforcing links between the school and the world outside is often seen as one important way to facilitate active learning. Learning at work favours active methods of self-directed learning, team work and self-evaluation. Hence the development of structured learning in the work environment, described in Section 4.2 above, is a key part of this approach. Often such programmes also involve general education students, who tend to have fewer opportunities for contextual and applied learning than vocational education students. For example in Sweden around one in six students in the general education programmes undertake work placements in order to gain a better understanding of the way that general education subjects relate to working life, or in order to undertake projects in a more realistic work setting.

Other interesting examples involve students being required to engage in active learning in community settings, and young people undertaking projects in the community to solve problems that are relevant to themselves, their community or their school. As an example, in the United States service learning – voluntary service provided to the community by students – has been used for a decade as a form of active and applied learning: to expand learning through experience beyond the classroom, to connect young people to careers and their communities, to teach responsibility and basic life skills such as problem solving, as well as to provide useful service to others (Sagawa, 1998). Currently 48 of the American states have bipartisan state commissions on service learning, and their efforts are supported by the federal Corporation for National Service, authorised by Congress in 1993. Perhaps half of all students in grades six to 12 have performed some form of community service, although not all of this is structured in such a way as to explicitly promote learning. In some states, such as Colorado and Vermont, service learning is being integrated into state performance-based educational standards, in a wide range of general education subjects. This can be a way to make active and applied learning part of mainstream education.

... and learning in the community.

Active learning strategies can also be integrated into students' career education as well as personal and career planning. Box 5.3 provides such an example from the United Kingdom.

Box 5.3. Transition Teams

Transition Teams are self managing teams of young people that:
- Investigate their own choices of post compulsory education and employment.
- Explore the issues and changes students will need to manage in their transition from school; and
- Present information about their investigation to other students.

Transition Teams enable young people to be both learners and teachers in an active career education program. Transition Teams enable young people to gain knowledge and understanding, to develop key work competencies, and to influence education and training providers to respond better to their needs. They aim to generate information and contacts that enhance schools' careers libraries, schools' knowledge of local employers and education providers, and the participation of community members in the curriculum. They aim to enhance students' enterprising skills by actively involving them in learning and project management.

Examples of Transition Team projects include:
- Researching what local Further Education colleges offer and what they expect of students, and then presenting the results to fellow students.
- Researching jobs available in the local labour market and writing articles for the local newspaper or giving local radio interviews on the results.
- Shadowing young workers in the workplace to understand the nature of their jobs, and presenting findings on the themes and problems emerging both to the young workers and to fellow students.

Source: CCDU Training and Consultancy (1995).

A key challenge for policy makers is how to make sure that pedagogical initiatives designed to motivate young people and to build the foundation skills for lifelong learning can work across education systems as a whole, as normal educational practice, rather than as impressive but isolated innovations. For example impressive though the Aalborg example is, it has had little impact

Moving innovation into the mainstream is a key challenge.

upon other Danish universities. A substantial part of the answer lies in the support and promotion of appropriate teaching and learning methods through organisational and institutional conditions that make them easier to adopt. Many such innovations require changes to be made to the curriculum, and to the ways that schools are organised and that teachers work. The school timetable and class sizes can be affected for example. Less classroom teaching, a closer involvement with the community, and more organising and mediating tasks for teachers can raise basic issues about teacher training, about what will be counted as teaching time, and about what constitutes normal duties for a teacher. The need for system-wide solutions to such problems has been recognised in a 1996 development agreement between the Swedish Association of Local Authorities – the principal employer of Sweden's teachers – and the Swedish Teachers' Union and the National Union of Teachers.[3] The agreement regulates the working conditions and salaries of teachers in a new way through addressing the organisation of schools and teachers' professional development. At its heart is a recognition of the need to shift from teaching time as the basic measure of teachers' working time to regulated hours of work – including teaching time, preparation time and other educational activities. This is intended to create more flexible working organisations that can promote better learning, including more active learning modes.

One of the most serious obstacles to more active and applied learning in the transition phase is provided by the signals that tests and examinations send to teachers and students about the priority that is attached to different learning outcomes. Too often these over-emphasise the assimilation of factual knowledge and theoretical reasoning, to the detriment of applied knowledge and the demonstration of practical skills. Under such circumstances teachers will be reluctant to apply pedagogical methods which they feel to be less than optimal in producing the expected results. What is more, such contradictions cannot be resolved by providing opportunities for active and applied learning, and related assessment of learning outcomes, only to so-called low-achievers or young people at risk, important as that may be. If this kind of pedagogy is only associated with an image of "second class" education it will not be able to penetrate the educational mainstream. All these are issues for central policy makers, not just for individual schools and teachers.

3. *On the Threshold of the 21st Century*, Svenska Kommunförbundet, Stockholm

Chapter 6

CONCLUSION

The last 20 years have seen major changes to the ways that young people make the transition from initial education to work. In fewer and fewer countries is it any longer the norm for most young people to permanently leave education at the end of compulsory schooling in order to enter the labour force. In fewer countries is the pathway that leads to work through tertiary education the preserve of only a small minority. At the end of the 1990s participation in at least some upper secondary education has become almost universal in OECD countries. In some countries the completion of at least upper secondary education or training is now the expected level of entry to the work force for all but a small and decreasing minority. More and more of those who once would have left school early are now staying on in upper secondary education; the duration of upper secondary education is rising in some countries; and the academic demands that are made by vocational education pathways are also rising. Together these trends are placing greater and greater pressures upon upper secondary education to find ways to motivate and raise the achievement levels of the least successful students. Upper secondary education faces the challenge of constructing flexible yet high quality and equitable pathways that have tight connections to students' post-school destinations. It faces the challenge of providing universal access to high quality, broad education that develops general, personal and work-related knowledge and skills in all young people, and of providing all of them with opportunities for learning outside of the classroom. These challenges need to be met if the transition phase is to be better able to lay a foundation for lifelong learning for all.

Transition patterns differ markedly from those that were the norm 20 years ago.

For more and more young people participation in tertiary education is now a prelude to work force entry. If current university-level entry rates extend into the future, one in three of today's youth will enter tertiary education at university level during their lives (OECD, 1998*a*). The proportion who can be expected to enrol in any form of tertiary education is even greater, and will be higher still given the extent of innovations in non-university tertiary education highlighted by the Thematic Review. However already entry to tertiary education does not occur, for many, immediately after leaving upper secondary education, but after a delay of one, two or more years. The increasing enrolment of adults in tertiary education has meant that the student body is less dominated by those in their late teens and early 20s than once was the case: in the eight countries participating in the Thematic Review for which data is available 20% or more of new university entrants are now aged 23 or more, and in Denmark, Finland, Hungary and Norway 20% are 25 or older.

More and more, it seems, periods of work and learning are being spread throughout life, rather than being concentrated in distinct and separated periods: education in the period up to the late teens and early 20s; work after that. A mingling of work with education is also being observed increasingly during the period

© OECD 2000

of initial education. Some of this has been stimulated by education systems, aware of the powerful motivating effect that applied and contextual learning can have upon young people. Students' part-time and holiday jobs are another large reason for this growing blurring between initial education and work. These jobs have arisen in large part as a result of new patterns of economic activity and a changing distribution of employment: away from agriculture, manufacturing and construction, and increasingly towards the service sector. In some countries these same types of jobs are also a factor in many young people's transition becoming more uncertain in the period immediately after leaving initial education: more likely to be temporary and part-time; less likely to be permanent and full-time. In other instances the possibility of combining such jobs with tertiary study has contributed to a longer period taken to complete a tertiary qualification.

Together these trends are helping to spread the transition to working life over a longer period. Young people's attitudes and values also play an important role in this lengthening. Young people appear to be astute in using existing transition pathways in often unexpected ways in order to maximise their advantages. In some countries young people appear in no hurry to settle into permanent work, or to be in no rush to move from one level of education to another. Travel, study abroad, working for a period before starting tertiary study: all are common ways for them to extend the transition period.

A spreading of education over a wider period of working life is one of the logical consequences of lifelong learning becoming a reality. In some countries we can see this emerging quite early: during the transition phase. These new and emerging transition patterns are not universal in all countries. However there are sufficient signs of them in sufficient countries for us to ask whether, in 20 years' time, we will be able to look back on present transition patterns and see them as being as unusual as we now regard the transition patterns of young people 20 years ago.

Effective transition arrangements are embedded in societies that value young people.

A limited number of common key features appear to be central in building effective transition systems for youth:

– A healthy economy.
– Well organised pathways that connect initial education with work and further study.
– Widespread opportunities to combine workplace experience with education.
– Tightly knit safety nets for those at risk.
– Good information and guidance; and
– Effective institutions and processes.

Although institutional frameworks differ, all effective transition systems appear to have one thing in common: underlying them are societies that assume responsibility for young people's transition from education to work. In different ways these societies make focused efforts to ensure that national transition arrangements are inclusive, so that as few young people as possible fall through the cracks. These are societies that believe young people important enough to be given a high priority among all of the many priorities that compete for attention on the public policy agenda. They are societies that believe specific transition policies are needed to ensure that young people do not have to compete for work unprepared, and that special arrangements – whether apprenticeships, safety nets, or efficient recruitment systems – are needed to ensure that they are able to compete on more equal terms. This appears to be the single most important lesson to have emerged from the Thematic Review.

REFERENCES

ABRAHART, A. and TZANNATOS, T. (1999),
"Australia: Confronting institutional impediments", in I. Gill, F. Fluitman and A. Dar (eds.), *Skills and Change: Constraints and Innovations in the Reform of Vocational Education and Training*, Oxford University Press for the World Bank, Oxford.

AGELL, J. (1999),
"On the benefits from rigid labour markets: Norms, market failures and social insurance", *The Economic Journal*, Vol. 109, pp. F143-F164, February.

AINLEY, J. and FLEMING, M. (1997),
School-Industry Programs National Survey 1996, Australian Student Traineeship Foundation, Sydney.

AMIRAULT, T. (1992),
"Training to qualify for jobs and improve skills", *Monthly Labor Review*, Vol. 115, No. 9, pp. 31-35.

BAILEY, T., HUGHES, K. and BARR, T. (1999),
Achieving Scale and Quality in School-to-Work Internships: Findings from an Employer Survey, National Center for Research in Vocational Education, Berkeley.

BALL, K. (1999),
"Participation in and outcomes from vocational education and training", in *Australia's Young Adults: The Deepening Divide*, Dusseldorp Skills Forum, Sydney.

BALL, K. and ROBINSON, C. (1998),
"Young people's participation in and outcomes from vocational education and training", in *Australia's Youth: Reality and Risk*, Dusseldorp Skills Forum, Sydney.

BARRELL, R. and GENRE, V. (1999),
"Employment strategies for Europe: Lessons from Denmark and the Netherlands", *National Institute Economic Review*, pp. 82-96, April.

BASSI, L., FEELEY, T., HILLMEYER, J. and LUDWIG, J. (1997),
Learning and Earning. An Employer's Look at School-to-Work Investments, American Society for Training and Development.

BENTLEY, T. and GURUMURTHY, R. (1999),
Destination Unknown. Engaging With the Problems of Marginalised Youth, Demos, London.

BERTRAND, O. (1999),
"Apprentisssage et formation en alternance", Conférence sur la formation professionelle et technique, Montreal.

BISHOP, J. (1996),
"Signalling the competences of high school students to employers", in L. Resnick and J. Wirt (eds.), *Linking School and Work: Roles for Standards and Assessment*, Jossey-Bass, San Francisco, pp. 79-124.

BISHOP, J. (1998),
"Welfare reform in the US: Is it successful. Myths about the history of American poverty policy", in *Employability and Exclusion: What Governments Can Do*, Centre for Economic Performance, University of London.

BLANCHARD, O. and PORTUGAL, P. (1998),
"What hides behind an unemployment rate: Comparing Portuguese and US unemployment", http://web.mit.edu/blanchar/www/articles.html.

BUCHMANN, M. and SACCHI, S. (1998),
"The transition from school to work in Switzerland: Do characteristics of the educational system and class barriers matter?", in Y. Shavit and W. Müller (eds.), *From School to Work. A Comparative Study of Educational Qualifications and Occupational Destinations*, Clarendon Press, Oxford, pp. 1-48.

BYRNE, E. and BEAVERS, E. (1993),
"Career education, career guidance and curriculum choice: A research review", *Australian Journal of Career Development*, Vol. 2, No. 3, pp. 23-26.

CARNEVALE, A. and ROSE, S. (1998),
The New Office Economy, Educational Testing Service, Princeton.

CASPI, A., WRIGHT, B., MOFFIT, T., and SILVA, P. (1998),
"Early failure in the labor market: Childhood and adolescent predictors of unemployment in the transition to adulthood", *American Sociological Review*, Vol. 63, June, pp. 424-451.

CCDU TRAINING AND CONSULTANCY (1995),
Introducing Transition Teams: A School-based Strategy for Developing Young People as Empowered Customers of Post-Compulsory Education and Training, University of Leeds and Department for Education and Employment, Leeds.

CHIOUSSE, S. and WERQUIN, P. (1999),
Lifelong Vocational Guidance: European Case Studies, CEDEFOP, Thessaloniki.

CONFERENCE BOARD OF CANADA (1992a),
Dropping Out: The Costs to Canada, Conference Board of Canada, Ottawa.

CONFERENCE BOARD OF CANADA (1992b),
Employability Skills Profile: What Are Employers Looking For?, Conference Board of Canada, Ottawa.

CONGER, D. (1994),
Policies and Guidelines for Educational and Vocational Guidance, UNESCO, Paris.

CONTINI, B., PACELLI, L. and VILLOSIO, C. (1999),
"Short employment spells in Italy, Germany and Great Britain: testing the 'Port-of entry' hypothesis", Discussion Paper, No. 42, University of London, Centre for Economic Performance.

CULPEPPER, P. (1999),
"The future of the high-skill equilibrium in Germany", *Oxford Review of Economic Policy*, Vol. 15, No. 1, pp. 43-59.

CUMMING, J. and CARBINES, B. (1997),
Reforming Schools Through Workplace Learning, National Schools Network, Sydney.

DEARING, R. (1996),
Review of Qualifications for 16-19 Year-Olds. SCAA, Hayes.

DORE, R. and SAKO, M. (1998),
How the Japanese Learn to Work, 2nd edition, Routledge, London.

DUSSELDORP SKILLS FORUM and CAREER EDUCATION ASSOCIATION OF VICTORIA (1997),
Career Education and Guidance for the Next Millennium, Dusseldorp Skills Forum, Sydney.

DWYER, P., HARWOOD, A., COSTIN, G., LANDY, M., TOWSTY, L. and WYN, J. (1999),
"Combined Study and Work Pathways in VET: Policy Implications and Analysis. Final Report", University of Melbourne, Youth Research Centre.

DWYER, P. and WYN, J. (1998),
"Post-compulsory education policy in Australia and its impact on participant pathways and outcomes in the 1990s", *Journal of Educational Policy*, Vol. 13 (3), pp. 285-300.

EUROPEAN COMMUNITIES (1999a),
The European Employment Strategy, Luxembourg.

EUROPEAN COMMUNITIES (1999b),
Employment Policies in the EU and in Member States, Joint Report 1998, Luxembourg.

EUROSTAT (1997),
Youth in the European Union. From Education to Working Life, European Communities, Luxembourg.

FINNIE, R. (1999a),
"The early years: Labour market outcomes of three recent cohorts of Canadian post-secondary graduates", Queens University School of Policy Studies and Business and Labour market Analysis Division, Statistics Canada, Ottawa, Ontario.

FINNIE, R. (1999b),
"The school-to-work transition of Canadian post-secondary graduates: A cross-cohort, longitudinal analysis using the national Graduate Surveys", Queens University School of Policy Studies and Business and Labour market Analysis Division, Statistics Canada, Ottawa, Ontario.

FRIEDLANDER, D., GREENBERG, D. and ROBINS, P. (1997),
"Evaluating government training programs for the economically disadvantaged", *Journal of Economic Literature*, Vol. 35, pp. 1809-1855, December.

GARDECKI, R. and NEUMARK, D. (1997),
"Order from chaos? The effects of early labor market experiences on adult labour market outcomes", NBER Working Paper, No. 5899.

GILL, I. FLUITMAN, F. and DAR, A. (1999),
Skills and Change: Constraints and Innovations in the Reform of Vocational Education and Training, Oxford University Press for the World Bank, Oxford.

GITTER, R. and SCHEUER, M. (1997),
"US and German youths: Unemployment and the transition from school to work", *Monthly Labor Review*, March, pp. 16-20.

GOLDING, B. (1999),
"Two way movement and recognition between university and technical and further education in Victoria between 1990 and 1996", Doctor of Philosophy Thesis, Centre for the Study of Higher Education, University of Melbourne.

GOSPEL, H. (1994a),
"The decline of apprenticeship training in Britain", Discussion Paper No. 189, Centre for Economic Performance, London School of Economics.

GOSPEL, H. (1994b),
"Whatever happened to apprenticeship training? A British, American and Australian comparison", Discussion Paper No. 190, Centre for Economic Performance, London School of Economics.

GREEN, A., WOLF, A. and LENEY, T. (1999),
Convergence and Divergence in European Education Systems, Institute of Education, University of London.

GROOTINGS, P. (1999),
"Constraints and innovations in vocational education and training reform in the Czech Republic", in I. Gill, F. Fluitman and A. Dar (eds.), *Skills and Change: Constraints and Innovations in the Reform of Vocational Education and Training*, Oxford University Press for the World Bank, Oxford.

GRUBB, N. (1999),
"Lessons from education and training for youth: Five precepts", in OECD *Preparing Youth for the 21st Century*, Paris.

HAGSTRÖM, T. and GAMBERALE, F. (1995),
"Young people's work motivation and value orientation", *Journal of Adolescence*, Vol. 18, pp. 475-490.

HAMILTON, M. and HAMILTON, S. (1997),
"When is work a learning experience?", *Phi Delta Kappan*, Vol. 78, No. 9, pp. 682-689.

HAMILTON, S. and LEMPERT, W. (1996),
"The impact of apprenticeship on youth: A prospective analysis", *Journal of Research on Adolescence*, Vol. 6, No. 4, pp. 427-455.

HAMMER, T. (1997),
"History dependence in youth unemployment", *European Sociological Review*, Vol. 13, No. 1, pp. 17-33.

HANNAN, D., RAFFE, D. and SMYTH, E. (1996),
"Cross-national research on school to work transitions: An analytical framework", Background paper prepared for the Planning Meeting for the Thematic Review of the Transition from Initial Education to Working Life, 26-27 September, OECD, Paris.

HANNAN, D. and WERQUIN, P. (1999),
"Education and labour market change: The dynamics of education to work transitions in Europe", paper presented to a TSER-European Socio-Economic Research conference, Brussels.

HEALY, G. (1999),
"Graduates get jobs in work alliance", *The Australian Higher Education Supplement*, June 30.

HOLLAND, J. (1997),
Making Vocational Choices : A Theory of Vocational Personalities and Work Environments, 3rd edition, Psychological Assessment Resources, New York.

HUGHES, K. (1998),
"Employer recruitment is not the problem: A study of school-to-work transition programs", IEE *Brief*, July, No. 21, pp. 1-4.

HUMMELUHR, N. (1997),
The Youth Guarantee in Nordic Countries, Copenhagen, December.

ILG, R. (1996),
"The nature of employment growth, 1989-95", *Monthly Labor Review*, June, pp. 29-36.

INDUSTRY IN EDUCATION (1996),
Towards Employability. Addressing the Gap between Young People's Qualities and Employers' Recruitment Needs, Industry In Education, London.

ISHIDA, H. (1998),
"Educational credentials and labour market outcomes in Japan", in Y. Shavit and W. Müller (eds.), *From School to Work. A Comparative Study of Educational Qualifications and Occupational Destinations*, Clarendon Press, Oxford, pp. 1-48.

JARVIS, H. (1994),
"Smoothing the transition to skilled employment: School-based vocational guidance in Britain and continental Europe", *National Institute Economic Review*, November, pp. 73-89.

JEONG, J. (1995),
"The failure of recent state vocational training policies in Korea from a comparative perspective", *British Journal of Industrial Relations*, Vol. 33, No. 2, pp. 237-252, June.

KARIYA, T. (1998),
"From high school and college to work in Japan: Meritocracy through institutional and semi-institutional linkages", in Y. Shavit and W. Müller (eds.), *From School to Work. A Comparative Study of Educational Qualifications and Occupational Destinations*, Clarendon Press, Oxford, pp. 1-48.

KARIYA, T. (1999),
"Transition from school to work and career formation of Japanese high school students", in D. Stern and D. Wagner (eds.), *International Perspectives on the School-to-Work Transition*, Hampton Press, Cresskill, N.J.

KJERSDAM, F. and ENEMARK, S. (1994),
The Aalborg Experiment: Project Innovation in University Education, Aalborg University Press, Aalborg.

KING, A. (1999),
"The cost to Australia of early school leaving", draft paper, National Centre for Social and Economic Modelling, University of Canberra.

KLERMAN, J. and KAROLY, L. (1995),
The Transition to Stable Employment: The Experience of US Youth in their Early Career, National Centre for Research in Vocational Education, Berkeley, CA.

KUCHAR, P. (1998),
"Problems with the placement of graduates after leaving schools", paper prepared for the Ministry of Education, Charles University, Prague.

LANDT, J. and SCOTT, P. (1998),
"Youth incomes", in Dusseldorp Skills Forum (ed), *Australia's Youth: Reality and Risk*, Dusseldorp Skills Forum, Sydney.

LANNERT, J. (1997),
Education in Hungary 1996, National Institute of Public Education, Budapest.

LANNERT, J. (1999),
"Building up partnership: The Hungarian experience", in D. Atchoarena (ed.), *Getting the Stakeholders Involved: Partnership at work in Three Countries from Africa, Asia and Eastern Europe*, UNESCO International Institute for Educational Planning, Paris, pp. 57-104.

LAPAN, R., GYSBERS, N. and SUN, Y. (1997),
"The impact of more fully implemented guidance programs on the school experiences of high school students: A Statewide evaluation study", *Journal of Counseling and Development*, Vol. 75, pp. 292-301.

LAYARD, R. (1998),
"Welfare to work", in *Employability and Exclusion: What Governments Can Do*, Centre for Economic Performance, University of London.

LAYARD, R., NICKELL, S. and JACKMAN, R. (1991),
Unemployment: Macroeconomic Performance and the Labour Market, Oxford University Press, Oxford.

LERMAN, R. (1997),
"Employment and training programs for out-of-school youth: Past efforts and lessons for the future", Urban Institute and American University.

LeTENDRE, G. (1999),
"The problem of Japan: Qualitative studies and international comparisons", *Educational Researcher*, Vol. 28, No. 2, pp. 38-45.

LIGHT, A. (1998),
"Estimating returns to schooling: When does the career begin?", *Economics of Education Review*, Vol. 17, No. 1, pp. 31-45.

LUCAS, R. and LAMMONT, N. (1998),
"Combining school and work: An empirical study of full-time students in school, college and university", *Journal of Education and Work*, Vol. 11, No. 1, pp. 45-56.

LUTZ, B. (1994),
"The difficult rediscovery of 'professionalism'", in OECD *Apprenticeship: Which Way Forward*, Paris.

McCLELLAND, A., MACDONALD, F. and MACDONALD, H. (1998),
"Young people and labour market disadvantage. The situation of young people not in education or full-time work", in Dusseldorp Skills Forum (ed.), *Australia's Youth: Reality and Risk*, Dusseldorp Skills Forum, Sydney.

McKENZIE, P. (1998),
"The transition from education to work in Australia compared to selected OECD countries", paper delivered to the Sixth International Conference on Post-compulsory Education and Training, Gold Coast, Queensland, December.

McPHERSON, M. and SCHAPIRO, M. (1998),
"An overview of trends and patterns in participation and financing in US higher education", Unpublished paper prepared for the OECD, Paris.

MADDY-BERNSTEIN, C. and CUNANAN, C. (1995),
Exemplary Career Education programs: What Should They Look Like?, National Center for Vocational Education Research, Berkeley, CA.

MALLEY, J., FRIGO, T. and ROBINSON, L. (1999),
Case Studies of Australian School-Industry Programs, Australian Student Traineeship Foundation, Sydney.

MARKS, G. and FLEMING, N. (1998a),
"Factors influencing youth unemployment in Australia: 1980-1994", Longitudinal Surveys of Australian Youth Research Report, No. 7, Australian Council for Educational Research, Melbourne.

MARKS, G. and FLEMING, N. (1998b),
"Youth earnings in Australia 1980-1994: A comparison of three youth cohorts", Longitudinal Surveys of Australian Youth Research Report, No. 8, Australian Council for Educational Research, Melbourne.

MARQUARDT, R. (1998),
"Labour market policies and programs affecting youth in Canada", Background paper prepared for the Thematic Review of the Transition from Initial Education to Working Life, Paris.

MARTIN, J. (1998),
"What works among active labour market policies: Evidence from OECD countries' experiences", Labour Market and Social Policy Occasional Papers, No. 35, OECD, Paris.

MAYER, E. (Chair) (1992),
Putting General Education to Work: The Key Competencies Report, Australian Education Council, Melbourne.

MILLER, S. (1998),
"Shortcut: High school grades as a signal of human capital", *Educational Evaluation and Policy Analysis*, Winter, Vol. 20, No. 4, pp. 299-311.

MINISTRY OF CULTURE AND EDUCATION HUNGARY (1996),
National Core Curriculum, Budapest.

MINISTRY OF EDUCATION (1997),
The Joy of Learning. A National Strategy for Lifelong Learning, Committee Report, No. 14, Helsinki.

MITANI, N. (1999),
"The Japanese employment system and youth labour market", in OECD *Preparing Youth for the 21st Century*, Paris.

MOELLER, G. and LJUNG, V. (1999),
"The Korsør Production School and the Danish Production Schools", in OECD *Preparing Youth for the 21st Century*, Paris.

MÜLLER, W. and SHAVIT, Y. (1998),
"The institutional embeddedness of the stratification process: A comparative study of qualifications and occupations in thirteen countries", in Y. Shavit and W. Müller (eds.), *From School to Work. A Comparative Study of Educational Qualifications and Occupational Destinations*, Clarendon Press, Oxford, pp. 1-48.

MUNBY, H., HUTCHINSON, N. and CHIN, P. (1998),
"'I know how to do it': Research priorities for co-operative and career education in Canada's secondary schools", Discussion paper prepared for the Council of Ministers of Education, Canada.

NICAISE, I. (1999),
"Labour market policies for disadvantaged young people in Europe", in OECD *Preparing Youth for the 21st Century*, Paris.

OECD (1977a),
Entry of Young People Into Working Life. General Report, Paris.

OECD (1977b),
Entry of Young People Into Working Life. Technical Reports, Paris.

OECD (1989),
Pathways for Learning. Education and Training From 16 to 19, Paris.

OECD (1992),
Education at a Glance. OECD Indicators, Paris.

OECD (1994a),
:   *Apprenticeship: Which Way Forward?*, Paris.

OECD (1994b),
:   *Employment Outlook*, Paris.

OECD (1994c),
:   *The OECD Jobs Study: Evidence and Explanations, Parts I and II*, Paris.

OECD (1994d),
:   *Vocational Education and Training for Youth: Towards Coherent Policy and Practice*, Paris.

OECD (1996a),
:   *Enhancing the Effectiveness of Labour Market Policies*, Paris.

OECD (1996b),
:   "Growing into work: Youth and the labour market over the 1980s and 1990s", *Employment Outlook*, Paris.

OECD (1996c),
:   *Lifelong Learning for All*, Paris.

OECD (1996d),
:   "Transition from school to work", *Education at a Glance: Analysis*, Paris, pp. 41-54.

OECD (1997a),
:   *Education at a Glance. OECD Indicators*, Paris.

OECD (1997b),
:   *Literacy Skills for the Knowledge Society*, Paris.

OECD (1997c),
:   *OECD Economic Surveys: Switzerland, 1997*, Paris.

OECD (1998a),
:   *Education at a Glance. OECD Indicators*, Paris.

OECD (1998b),
:   *Employment Outlook*, Paris.

OECD (1998c),
:   *Overcoming Failure at School*, Paris.

OECD (1998d),
:   *Pathways and Participation in Vocational and Technical Education and Training*, Paris.

OECD (1998e),
:   *Redefining Tertiary Education*, Paris.

OECD (1998f),
:   *Reviews of National Policies for Education: Korea*, Paris.

OECD (1998g),
:   *Reviews of National Policies for Education: Sweden*, Paris.

OECD (1998h),
:   "Supporting youth pathways", *Education Policy Analysis*, Paris.

OECD (1998i),
:   "Thematic Review of the Transition for Initial Education to Working Life: Interim Comparative Report", DEELSA/ED(98)11, Paris.

OECD (1999a),
:   *Employment Outlook*, Paris.

OECD (1999b),
:   "Preparing youth for the 21st century: The policy lessons from the past two decades", in OECD *Preparing Youth for the 21st Century*, Paris.

OECD (1999c),
:   "Study on Local partnerships – Project Methodology", DT/LEED/DC(99)1, Paris.

OECD/CERI (1992),
:   *Schools and Business. A New Partnership*, Paris.

OECD/CERI (1996),
:   *Mapping the Future. Young People and Career Guidance*, Paris.

OECD/CERI (1999),
:   *Innovating Schools*, Paris.

PICHELMANN, K. and HOFER, H. (1999),
"Austria: Long-term success through social partnership", Prepared for an ILO symposium on Social Dialogue and Employment Success, Geneva.

PLANAS, J. (1999),
"School-to-work transition in Spain", in D. Stern and D. Wagner (eds.), *International Perspectives on the School-to-Work Transition*, Hampton Press, Cresskill, N.J., pp. 413-442.

RAFFE, D. (1998),
"Where are pathways going? Conceptual and methodological lessons from the pathways study", in OECD (1998), *Pathways and Participation in Vocational and Technical Education and Training*, Paris.

RAIZEN, S. (1994),
"Learning and work: The research base", in OECD *Vocational Education and Training for Youth: Towards Coherent Policy and Practice*, Paris, pp. 69-114.

ROBERTS, K. (1998),
"School-to-work transitions in former communist countries", *Journal of Education and Work*, Vol. 11, No. 3, pp. 221-238.

ROBINSON, L. (1999),
"The effects of part-time work on school students", Research Report, No. 9, Australian Council for Educational Research, Melbourne.

ROSENBAUM, J. (1999),
"Preconditions for effective school-to-work linkages in the United States", in D. Stern and D. Wagner (eds.), *International Perspectives on the School-to-Work Transition*, Hampton Press, Cresskill, N.J., pp. 503-538.

ROYAL MINISTRY OF EDUCATION, RESEARCH AND CHURCH AFFAIRS (1997),
Core Curriculum for Primary, Secondary and Adult Education, Oslo.

RUMBERGER, R. and LAMB, S. (1998),
"The early employment and further education experiences of high school drop-outs: A comparative study of the United States and Australia", Background paper prepared for the Thematic Review of the Transition from Initial Education to Working Life, OECD, Paris.

RYAN, P. (1998),
"Is apprenticeship better? A Review of the economic evidence", *Journal of Vocational Education and Training*, Vol. 50, No. 2, pp. 289-325.

RYAN, P. (1999),
"The school-to-work transition twenty years on: Issues, evidence and conundrums", in OECD *Preparing Youth for the 21st Century*, Paris.

RYAN, P. and BUECHTEMANN, C. (1996),
"The school to work transition", in G. Schmid, J. O'Reilly and K. Schomann (eds.), *International Handbook of Labour Market Policy and Evaluation*, Elgar, Cheltenham, England, pp. 308-347.

SAGAWA, S. (1998),
"Ten years of youth in service to America", in S. Halperin (ed.), *The Forgotten Half Revisited: American Youth and Young Families 1988-2008*, American Youth Policy Forum, Inc., Washington.

SCHRAMMEL, K. (1998),
"Comparing the labor market success of young adults from two generations", *Monthly Labor Review*, February, pp. 3-9.

SCHRÖDER, L. (1996),
"Dead end jobs and upgrading plans. An evaluation of job creation programmes", in E. Wadensjö (ed.), *The Nordic Labour Markets in the 1990s*, Part 2, Elsevier, Amsterdam, pp. 107-130.

SEAVEY, D. and KAZIS, R. (1994),
Skills Assessment, Job Placement, and Training: What Can Be Learned from the Temporary Help/Staffing Industry? An Overview of the Industry and a Case Study of Manpower, Jobs for the Future, Boston.

SECRETARY'S COMMISSION ON ACHIEVING NECESSARY SKILLS (1991),
What Work Requires of Schools: A SCANS Report for America 2000, US Department of labor, Washington.

SHAVIT, Y. and MÜLLER, W. (eds.) (1998),
From School to Work. A Comparative Study of Educational Qualifications and Occupational Destinations, Clarendon Press, Oxford.

SILVERBERG, M., HAIMSON, J., and HERSHEY, A. (1998),
Building Blocks for a Future School-to-Work System: Early National Implementation Results, Mathematica Policy Research Inc., Princeton, N.J., MPR 8292-650.

STATISTICS SWEDEN (1997),
Avgångna från gymnasieskolans program. Elever som avgick från gymnasieskolan 1996, Örebro.

STASZ, C. and KAGANOFF, T. (1997),
Learning How to Learn at Work: Lessons from Three High School Programs, National Center for Research in Vocational Education, Berkeley, CA.

STEEDMAN, H., GOSPEL, H. and RYAN, P. (1998),
Apprenticeship: A Strategy for Growth, Centre for Economic Performance, University of London.

STERN, D., FINKELSTEIN, N., STONE, J., LATTING, J. and DORNSIFE, C. (1994),
Research on School-to Work programs in the United States, National Centre for Research in Vocational Education, Berkeley, CA.

STERN, D., FINKELSTEIN, N., URQUIOLA, M. and CAGAMPANG, H. (1997),
"What difference does it make if school and work are connected? Evidence on co-operative education in the United States", *Economics of Education Review*, Vol. 16, No. 3, pp. 213-229.

STERN, D. and HUBER, G. (eds.) (1997),
Active Learning for Students and Teachers. Reports from Eight Countries, Peter Lang, Frankfurt am Main.

STERN, D. and WAGNER, D. (eds.) (1999),
International Perspectives on the School-to-Work Transition, Hampton Press, Cresskill, N.J.

SWEDISH MINISTRY OF EDUCATION AND SCIENCE (1994),
1994 Curriculum for Compulsory Schools (Lpo 94), Stockholm.

SWEET, R. (1995),
"The naked emperor: Training reform, initial vocational preparation and youth wages", *Australian Economic Review*, July, pp. 101-108.

TAYLOR, A. (1999),
"Spitting in the Wind? The Demise of a School-Business Partnership", Working Paper, No. 99.05, Western research Network on Education and Training, University of British Columbia.

TEESE, R., DAVIES, M. and RYAN, C. (1997),
Workplace Experience: The Student Perspective, Educational Outcomes Unite, University of Melbourne.

URQUIOLA, M., STERN, D., HORN, I., DORNSIFE, C. and CHI, B. (1997),
School to Work, College and Career: A Review of Policy, Practice and Results, 1993-1997, National Centre for Research in Vocational Education, Berkeley, CA.

VILLENEUVE, J. and GRUBB, N. (1996),
Indigenous School-to-Work Programs: Lessons from Cincinnati's Co-op Education, National Center for Research in Vocational Education Berkeley, CA.

WATTS, A.G. (1994),
Educational and Vocational Guidance in the European Community, Commission of the European Communities, Brussels.

WERNER, H. (1999),
"Countries With Successful Employment Policies – What Is Behind Their Success?", *Labour Market Research Topics*, No. 33, Nuremberg, Institute for Employment Research.

WERQUIN, P. and CHIOUSSE, S. (1999),
Lifelong Vocational Guidance: European Case Studies, European Communities, Luxembourg.

WOODEN, M. (1998),
"The labour market for young Australians", in Dusseldorp Skills Forum (ed.), *Australia's Youth: Reality and Risk*, Dusseldorp Skills Forum, Sydney.

WOODEN, M. (1999),
"The labour market for young adults", in Dusseldorp Skills Forum (ed.), *Australia's Young Adults: The Deepening Divide*, Dusseldorp Skills Forum, Sydney.

WYN, J. and DWYER, P. (1999),
"New directions in research on youth in transition", *Journal of Youth Studies*, Vol. 2, No. 1, pp. 5-21.

YOSHIMOTO, K. (1996),
"Transition from school to work in Japan", Background paper prepared for the Thematic Review of the Transition from Initial Education to Working Life, OECD, Paris.

Appendix 1

NATIONAL CO-ORDINATORS AND REVIEW TEAM MEMBERS

AUSTRALIA

National Co-ordinator

Mr Tony Greer
Vocational Education and Training Division
Department of Education, Training and Youth Affairs
Canberra

OECD Reviewers for the visit 18-27 March, 1997

Mr Abrar Hasan
Head of Division
Directorate for Education, Employment, Labour
and Social Affairs
OECD
Paris, France

Mr Phillip McKenzie
Principal administrator
Directorate for Education, Employment, Labour
and Social Affairs
OECD
Paris, France

Mr Erik Nexelmann
Division of Vocational Education and Training
Ministry of Education and Research
Copenhagen, Denmark

Mr Robert Schwartz (Rapporteur)
Graduate School of Education
Harvard University
Cambridge, United States of America

AUSTRIA

National Co-ordinator

Ms Eleonora Schmid
General Directorate for Technical
and Vocational Education
Federal Ministry of Education and Cultural Affairs
Vienna

OECD Reviewers for the visit 18-28 November, 1997

Ms Marianne Durand-Drouhin
Principal Administrator
Directorate for Education, Employment, Labour
and Social Affairs
OECD
Paris, France

Mr Damian Hannan
Economic and Social Research Institute
Dublin, Ireland

Ms Jana Hendrichova
Ministry of Education, Youth and Sports
Prague, Czech Republic

Ms Lena Schröder (Rapporteur)
Swedish Institute for Social Research
Stockholm University
Stockholm, Sweden

CANADA

National Co-ordinator

Mr Pierre Brodeur
Direction aux affaires internationales et canadiennes
Ministère de l'Éducation
Québec

OECD Reviewers for the visit 1-10 October, 1997

Ms Marianne Durand-Drouhin
Principal Administrator
Directorate for Education, Employment, Labour
and Social Affairs
OECD
Paris, France

Mr Abrar Hasan
Head of Division
Directorate for Education, Employment, Labour
and Social Affairs
OECD
Paris, France

Ms Claudine Romani
Cabinet du Premier ministre
Paris, France

Ms Hilary Steedman (Rapporteur)
London School of Economics
London, United Kingdom

© OECD 2000

CZECH REPUBLIC

National Co-ordinator

Ms Vera Czesaná, National Training Fund

OECD Reviewers for the visit 20-30 May, 1997

Ms Marianne Durand-Drouhin
Principal Administrator
Directorate for Education, Employment, Labour
and Social Affairs
OECD
Paris, France

Mr Niels Hummeluhr
Ministry of Education
Copenhagen, Denmark

Mr Phillip McKenzie
Principal Administrator
Directorate for Education, Employment, Labour
and Social Affairs
OECD
Paris, France

Mr Gregor Ramsey (Rapporteur)
TASA
Sydney, Australia

DENMARK

National Co-ordinator

Mr Erik Nexelmann, Ministry of Education and Research

OECD Reviewers for the visit, 24 August-2 September, 1998

Mr Gábor Halász
Head of Research Department
National Institute of Public Education
Budapest, Hungary

Mr Erland Ringborg
Director General
Swedish Institute
Stockholm, Sweden

Mr Richard Sweet
Principal Administrator
Directorate for Education, Employment, Labour
and Social Affairs
OECD
Paris, France

Mr Marc Tucker (Rapporteur)
President and Chief Executive Officer
National Center on Education and the Economy
Washington, DC, USA

FINLAND

National Co-ordinator

Ms Tarja Riihimäki, Ministry of Education

OECD Reviewers for the visit, 2-11 November, 1998

Ms Marianne Durand-Drouhin
Principal Administrator
Directorate for Education, Employment, Labour
and Social Affairs
OECD
Paris, France

Mr. Lorenz Lassnigg (Rapporteur)
Assistant Professor
Institute for Advanced Studies, Department of Sociology
Vienna, Austria

Dr Cathleen Stasz
Researcher
RAND Corporation
Santa Monica, USA

Ms Karin Wagner
Professor
FHTW (Fachhochschule für Tecknik und Wirtschaft)
Berlin, Germany

HUNGARY

National Co-ordinators

Professor János Tímár
Budapest University of Economics

OECD Reviewers for the visit, 8-17 June, 1998

Dr Margarida Abecasis
Deputy Director General
Ministry of Work and Solidarity
Lisbon, Portugal

Mr Olivier Bertrand (Rapporteur)
Consultant
Previously of the Centre d'Études et de Recherches
sur les Qualifications (CEREQ)
Paris, France

Dr Richard Koch
Head, Department for International Comparisons
of Vocational Training
Federal Institute for Vocational Training
Berlin, Germany

Mr Richard Sweet
Principal Administrator
Directorate for Education, Employment, Labour
and Social Affairs
OECD
Paris, France

Appendix 1: National Co-ordinators and Review Team Members

JAPAN

National Co-ordinator

Mr Muneharu Iwamoto
Ministry of Education, Science, Sports and Culture

**OECD Reviewers for the visit,
28 September-7 October 1998**

Mr Chon Sun Ihm
Professor and Dean, College of Liberal Arts
Seoul, Korea

Mr Arvo Jäppinen
Ministry of Education and Science
Helsinki, Finland

Mr Phillip McKenzie
Principal Administrator
Directorate for Education, Employment, Labour
and Social Affairs
OECD
Paris, France

Mr David Raffe (Rapporteur)
Centre for Educational Sociology
University of Edinburgh, Scotland, UK

NORWAY

National Co-ordinator

Ms Inger Iversen
Department of Upper Secondary Education
Ministry of Education, Research and Church Affairs

**OECD Reviewers for the visit to Norway
15-24 October, 1997**

Mr Phillip McKenzie
Principal Administrator
Directorate for Education, Employment, Labour
and Social Affairs
OECD
Paris, France

Ms Eleonora Schmid
General Directorate for Technical and Vocational Education
Federal Ministry of Education and Cultural Affairs
Vienna, Austria

Mr David Stern
National Center for Research in Vocational Education
University of California
Berkeley, United States of America

Mr Richard Sweet (Rapporteur)
Dusseldorp Skills Forum
Sydney, Australia

PORTUGAL

National Co-ordinator

Mr Domingos Fernandes,
Department of Secondary Education, Ministry of Education

OECD Reviewers for the visit 3-12 December, 1997

Mr Per Olaf Aamodt
Norwegian Institute for Studies in Research and Higher Education
Oslo, Norway

Mr Phillip McKenzie
Principal Administrator
Directorate for Education, Employment, Labour
and Social Affairs
OECD
Paris, France

Ms Nevzer Stacey (Rapporteur)
Office for Educational Research and Innovation
United States Department of Education
Washington DC, USA

Mr Patrick Werquin
Ingénieur de recherche chargé d'études
Centre d'études et de recherches sur les qualifications
Marseille, France

SWEDEN

National Co-ordinator

Mr Sten Ljungdahl
Ministry of Education and Science

OECD Reviewers for the visit, 25 January-3 February 1999

Ms Merete Pedersen
Chief Adviser, Ministry of Education and Research
Copenhagen, Denmark

Mr Richard Sweet
Principal Administrator
Directorate for Education, Employment, Labour
and Social Affairs
OECD
Paris, France

Mr Jan van Ravens
Co-ordinator, International Strategy
Ministry of Education, Culture and Science
Zoetermeer, The Netherlands

Ms Margaret Vickers (Rapporteur)
Dean of Education
University of Western Sydney
Sydney, Australia.

© OECD 2000

SWITZERLAND

National Co-ordinator

Ms Stéphanie Vanhooydonck
Office fédéral de la formation professionnelle
et de la technologie
Berne

OECD Reviewers for the visit, 11-20 January 1999

Mr Patrice de Broucker (Rapporteur)
Centre for Education Statistics
Statistics Canada
Ottawa, Canada

Mr Werner Clement
Institut für Volkswirtschaftstheorie und politik
Vienna, Austria

Ms Marianne Durand-Drouhin
Principal Administrator
Directorate for Education, Employment, Labour
and Social Affairs
OECD
Paris, France

Ms Marinella Giovine
ISFOL (Istituto per lo sviluppo della formazione
professionale dei lavoratori)
Roma, Italy

UNITED KINGDOM

National Co-ordinator

Mr Philip Lomas
Department for Education and Employment

OECD Reviewers for the visit, 14-25 September 1998

Ms Marianne Durand-Drouhin
Principal Administrator
Directorate for Education, Employment, Labour
and Social Affairs
OECD
Paris, France

Mr Peter Grootings
Consultant
Poland

Mr Ted Hanisch
Director, Arbeidsdirectoratet
Oslo, Norway

Mr Claude Pair (Rapporteur)
Professor at the IUFM (Institut universitaire de formation
des maîtres) of Lorraine, former Chief Education Officer,
Lille
France

UNITED STATES

National Co-ordinator

Ms Nevzer Stacey
Office of Educational Research and Improvement
U.S. Department of Education

OECD Reviewers for the visit, 19-30 October 1998

Mr Ole Briseid
Director General
Royal Norwegian Ministry of Education, Research
and Church Affairs
Oslo, Norway

Dr Ute Laur-Ernst
Head, Directorate 5
Federal Institute for Vocational Training
Berlin, Germany

Mr Richard Sweet
Principal Administrator
Directorate for Education, Employment, Labour
and Social Affairs
OECD
Paris, France

Professor Alison Wolf (Rapporteur)
Professor of Education and Director, International Centre
for Research on Assessment
Institute of Education
University of London
London, United Kingdom

Appendix 2
CONSULTANTS' PAPERS

AINLEY, J. (1996),
Learning about Work in General Secondary Schools, Australian Council for Educational Research, Melbourne, September.

HANNAN, D., RAFFE, D. and SMYTH, E. (1996),
Cross-National Research on School to Work Transitions: An Analytical Framework, Economic and Social Research Institute, Dublin, September.

HUMMELUHR, N. (1997),
The Youth Guarantee in Nordic Countries, Copenhagen, December.

LASSNIGG, L. (1998),
Youth Labour Market Policy in Austria, Institute for Advanced Studies, Vienna, March.

MARQUARDT, R. (1998),
Labour Market Policies and Programs Affecting Youth in Canada, Ottawa, April.

RUMBERGER, R. and LAMB, S. (1998),
The Early Employment and Further Education Experiences of High School Drop-Outs: A Comparative Study of the United States and Australia, University of California, Santa Barbara, May.

YOSHIMOTO, K. (1996),
Transition from School to Work in Japan, Kyushu University, September.

Appendix 3
STATISTICAL TABLES

Table 1.1. **Some contextual features of the countries participating in the Thematic Review**

	AUS	AUT	CAN	CZE	DNK	FIN	HUN	JPN	NOR	PRT	SWE	CHE	UKM	USA
Population '000 (1997)	18 532	8 072	30 287	10 304	5 284	5 140	10 155	126 166	4 493	9 950	8 848	7 087	59 009	266 792
Area '000 sq. km	7 687	84	9 976	79	43	338	93	378	324	92	450	41	245	9 372
Population density	2	96	3	131	123	15	109	334	14	108	20	172	241	28
Federal system of government	Yes	No	Yes	No	No	No	No	No	No	No	No	Yes	Yes	Yes
Per cent of educational decisions taken at the school level, 1998	m	25	m	52	31	36	65	m	9	24	66	m	62[2]	29
GDP per capita, 1998 (USD)	22 689	23 985	24 468	13 137	26 280	21 659	10 524	24 109	27 497	15 266	21 213	26 576	21 170	30 514
– as per cent of OECD average	108	114	116	62	125	103	50	115	131	73	101	126	101	145
GDP growth, 1997-98	3.6	3.1	3.0	-0.7	2.4	5.0	5.1	-2.6	2.3	4.0	2.8	1.7	2.7	3.5
Average GDP per capita, 1990-98 (USD)[1]	18 158	21 512	20 524	2 457	27 767	25 536	3 128	25 306	30 397	7 466	26 363	32 538	17 302	22 983
Average annual GDP growth, 1990-98[1]	2.81	2.33	1.59	0.04	2.52	0.92	-0.74	2.14	3.67	2.51	0.86	0.64	1.59	2.40
Educational participation at age 16, 1996	97	91	91	99	93	93	88	98	94	78	97	87	83	86
Educational participation at age 18, 1996	67	68	68	54	74	83	52	m	83	56	94	78	55	58
Educational participation at age 22, 1996	30	23	32	19	37	46	16	m	39	30	34	23	23	29
1990-96 change in tertiary education enrolments (1990 = 100)	129	120	118	149	121	130	185	121	139	244	141	112	181	106
Unemployment rate, 1998	8.0	4.7	8.3	6.5	5.1	11.4	8.0	4.1	3.3	4.9	8.2	4.2	6.3	4.5
Average unemployment, 1990-97	9.1	4.1	10.1	4.1	8.1	12.1	9.6	2.8	5.3	6.1	7.4	3.4	8.7	6.2
Labour force participation rate, age 15-24, 1998	67.6	58.5	62.0	49.0	71.5	49.7	40.8	48.3	63.8	47.4	50.0	67.2	69.5	65.9
Labour force participation rate, age 25-54, 1998	80.0	84.7	84.3	88.6	87.4	87.1	77.8	82.1	87.8	83.8	88.0	87.8	83.3	84.1
Expenditure on employment services and labour market programmes[3]	0.21	0.30	0.18	0.06	1.10	0.35	0.09	0.12	0.44	0.26	0.47	0.48	m	0.10
Trade union density, 1994	35	42	38	m	76	81	m	24	58	32	91	27	34	16
Collective bargaining coverage, 1994	80	98	36	m	69	95	m	21	74	71	89	50	47	18

m: Missing data.
1. At 1990 price levels and exchange rates.
2. Refers to England. The figure for Scotland is 40%. Refers to public lower secondary education.
3. Per cent of GDP spent on employment and labour market services for every one per cent of unemployment.

Sources: OECD education, labour force and economic databases; OECD (1994b, 1998a and 1999a).

Appendix 3: Statistical Tables

Table 2.1a. **Indicators of transition outcomes by dominant pathway types in OECD countries**

Dominant pathway type[1]

Indicators	App. CHE	App. DEU	Mixed pathways AUT	Mixed pathways DNK	Mixed pathways NLD	Mixed pathways NOR	School-based vocational BEL	School-based vocational CZE	School-based vocational FIN	School-based vocational FRA	School-based vocational HUN	School-based vocational ITA	School-based vocational POL	School-based vocational SWE	School-based vocational UKM	General education AUS	General education CAN	General education GRC	General education IRL	General education JPN	General education KOR	General education NZL	General education PRT	General education ESP	General education USA
1. Unemployment to population ratio, 15-19 year-olds	✓	✓	✓				✓								X	X	X			✓	✓	X		X	
2. Non-student unemployed as a percentage of all 15-19 year-olds	✓	✓				✓	✓		X	✓					X	X								X	✓
3. Long term unemployment, 15-19 year-olds					X	✓			✓	✓		X		✓				X	X		✓				✓
4. Unemployment to population ratio, 20-24 year-olds	✓		✓	✓	✓	✓			X	X		X						X	X					X	✓
5. Long term unemployment, 20-24 year-olds			✓	✓	X	✓	X		✓			X	X					X	X		✓				
6. Employment to population ratio, 20-24 year-olds	✓		✓	✓		✓	✓	✓	X			X				✓		X						X	X
7. Percentage of non students aged 20-24 employed	✓	✓	✓	✓		X	✓					X				✓		X	✓					X	
8. Youth to adult unemployment ratio						✓	✓	✓	✓			X		✓	✓	✓	X	X	X	✓					X
9. Percentage not in education one year after the end of compulsory schooling																		X							
10. Apparent upper secondary graduation rates	✓						✓	✓	✓	✓	X	X	X	✓			X	X	X	✓		X		X	X
11. 16-25 year-olds at document literacy level 4/5				X	X										✓		✓		X						X
12. Percentage of 20-24 year olds with low qualifications					✓	✓		✓			X	✓		✓		✓		X		✓	✓	✓		X	✓
13. Relative disadvantage of low qualified 20-24 year-olds			X					X			X		✓		✓		X	X	X	✓	✓	X	X	X	X
14. Percentage tertiary qualified at age 25-29		X	X		✓	✓	✓	X			X	X	X		X		✓	✓	✓	✓	✓	X	X	✓	✓

Key: ✓: In the top (most favourable) quartile of OECD countries. X: In bottom (least favourable) quartile of OECD countries. m: Missing. ▨: Countries of the Thematic Review.
1. Table 2.2 gives the data upon which this grouping is based.
Sources: See Table 2.1b.

© OECD 2000

Table 2.1b. **Transition outcome indicators: values, sources and notes**

Indicator values

	1	2	3	4	5	6	7	8	9	10	11	12	13	14
Australia	10.1	6.0	41.9	9.6	45.0	71.4	78.0	2.3	3.3	m	19.2	26.1	1.8	25.1
Austria	3.0	2.0	50.6	3.3	21.4	69.4	84.9	1.4	8.8	86	m	18.4	1.9	7.6
Belgium	2.3	1.6	57.1	10.9	71.3	46.3	70.0	2.4	0.0	117	25.0	22.3	1.7	34.0
Canada	9.6	3.7	m	9.3	m	66.7	70.3	2.1	19.8	73	31.0	14.7	2.1	55.4
Czech Republic	5.6	3.1	33.0	6.4	46.1	64.2	84.8	2.3	0.7	83	m	7.2	3.4	10.2
Denmark	5.6	2.3	16.2	4.7	27.0	73.2	73.8	1.6	18.3	81	m	33.7	1.6	20.4
Finland	9.1	3.2	13.0	12.7	19.3	54.7	63.2	2.5	7.6	98	m	20.5	1.8	22.9
France	1.9	1.6	59.0	12.7	54.8	36.9	64.3	2.3	m	85	m	21.8	1.6	28.9
Germany	2.6	1.6	50.8	6.9	55.2	63.1	77.9	1.1	2.0	86	22.8	22.7	1.8	16.7
Greece	7.1	5.9	71.3	19.1	70.3	45.1	60.3	3.3	19.0	80	m	24.6	0.6	29.0
Hungary	3.9	m	57.1	6.8	62.6	54.7	m	2.1	25.9	86	m	19.8	1.9	12.8
Ireland	3.9	m	63.6	7.6	66.1	65.4	m	1.6	10.0	79	13.2	22.4	2.3	34.5
Italy	7.4	6.3	79.6	17.1	83.4	35.9	50.2	3.6	m	79	m	36.9	0.8	7.1
Japan	1.9	m	m	5.3	m	68.6	m	2.3	2.0	99	m	m	m	m
Korea	2.2	m	6.8	8.6	13.8	49.7	m	2.5	8.0	91	m	4.9	1.3	30.8
Netherlands	6.7	m	89.6	4.6	83.3	74.7	m	2.2	7.0	81	26.0	30.4	1.4	25.5
New Zealand	9.4	m	m	9.6	m	67.1	m	2.4	19.8	93	20.6	28.7	1.6	22.4
Norway	6.6	m	0.0	5.6	18.8	69.4	m	4.1	7.4	117	m	12.3	1.7	30.2
Poland	3.4	m	31.8	13.8	55.3	49.1	m	2.5	m	94	8.5	m	m	m
Portugal	3.3	m	49.0	5.8	56.2	57.9	m	2.3	9.6	91	m	55.6	0.8	16.2
Spain	10.9	9.1	55.1	19.4	65.3	41.4	59.6	2.1	23.9	73	m	38.7	0.9	32.4
Sweden	6.1	1.8	15.3	10.1	33.4	55.3	69.7	2.2	3.5	81	40.7	14.1	1.7	27.8
Switzerland	2.2	0.9	m	5.4	m	64.8	87.4	1.7	12.6	81	26.2	20.8	1.8	18.9
United Kingdom	9.6	7.2	30.8	7.7	36.9	68.3	74.3	2.4	26.0	m	21.5	10.8	2.6	23.5
United States	7.7	2.8	7.3	6.1	11.1	71.4	75.8	3.0	18.0	72	16.1	14.2	2.2	35.4

m: Missing data.

Appendix 3: Statistical Tables

Table 2.1b. **Key to Table 2.1b** (cont.)

Indicator	Description	Sources	Notes
1.	Unemployment to population ratio, 15-19 year-olds, 1998	OECD labour force database; Switzerland INES Network B transition collection	Switzerland subject to high sampling variability
2.	Non-student unemployed as a per cent of all 15-19 year-olds, 1996	INES Network B 1998 special transition collection	Switzerland subject to high sampling variability
3.	Per cent of unemployed 15-19 year-olds unemployed for six months or more, 1998	OECD labour force database	Ireland 1997
4.	Unemployment to population ratio, 20-24 year-olds, 1998	OECD labour force database; Switzerland INES Network B transition collection	
5.	Per cent of unemployed 20-24 year-olds unemployed for six months or more, 1998	OECD labour force database	Ireland 1997
6.	Employment to population ratio, 20-24 year-olds, 1998	OECD labour force database; Switzerland INES Network B transition collection	
7.	Per cent of non-students employed, age 20-24, 1996	INES Network B 1998 special transition collection	Italy 25-59 year-olds
8.	Ratio of the unemployment rate among 15-24 year-olds to the unemployment rate among 25-54 year-olds, 1998	OECD labour force database	
9.	Per cent not in education one year after the end of compulsory schooling	OECD education database	Belgium, Germany, Netherlands: per cent not in full-time education one year after the end of compulsory schooling
10.	Apparent upper secondary graduation rates	OECD (1998), *Education at a Glance. OECD Indicators*, Paris, Table C2.3	1. Refers to first educational programmes 2. Belgium Flemish Community
11.	Per cent of 16-25 year-olds at document literacy level 4/5, 1994-95	OECD (1997), *Literacy Skills for the Knowledge Society*, Paris, Table 1.6	1. Belgium Flemish community 2. Switzerland average of French and German communities
12.	Per cent of 20-24 year-olds whose highest level of education is lower secondary school (ISCED 0, 1, 2), 1996	OECD education database	New Zealand 1997
13.	Ratio of low qualified 20-24 year-olds' share of total unemployment to their share of total employment	OECD education database	1. See Appendix 6 2. New Zealand 1997
14.	Per cent of 25-29 year-olds with tertiary qualifications, 1996	OECD education database	

INES: Indicators of International Education Systems.

From Initial Education to Working Life

Table 2.2. **Estimated distribution of upper secondary students by the main education and training pathways after compulsory education (1996 or closest year)**

	Pathway		
	Apprenticeship-type	School-based vocational	General education
Thematic Review countries			
Australia	3	2	94
Austria	41	37	22
Canada	1	5	94
Czech Republic	x	82	18
Denmark	44	14	42
Finland	5	47	48
Hungary	x	68[1]	32
Japan	a	26	74
Norway	25	27	48
Portugal	4	32	64
Sweden	n	60	40
Switzerland	60	9	31
United Kingdom	24	33	43
United States	n	12	88
Other countries			
Belgium	3	65	32
France	11	43	46
Germany	52	24	24
Greece	n	32	68
Ireland	5	15	80
Italy	a	72	28
Korea	a	42	58
Netherlands	23	47	30
New Zealand	8	30	62
Poland	m	69	31
Spain	2	37	61

a: Not applicable.   *m*: Data not available.   *n*: Magnitude either negligible or zero.   *x*: Included in another column.

1. In Hungary some one in four upper secondary students are found in lower vocational (trade) schools, and are often referred to in national sources (see for example Lannert, 1997) as apprentices, although the combinations of school-based and practical training that they undertake is often more similar to school-based vocational programmes in which the young person has the status of a student than to apprenticeships in which the young person has the status of an employee and takes part in a contract of employment and training. The closure of many former state-owned enterprises whose facilities were formerly used for practical training resulted in some two thirds of all workshop training occurring in school in the mid 1990s, compared to less than one third in 1990. Growth in the number of small firms, on the other hand, has created new opportunities for practical training by self-employed craftsmen. It is not clear how many of the latter category are formally indentured as apprentices. As a result they are included in the school-based vocational category.

Sources: **Australia:** Country note, Background Report, and Ball and Robinson (1998). Refers to 16 year-olds. Note that the proportion entering the school-based vocational and apprenticeship-type pathways rises between the ages of 16 and 19, and for the 15-19 age group as a whole is roughly 20%. **Canada:** OECD (1998i). **Czech Republic:** OECD (1998i). Refers to new upper secondary entrants. **Denmark:** Background Report. Refers to the destinations of those leaving compulsory school. The school-based vocational category refers to HHX and HTX programmes which also share many of the characteristics of general education programmes. **Japan:** Background Report. Refers to total students. **Norway:** Country note. Refers to first year of upper secondary education. Proportions in the general pathway rise somewhat by the third and final year of upper secondary education. **Portugal:** OECD (1998i). **Sweden:** Background Report. Refers to upper secondary entrants. **United Kingdom:** Background Report. Refers to England and Wales. **United States:** Background Report. Refers to 1992. **All other countries:** OECD (1998a), Table C2.1.

Appendix 3: Statistical Tables

Table 2.3. **Indices of relative labour market advantage by level of education, 1996**

	University vs. lower secondary			University vs. upper secondary			Upper secondary vs. lower secondary		
	Unemployment	Employment	Earnings	Unemployment	Employment	Earnings	Unemployment	Employment	Earnings
	Age 25-29	Age 25-29	Age 30-44	Age 25-29	Age 25-29	Age 30-44	Age 25-29	Age 25-29	Age 30-44
Australia	286	137	169	169	109	145	169	125	116
Austria	200	115	m	86	97	m	232	118	m
Canada	372	156	190	205	116	158	181	134	120
Czech Republic	1 627	164	245	327	107	162	497	153	152
Denmark	300	134	157	117	102	132	255	131	119
Finland	375	149	190	224	122	173	168	122	110
Hungary	507	161	225	244	113	162	208	143	139
Norway	202	122	162	112	103	138	181	119	118
Portugal	102	106	310	99	120	183	103	88	169
Sweden	447	144	164	267	113	149	168	128	110
Switzerland	m	111	164	m	84	149	m	133	124
United Kingdom	443	177	231	194	117	185	228	152	125
United States	579	152	282	254	113	186	228	135	152
Average	**453**	**141**	**207**	**191**	**109**	**160**	**218**	**129**	**130**

The *unemployment index* is the unemployment rate among those with the lower of each pair of education levels divided by the unemployment rate among those with the higher of each pair, times 100. Austria, 1995. *Source:* OECD (1998a), Table D4.1a.
The *employment index* is the employment to population ratio among those with the higher of each pair of education levels divided by the employment to population ratio among those with the lower of each pair, times 100. Austria, 1995. *Source:* OECD (1998a), Table D4.2a.
The *earnings index* is the mean pre-tax earnings from work of those with the higher of each pair of education levels divided by the mean pre-tax earnings from work of those with the lower of each pair, times 100. Australia and Finland, 1995. *Source:* OECD (1998a), Table F7.2.

© OECD 2000

Table 2.4. **School leaving shortly after the end of compulsory education, 1996**

	Ending age of compulsory schooling	Per cent not in education one year after the ending age of compulsory schooling
Thematic Review countries		
Australia	15	3
Austria	15	9
Canada	16	20
Czech Republic	15	1
Denmark	16	18
Finland	16	8
Hungary	16	26
Japan	15	2
Norway	16	7
Portugal	14	10
Sweden	16	4
Switzerland	15	13
United Kingdom	16	26
United States	17	18
Other countries		
Belgium[1]	15	0
Belgium[2]	18	73
France	16	8
Germany[1]	15	2
Germany[2]	18	65
Greece	14.5	19
Ireland	15	10
Korea	14	12
Mexico	16	60
Netherlands[1]	16	7
Netherlands[2]	18	70
New Zealand	16	20
Poland	15	6
Spain	16	24

1. The first age at which full-time education is not compulsory.
2. The first age at which education is not compulsory.
Source: OECD education database.

Appendix 3: Statistical Tables

Table 2.5. **Relationship between youth and adult unemployment**[1]

	15-19 year-olds with 25-54 year-olds		20-24 year-olds with 25-54 year-olds		Period
	Linear fit	Polynomial second order fit	Linear fit	Polynomial second order fit	
Thematic Review countries					
Australia	.81	.91	.97	.98	1966-1997
Canada	.83	.88	.93	.94	1953-1997
Denmark	.03	.06	.79	.80	1983-1997
Finland	.79	.89	.97	.97	1963-1997
Japan	.73	.76	.94	.95	1968-1997
Norway	.71	.77	.97	.97	1972-1997
Portugal	.05	.21	.35	.46	1974-1997
Sweden	.47	.62	.96	.97	1963-1997
United Kingdom	.73	.78	.89	.90	1984-1997
United States	.80	.81	.88	.89	1957-1997
Average	**.60**	**.67**	**.87**	**.88**	
Other countries					
Belgium	.41	.50	.84	.85	1983-1997
France	.00	.64	.78	.92	1968-1997
Germany	.40	.66	.79	.85	1970-1997
Greece	.03	.11	.76	.83	1983-1997
Ireland	.12	.18	.95	.95	1961-1997
Italy	.19	.90	.73	.97	1970-1997
Korea	.76	.88	.80	.82	1980-1997
New Zealand	.97	.97	.97	.97	1986-1997
Spain	.23	.67	.79	.94	1972-1997
Average	**.35**	**.61**	**.82**	**.90**	

1. The table shows multiple correlation coefficients between annual unemployment to population ratios for each of the two youth age groups on the one hand and annual unemployment to population ratios for 25-54 year-olds on the other. The period covered is shown in the right hand column. In each case both a linear trend line and a second order polynomial trend line were fitted to the data. Both are shown in the table. The extent to which the second order polynomial coefficient exceeds the corresponding linear coefficient indicates the extent to which the fit between the two sets of data is best described by a curvilinear rather than a linear relationship. An example of a curvilinear relationship is 15-19 year-olds in Sweden. Here the per cent of youth unemployed has risen as adult unemployment has risen up to a certain level, and remained relatively constant with increases in adult unemployment beyond that point. An example of a linear relationship is 20-24 year-olds in the United States. Here the per cent of youth unemployed is low when adult unemployment is low, average when it is average, and high when it is high.
Source: OECD labour force database.

From Initial Education to Working Life

Table 2.6. **Ratios of the relative difference between males and females on 14 indicators of transition outcomes and on two composite indices of gender equity in transition outcomes**[1]

						Indicator[2]										Index	
	1	2	3	4	5	6	7	8	9	10	11	12	13	14		E[3]	LM[4]
Thematic Review countries																	
Australia	1.22	1.59	1.10	1.33	1.05	1.11	1.12	1.01	2.00	m	m	1.09	1.44	1.11		1.40	1.22
Austria	1.37	1.48	1.31	1.08	1.70	1.06	1.02	1.20	1.81	1.06	m	1.20	1.36	1.12		1.30	1.29
Canada	1.18	1.55	m	1.37	m	1.05	1.08	1.18	1.05	1.10	1.01	1.37	1.13	1.10		1.13	1.22
Czech Republic	1.03	1.19	1.03	1.04	1.06	1.38	1.15	1.33	1.78	1.04	m	1.32	1.21	1.34		1.37	1.16
Denmark	1.23	1.34	2.05	1.07	1.88	1.06	1.14	1.65	1.08	1.14	m	1.24	1.35	1.15		1.15	1.42
Finland	1.19	1.27	1.00	1.09	1.58	1.24	1.14	1.09	1.16	1.12	m	1.08	1.04	1.17		1.13	1.18
Hungary	1.27	m	1.08	1.97	1.19	1.29	m	1.12	1.22	m	m	1.03	1.07	1.51		1.25	1.28
Japan	1.43	m	m	1.08	m	1.01	m	1.38	m	1.07	m	m	m	m		1.07	1.22
Norway	1.05	m	1.00	1.25	1.56	1.13	m	1.01	1.04	m	m	1.11	1.02	1.29		1.15	1.14
Portugal	1.81	m	1.80	1.19	1.05	1.14	m	1.08	1.48	m	m	1.29	1.01	1.52		1.43	1.30
Sweden	1.10	1.09	1.06	1.28	1.18	1.11	1.03	1.02	1.04	1.02	1.09	1.05	1.27	1.07		1.06	1.13
Switzerland	1.21	3.07	m	1.50	m	1.12	1.02	1.04	2.00	1.12	1.06	1.20	1.10	2.45		1.57	1.44
United Kingdom	1.30	1.74	1.45	1.70	1.21	1.13	1.12	1.09	1.22	m	1.32	1.02	1.03	1.11		1.17	1.31
United States	1.27	1.40	1.00	1.17	1.33	1.12	1.25	1.32	1.02	1.10	1.13	1.02	2.09	1.12		1.08	1.33
Other countries																	
Belgium	1.12	1.12	1.70	1.06	1.01	1.25	1.19	1.28	1.28	m	1.07	1.44	1.51	1.35		1.28	1.25
France	1.47	1.39	m	1.18	m	1.27	1.28	1.00	m	1.01	m	1.17	1.11	1.16		1.12	1.24
Germany	1.08	1.24	1.02	1.44	1.24	1.02	1.15	1.51	1.02	1.00	1.36	1.09	1.04	1.06		1.11	1.19
Greece	1.67	1.79	1.09	1.47	1.20	1.58	1.65	1.20	2.06	1.14	m	1.42	1.20	1.34		1.49	1.43
Ireland	1.14	m	1.08	1.35	1.17	1.09	m	1.07	1.89	1.12	1.37	1.64	1.70	1.06		1.42	1.23
Italy	1.03	1.04	1.05	1.10	1.02	1.38	1.27	1.40	m	1.09	m	1.25	1.01	1.22		1.18	1.14
Korea	1.10	m	1.41	1.47	1.00	1.23	m	1.11	1.02	1.00	m	2.26	1.58	1.06		1.34	1.27
Netherlands	1.37	m	1.05	1.30	1.03	1.03	m	1.55	1.24	m	1.44	1.28	1.32	1.06		1.25	1.24
New Zealand	1.06	m	m	1.51	m	1.11	m	1.18	1.36	1.15	1.05	1.00	1.08	1.22		1.16	1.19
Poland	1.19	m	1.07	1.04	1.17	1.27	m	1.20	m	m	1.28	m	m	m		1.28	1.16
Spain	1.04	1.02	1.17	1.38	1.13	1.48	1.29	1.30	1.40	1.25	m	1.36	1.08	1.23		1.31	1.21

m: Missing data.
1. For all entries in the table a value of 1.00 indicates no difference between males and females. Values that are greater than 1.00 indicate the extent to which one or other gender is greater than the other on the indicator or index.
2. The 14 indicators correspond to indicators 1 to 14 in Table 2.1a.
3. Index of gender equity in education transition outcomes.
4. Index of gender equity in labour market transition outcomes.
Source: See Table 2.1a.

174

© OECD 2000

Appendix 3: Statistical Tables

Table 2.7. **Unemployment to population ratios, 1998**

	15-19 year-olds	20-24 year-olds	20-24 ratio as a per cent of 15-19 ratio
Thematic Review countries			
Australia	10.1	9.6	95
Austria	3.6	3.5	95
Canada	9.6	9.3	97
Czech Republic	5.6	6.4	115
Denmark	5.6	4.7	84
Finland	9.1	12.7	139
Hungary	3.9	6.8	173
Japan	1.9	5.3	275
Norway	6.6	5.6	86
Portugal	4.3	10.2	237
Sweden	6.1	10.1	165
Switzerland	m	5.4	m
United Kingdom	9.6	7.7	80
United States	7.7	6.1	80
Other countries			
Belgium	2.3	10.9	471
France	1.9	12.7	673
Germany	2.6	6.9	272
Greece	7.1	19.1	269
Ireland	3.9	7.6	196
Italy	7.4	17.1	232
Korea	2.2	8.6	387
Netherlands	6.7	4.5	67
New Zealand	9.4	9.6	102
Poland	3.4	13.8	407
Spain	10.9	19.4	178
Turkey	4.6	8.2	179
Average	**5.8**	**9.3**	**206.2**

m: Missing data.
Sources: OECD labour force database and for Switzerland INES Network B special transition collection.

Table 2.8. **Youth to adult unemployment ratios, 1990-98 (Thematic Review countries)**

	1990	1991	1992	1993	1994	1995	1996	1997	1998
Australia	2.6	2.3	2.4	2.2	2.2	2.3	2.2	2.4	2.3
Austria	m	m	m	m	1.4	1.5	1.7	1.6	m
Canada	1.7	1.7	1.7	1.7	1.7	1.8	1.8	2.0	2.1
Czech Republic	m	m	m	2.3	2.6	2.4	2.3	2.1	2.3
Denmark	1.5	1.3	1.5	1.4	1.3	1.6	1.8	1.7	1.6
Finland	4.3	2.9	2.5	2.2	2.2	2.0	2.0	2.2	2.3
Hungary	m	m	2.0	2.1	2.1	2.1	2.1	2.1	2.1
Japan	2.6	2.8	2.6	2.5	2.3	2.4	2.5	2.4	2.3
Norway	2.8	2.5	2.8	2.7	2.8	2.9	3.2	3.4	4.1
Portugal	2.6	2.7	3.1	2.8	2.4	2.5	2.6	m	m
Sweden	3.6	3.2	2.9	3.0	2.9	2.6	2.6	2.5	2.2
Switzerland	m	2.0	1.8	2.0	1.7	1.8	1.3	1.5	1.7
United Kingdom	1.8	1.9	1.8	2.0	2.0	2.1	2.1	2.3	2.4
United States	2.4	2.4	2.2	2.3	2.5	2.7	2.8	2.9	3.0
Average	**2.6**	**2.3**	**2.3**	**2.2**	**2.2**	**2.2**	**2.2**	**2.2**	**2.4**

m: Missing data.
The table shows the ratio of the unemployment rate among 15-24 year-olds to the unemployment rate among 25-54 year-olds.
Source: OECD labour force database.

© OECD 2000

Table 2.9a. **Relative labour market disadvantage of 15-19 year-olds, 1990-1998[1]**

	1990	1991	1992	1993	1994	1995	1996	1997	1998
Thematic Review countries									
Australia	2.6	2.5	2.8	2.5	2.5	2.8	2.6	2.6	2.7
Austria	m	m	m	m	1.5	1.7	1.7	2.2	m
Canada	1.8	1.7	1.9	2.0	2.0	2.1	2.3	2.7	2.7
Czech Republic	m	m	m	3.1	3.7	3.6	3.8	3.8	4.8
Denmark	1.1	0.8	0.9	0.9	0.9	1.3	1.7	1.5	1.8
Finland	5.0	3.8	3.4	2.9	2.8	2.4	2.4	2.9	3.0
Hungary	m	m	3.4	3.7	3.5	4.0	4.0	4.2	4.0
Japan	3.2	3.2	3.2	2.8	2.7	2.7	3.0	2.7	2.7
Norway	3.5	3.3	3.1	3.4	3.6	3.6	4.3	4.6	4.6
Portugal	2.2	2.2	2.6	2.6	2.3	2.5	2.7	m	m
Sweden	4.1	3.5	3.0	3.3	3.0	2.6	2.6	2.8	2.8
United Kingdom	1.8	1.9	1.8	2.0	2.1	2.2	2.4	2.5	2.8
United States	3.1	3.1	3.1	3.1	3.3	3.5	3.5	3.6	3.6
Average	**2.8**	**2.6**	**2.6**	**2.7**	**2.6**	**2.7**	**2.8**	**3.0**	**3.2**
Other countries									
Belgium	3.5	3.7	3.8	5.1	4.9	4.8	3.1	4.7	4.2
France	2.3	3.0	2.6	2.9	2.5	2.4	2.4	2.5	2.4
Germany	0.8	0.9	0.7	0.7	0.7	0.8	0.9	0.8	0.9
Greece	4.4	4.4	4.8	5.1	5.0	5.1	6.3	5.7	5.0
Ireland	2.3	2.3	2.3	2.6	2.7	2.8	2.4	2.3	1.9
Italy	4.9	4.9	5.2	4.6	4.3	4.2	4.0	3.9	4.1
Korea	1.5	1.4	1.5	1.4	1.4	1.4	1.3	1.4	3.5
Netherlands	2.2	2.4	1.8	2.0	1.9	2.9	3.1	3.0	3.0
New Zealand	2.5	2.4	2.4	2.6	2.6	2.8	2.8	2.6	2.6
Poland	m	m	2.7	3.1	4.2	4.4	3.9	3.6	3.6
Spain	2.4	2.2	2.3	2.8	2.8	2.7	2.9	3.2	3.0
Turkey	2.1	1.9	1.8	1.9	1.9	2.0	1.9	2.2	2.0
OECD average	**2.7**	**2.6**	**2.7**	**2.8**	**2.8**	**2.9**	**2.9**	**3.0**	**3.1**

m: Missing data.
1. The ratio of the age group's share of total unemployment divided by its share of total employment.
Source: OECD labour force database.

Table 2.9b. **Relative labour market disadvantage of 20-24 year-olds, 1990-1998**[1]

	1990	1991	1992	1993	1994	1995	1996	1997	1998
Thematic Review countries									
Australia	1.6	1.6	1.6	1.6	1.6	1.4	1.4	1.7	1.6
Austria	m	m	m	m	1.3	1.2	1.4	1.1	m
Canada	1.5	1.6	1.5	1.5	1.5	1.5	1.5	1.5	1.5
Czech Republic	m	m	m	1.4	1.3	1.4	1.3	1.3	1.5
Denmark	1.7	1.7	1.8	1.9	1.6	1.6	1.5	1.5	1.2
Finland	2.1	1.9	2.1	2.0	2.0	1.8	1.8	1.7	1.8
Hungary	m	m	1.5	1.5	1.6	1.5	1.6	1.6	1.5
Japan	1.7	1.9	1.7	1.8	1.7	1.8	1.8	1.8	1.7
Norway	2.0	1.9	2.2	2.1	2.1	2.2	2.2	2.1	2.4
Portugal	2.1	2.2	2.3	2.2	2.1	2.2	2.3	m	m
Sweden	1.9	2.1	2.4	2.6	2.6	2.3	2.4	2.2	2.0
United Kingdom	1.4	1.6	1.6	1.7	1.6	1.7	1.7	1.7	1.7
United States	1.6	1.6	1.6	1.6	1.6	1.7	1.8	1.8	1.8
Average	**1.7**	**1.8**	**1.8**	**1.8**	**1.8**	**1.7**	**1.7**	**1.7**	**1.7**
Other countries									
Belgium	2.0	2.0	1.9	2.3	2.4	2.5	2.4	2.5	2.3
France	2.3	2.3	2.3	2.6	2.7	2.7	2.6	2.8	2.6
Germany	0.9	1.0	1.0	1.1	1.1	1.1	1.1	1.1	1.1
Greece	3.7	3.6	3.5	3.4	3.5	3.4	3.6	3.7	3.1
Ireland	1.0	1.3	1.4	1.5	1.4	1.3	1.4	1.4	1.3
Italy	3.1	3.2	3.2	3.3	3.3	3.4	3.5	3.4	3.3
Korea	0.6	0.5	0.5	0.5	0.6	0.5	0.6	0.6	2.3
Netherlands	1.3	1.2	1.3	1.4	1.4	1.4	1.4	1.2	1.3
New Zealand	1.5	1.7	1.7	1.6	1.6	1.5	1.5	1.7	1.8
Poland	m	m	2.3	2.4	2.5	2.6	2.5	2.3	2.3
Spain	2.2	2.1	2.1	2.2	2.2	2.1	2.2	2.0	2.0
Turkey	2.2	2.3	2.5	2.5	2.2	2.5	2.6	2.6	2.6
OECD average	**1.8**	**1.9**	**1.9**	**1.9**	**1.9**	**1.9**	**1.9**	**1.9**	**1.9**

m: Missing data.
1. The ratio of the age group's share of total unemployment divided by its share of total employment.
Source: OECD labour force database.

Table 2.10. **Percentage of unemployed 15-19 and 20-24 year-olds unemployed for six months or more, 1990-98**

	1990	1991	1992	1993	1994	1995	1996	1997	1998
Aged 15-19									
Australia	35.5	44.7	47.7	46.9	44.5	40.4	40.4	38.2	41.9
Austria	m	m	m	m	4.7	34.5	38.8	50.2	51.6
Czech Republic	m	m	m	27.5	27.5	41.7	37.7	32.5	33.0
Denmark	32.9	36.4	23.4	28.7	22.6	18.6	25.8	19.0	16.2
Finland	m	m	m	m	m	14.8	15.7	9.7	13.0
Hungary	m	m	30.8	39.5	44.0	57.6	61.5	58.6	57.1
Norway	21.4	20.8	22.6	30.8	20.6	30.0	0.0	0.0	0.0
Portugal	61.5	53.7	24.2	36.6	36.5	40.7	51.5	34.7	49.0
Sweden	22.4	18.3	21.3	17.6	22.3	29.8	25.3	22.3	23.3
United Kingdom	28.8	34.4	41.0	50.6	45.0	39.3	39.4	35.7	30.8
United States	3.2	4.0	6.7	6.0	9.4	8.8	8.7	8.1	m
Country average	**29.4**	**30.3**	**27.2**	**31.6**	**27.7**	**32.4**	**31.3**	**28.1**	**31.6**
OECD average	**24.7**	**23.0**	**19.9**	**21.4**	**24.6**	**22.0**	**23.8**	**24.6**	**24.9**
Aged 20-24									
Australia	37.4	48.1	57.7	53.9	56.2	47.5	44.8	50.5	45.0
Austria	m	m	m	m	12.2	31.8	33.0	32.7	19.3
Czech Republic	m	m	m	29.9	35.2	45.2	43.7	42.9	46.1
Denmark	43.5	39.6	37.0	31.8	36.4	25.7	22.5	21.1	27.0
Finland	m	m	m	m	m	40.2	33.1	27.6	20.4
Hungary	m	m	44.8	53.4	60.2	70.5	69.4	68.4	62.6
Norway	35.0	35.8	33.5	39.1	35.5	27.8	26.1	15.8	18.8
Portugal	56.7	54.2	33.3	34.4	48.0	57.4	56.3	55.9	56.2
Sweden	11.8	18.3	23.4	31.0	40.9	38.5	42.3	41.7	44.6
United Kingdom	41.0	42.3	55.1	58.6	61.6	54.6	51.6	46.7	36.9
United States	5.8	8.1	11.6	11.6	14.0	12.7	12.9	12.3	m
Country average	**33.0**	**35.2**	**37.0**	**38.2**	**40.0**	**41.1**	**39.6**	**37.8**	**37.7**
OECD average	**49.1**	**48.6**	**49.1**	**50.9**	**52.5**	**51.7**	**51.3**	**49.7**	**48.5**

m: Missing data.
Source: OECD labour force database.

Appendix 3: Statistical Tables

Table 3.1. **Size of general education pathways and tertiary participation**

	Percentage of upper secondary students in general education pathways	Tertiary education participation rate at the first age at which tertiary participation is at a maximum, 1996			First age at which tertiary participation is at a maximum, 1996
		University	Non-university	Total	
Australia	94	25	10	35	19
Austria	22	17	3	20	20
Belgium	32	19	25	44	20
Canada	94	25	22	47	19
Czech Republic	18	15	6	21	19
Denmark	42	23	2	25	23
Finland	48	25	8	33	21
Germany	24	16	2	18	22
Greece	68	38	11	49	19
Hungary	30	16	< 1	16	20
Korea	58	29	19	48	19
New Zealand	62	27	6	33	20
Norway	48	18	11	29	21
Portugal	64	17	6	23	21
Spain	61	29	2	31	20
Switzerland	31	11	6	17	22
United Kingdom	40	25	6	31	19
United States	88	21	16	37	19

Sources: Table 2.2 and OECD education database.

© OECD 2000

Table 3.2. **Duration and composition of the transition, 1996**

	First age at which education is not compulsory (A)	Age of leaving education (B)	Age of entering work (C)	Transition duration Total (C – A)	Transition duration In education (B – A)	Transition duration Not in education (C – B)
Thematic Review countries						
Australia	15	19.8	21.4[1]	6.4	4.8	1.6
Austria	15	18.6	m	–	3.6	–
Canada	16	20.4	22.8[2]	6.8	4.4	2.4
Czech Republic	15	18.2	m	–	3.2	–
Denmark	16	19.4	24.3[3]	8.3	3.4	4.9
Finland	16	18.8	m	–	2.8	–
Hungary	16	18.1	21.9[3]	5.9	2.1	3.8
Japan	15	m	m	–	–	–
Norway	16	19.0	24.6[3]	8.6	3.0	5.6
Portugal	14	18.5	22.7[2]	8.7	4.5	4.2
Sweden	16	18.7	23.6[6]	7.6	2.7	4.9
Switzerland	15	19.3	21.0[7]	6.0	4.3	1.7
United Kingdom	16	18.6	21.0[1]	5.0	2.6	2.4
United States	17	18.5	22.0[2]	5.0	1.5	3.5
Other countries						
Belgium	15	20.9	22.7[2]	7.7	5.9	1.8
France	16	21.5	23.2[2]	7.2	5.5	1.7
Germany	15	19.8	22.2[2]	7.2	4.8	2.4
Greece	14.5	19.4	23.0[2]	8.5	4.9	3.6
Ireland	15	19.9	21.2[2]	6.2	4.9	1.3
Italy	14	m	25.3[2]	11.3	–	–
Netherlands	16	20.9	23.4[2]	7.4	4.9	2.5
Spain	16	20.3	25.6[2]	9.6	4.3	5.3

m: Missing data.

Column A: The first age at which educational attendance is not compulsory: for Belgium, Germany and the Netherlands the first age at which full-time educational attendance is not compulsory. For each of these three countries 18 is the first age at which educational attendance is not compulsory. *Sources:* OECD (1998a), Paris; European Communities (1998), *Education Across the European Union*, Brussels.
Column B: The first age, in 1996, at which 50% or more of the cohort were not studying. *Source:* OECD education database.
Column C: The first age, in 1996 or the nearest year, at which 50% of the cohort were employed but not studying.
Sources:
1. Australian Bureau of Statistics data supplied to the Thematic Review.
2. For all countries except the United States, for which the Current Population Survey is the source, the source is the monthly *Labour Force Survey*, and, in the case of European Community members, the *European Labour Force Survey*.
3. Statistics Denmark Labour Force Survey data supplied to the *Thematic Review*.
4. Hungarian Background Report, Table 4, derived from the 1997 first quarter *Labour Force Survey*.
5. Norwegian Background Report, Annex I, Appendix I, Table 1, derived from Statistics Norway 1994 quarterly surveys.
6. Statistics Sweden Labour Force Survey data supplied to the Thematic Review.
7. Swiss Federal Statistical Office Labour Force Survey data supplied to the Thematic Review.

Appendix 3: Statistical Tables

Table 3.3. **Change in the duration and composition of the transition, 1990-96**

	First age at which education is not compulsory	Age at which 50% are not in education 1990	Age at which 50% are not in education 1996	Age at which 50% are employed and not in education 1990	Age at which 50% are employed and not in education 1996	Total duration of the transition in years 1990	Total duration of the transition in years 1996
Thematic Review countries							
Australia	15	17.9	19.5	19.7	21.4	4.7	6.4
Canada	16	19.4	20.2	21.2	22.8	5.2	6.8
Denmark	16	18.9[1]	20.2	21.0[1]	24.3	5.0[1]	8.3
Portugal	14	17.6	19.9	19.0	22.7	5.0	8.7
Sweden	16	18.4	19.6	18.7	23.6	2.7	7.6
Switzerland	15	20.0	20.0	20.0[2]	21.0	5.0	6.0
United Kingdom	16	17.0	17.8	18.9	21.0	2.9	5.0
United States	17	19.1	19.8	21.4	22.0	4.4	5.0
Other countries							
Belgium	15	20.5	20.9	21.5	22.7	6.5	7.7
France	16	20.0	21.6	21.4	23.2	5.4	7.2
Germany	15	19.8	20.3	20.5	22.2	5.5	7.2
Greece	14.5	19.0	19.8	22.7	23.0	8.2	8.5
Ireland	15	18.7	19.5	20.0	21.2	5.0	6.2
Italy	14	19.0	19.7	22.0	25.3	8.0	11.3
Netherlands	16	21.6	21.9	23.1	23.4	7.1	7.4
Spain	16	19.4	21.1	23.5	25.6	7.5	9.6
Average		**19.1**	**20.1**	**21.0**	**22.9**	**5.5**	**7.4**

1. 1989.
2. 1991.
Sources: Because of data gaps for 1990 the age at which 50% are not in education is calculated from *Labour Force Survey* data for both 1990 and 1996. In some cases this leads to slight differences in the estimated period spent in post-compulsory education for 1996 compared to Table 3.2. The source for the age at which 50% are employed and not in education is as for Table 3.2.

Table 3.4. **Duration of the transition through upper secondary education to tertiary study, (Thematic Review countries), 1996**

	First age at which education is not compulsory (A)	First age at which tertiary participation is at a maximum, 1996[1] (B)	Difference (B) − (A)
Australia	15	19 (35)	4
Austria	15	20 (20)	5
Canada	16	19 (47)	3
Czech Republic	15	19 (33)	4
Denmark	16	23 (25)	7
Finland	16	22 (33)	6
Hungary	16	20 (16)	4
Norway	16	21 (29)	5
Portugal	14	21 (23)	7
Sweden	16	21 (22)	5
Switzerland	15	22 (17)	7
United Kingdom	16	19 (31)	3
United States	17	19 (37)	2

1. Actual participation rates at the indicated age are shown in brackets.
Source: OECD education database.

© OECD 2000

From Initial Education to Working Life

Table 4.1. **Percentage of students employed,**[1,2] **1996**

	Aged 15-19	Aged 20-24	Aged 25-29
Australia	39.7	62.9	75.7
Austria	1.3	19.3	43.5
Belgium	0.8	6.4	52.9
Canada	31.6	43.5	53.7
Czech Republic	3.3	5.5	23.1
Denmark	41.6	32.5	43.0
Finland	10.3	24.9	45.7
France	0.4	6.1	35.5
Germany	2.0	11.3	28.5
Greece	0.7	4.6	23.9
Italy	0.8	3.1	10.2
Spain	2.2	9.8	30.2
Sweden	14.5	19.7	40.8
Switzerland	13.4	44.8	79.2
United Kingdom	36.2	41.3	64.0
United States	31.7	59.4	72.3
Country average	**14.4**	**24.7**	**45.1**

1. Excludes those in apprenticeship-type programmes.
2. Figures are based upon *Labour Force Survey* first quarter data.

Source: INES Network B 1998 special transition collection.

Table 4.2. **Percentage of 18 and 22 year-olds combining study with work, 1984 and 1997**

	18 year-olds		22 year-olds	
	1984	1997	1984	1997
Men	16.5	19.6	7.0	10.6
Women	11.3	17.3	6.2	11.5
Total	**13.9**	**18.4**	**6.6**	**11.1**

Source: OECD (1999b), Table 8.

Appendix 3: Statistical Tables

Table 4.3. **Percentage of employed 15-19 year-olds working part-time,[1] 1990 and 1998**

	1990	1998
Thematic Review countries		
Australia	41.7	64.6
Austria	m	5.6
Canada	64.6	71.1
Czech Republic	m	8.1
Denmark	30.7	56.3
Finland	30.7	56.3
Hungary	m	5.3
Norway	65.2	69.3
Portugal	5.3	8.1
Sweden	42.2	65.6
Switzerland	47.2[2]	49.7
United Kingdom	33.0	53.8
United States	62.4	67.1
Other countries		
Belgium	24.0	29.9
France	23.4	22.2
Germany	4.2	10.0
Greece	7.1	14.1
Italy	5.2	9.8
Netherlands	69.8	84.5
New Zealand	43.1	62.9
Poland	m	34.9
Spain	8.7	14.5

m: Missing data.
1. Refers to persons who normally worked for 30 hours or less per week. Includes both students and non-students.
2. 1991.
Sources: OECD labour force database and Swiss Federal Statistical Office Labour Force Survey data supplied to the Thematic Review.

Table 4.4. **Percentage of the population unemployed and not in education, 15-19 and 20-24 year-olds, 1996**

	15-19	20-24
Australia	6.0	7.5
Austria	1.9	3.7
Belgium	1.6	10.4
Canada	3.7	9.3
Czech Republic	3.1	3.0
Denmark	2.3	7.3
Finland	3.2	12.4
France	1.6	12.6
Germany	1.6	6.8
Greece	5.9	16.5
Italy	6.3	16.6
Spain	9.1	17.6
Sweden	1.8	8.8
Switzerland	0.9[1]	2.4[1]
United Kingdom	7.2	8.5
United States	2.8	5.5
Country average	**3.9**	**9.8**

1. Subject to high sampling variability.
Source: INES Network B 1998 special transition collection.

Table 4.5. **Proportion of young people in total population, 1980, 1990, 1998 and 2005**
(Thematic Review countries)

		1980	1990	1998	2005
Australia	Age 15-19	8.8	8.2	7.0	6.9
	Age 20-24	8.7	8.0	7.1	6.8
	Age 25-29	8.2	8.3	7.6	6.8
Austria	Age 15-19	8.7	6.4	6.1	6.1
	Age 20-24	7.8	8.3	6.3	6.4
	Age 25-29	6.7	9.0	7.7	6.4
Canada	Age 15-19	9.9	7.0	6.7	6.6
	Age 20-24	9.9	7.7	6.7	6.6
	Age 25-29	9.0	9.4	7.1	6.8
Czech Republic	Age 15-19	6.7	8.1	7.4	6.4
	Age 20-24	6.8	6.6	8.6	6.8
	Age 25-29	8.1	6.6	7.5	8.6
Denmark	Age 15-19	7.7	7.2	5.4	5.6
	Age 20-24	7.3	7.7	6.5	5.2
	Age 25-29	7.3	7.8	7.4	6.1
Finland	Age 15-19	8.0	6.1	6.5	6.1
	Age 20-24	8.0	7.0	6.1	6.4
	Age 25-29	8.5	7.6	6.2	6.3
Hungary	Age 15-19	6.0	7.6	7.1	6.2
	Age 20-24	7.3	6.6	8.3	6.5
	Age 25-29	8.4	5.9	7.4	8.4
Japan	Age 15-19	7.1	8.1	6.2	5.1
	Age 20-24	6.8	7.1	7.3	5.8
	Age 25-29	7.8	6.5	7.6	6.7
Norway	Age 15-19	7.7	7.4	5.9	6.3
	Age 20-24	7.6	8.0	6.5	5.8
	Age 25-29	7.4	7.6	7.5	6.0
Portugal	Age 15-19	9.3	8.6	7.1	5.5
	Age 20-24	8.4	7.8	8.3	6.6
	Age 25-29	7.7	7.4	8.1	8.0
Sweden	Age 15-19	6.8	6.6	5.5	6.4
	Age 20-24	6.7	7.1	6.0	5.7
	Age 25-29	7.0	7.1	6.8	5.8
Switzerland	Age 15-19	8.0	6.2	5.6	6.0
	Age 20-24	7.4	7.8	5.9	5.8
	Age 25-29	7.3	8.8	7.2	5.9
United Kingdom	Age 15-19	8.2	6.6	6.1	6.5
	Age 20-24	7.3	7.6	6.2	6.2
	Age 25-29	6.8	7.9	6.9	6.0
United States	Age 15-19	9.2	6.9	6.8	7.1
	Age 20-24	9.4	7.5	6.5	6.9
	Age 25-29	8.8	8.7	6.8	6.5

Notes: Data for the 1950-1995 period are United Nations demographic estimates. Data for the 1996-2050 period are from the United Nations Population Division's medium variant population projections.
Source: United Nations, World Population Prospects 1950-2050 (1998 revision).

Appendix 4

USING LABOUR MARKET INDICATORS OF TRANSITION OUTCOMES IN COMPARATIVE STUDIES
NATIONAL TRANSITION INDICATORS

In some respects the effectiveness at the national level of the transition from initial education to working life can be judged by education indicators. Such indicators might include upper secondary graduation rates, educational attainment levels, rates of transition between lower- and upper-secondary education, or rates of participation in tertiary education. Ultimately, however, it is in the labour market that the effectiveness of young people's preparation for work must be judged. This Appendix discusses the merits, within international comparative studies, of a variety of broad labour market indicators in assessing the transition outcomes achieved by young people. It concentrates upon indicators that can be obtained fairly readily from standard labour force surveys, rather than upon indicators – such as the proportion of time in the first five years out of education spent in employment – that require special surveys or longitudinal studies. Employment, unemployment, activity or inactivity are its main focus, as these have been the principal national indicators used within public policy debates to assess young people's success or otherwise in moving from initial education to working life. Other indicators such as earnings, labour turnover or the utilisation of skills are not included. Nor does the discussion cover indicators such as job satisfaction or self-esteem that look at the success or otherwise of transitions from the young person's perspective.

Teenage unemployment rates or unemployment to population ratios?

The unemployment rate among teenagers has been used widely, in the media as well as in public policy debates, as a key indicator of the difficulties that young people experience in the transition from initial education to working life. It framed much of the analysis of transition difficulties in the OECD's examination of the entry of young people into working life in the 1970s (OECD, 1977*a* and 1977*b*). Typically derived from national monthly labour force surveys, it measures the proportion of 15-19 year-olds in the labour force who are seeking work and who are available for work. As an indicator of difficulties in the transition from initial education to working life it has its greatest value when labour force participation rates are high among 15-19 year-olds (and conversely when education participation rates are low) and when the transition from education to the labour force is fairly sharp, with little overlap occurring between education and working life.

The first of these conditions certainly applied in the mid-1970s, with full-time educational enrolments rates among 17 year-olds averaging 45% among 20 OECD Member countries in 1974, compared to total enrolment rates for 17 year-olds in the same group of countries that averaged 86% in the mid-1990s.[1] The second condition is more likely to have applied in the mid-1970s than in the mid-1990s, not the least because twenty years ago opportunities for students to hold part-time jobs and otherwise to combine learning with earning were substantially fewer in many countries than they are at present. In the mid 1980s it is certainly true that these opportunities were less than at present (OECD, 1996*b*). While a key indicator in the mid-1970s, the unemployment rate among teenagers has become of less value as a measure of transition difficulties as education participation rates have risen, and as the boundaries between education and the labour market have become more blurred.

As the proportion of young people who are in the labour force falls, most commonly because of rising participation in full-time education, the teenage unemployment rate applies to an increasingly small proportion of youth. For example, while the unemployment rate among 15-19 year-olds in France in 1998 was 24%, only 8% of 15-19 year-olds were in the labour force (Table A4.1). In Canada the unemployment rate among 15-19 year-olds in 1998 was 20%, but 48% of the age group were in the labour force, six times the proportion observed in France. In the case of France only 2% of the total age group were seeking work. In the case of Canada 10% of the age group, or five times the proportion, wanted work but were unable to find it. Conversely, the teenage unemployment rate in Spain in 1998 was, at 41%,

---
1. *Sources*: OECD (1977*a*), Table 2 and OECD (1998*a*), Table C1.2.

Table A4.1. **Labour force participation rates, unemployment rates and unemployment to population ratios, 15-19 year-olds, 1998**

	Labour force participation rate	Unemployment rate	Unemployment to population ratio
Australia	54	19	10
Austria[1]	39	9	4
Belgium	8	30	2
Canada	48	20	10
Czech Republic	23	25	6
Denmark	65	9	6
Finland	32	28	9
France	8	24	2
Germany	31	8	3
Greece	18	41	7
Hungary	16	25	4
Iceland	52	8	4
Ireland	27	14	4
Italy[2]	20	37	7
Japan	18	11	2
Korea	11	21	2
Luxembourg	10	11	1
Mexico	45	6	2
Netherlands	56	12	7
New Zealand	56	16	9
Norway[3]	49	14	7
Poland	11	31	3
Portugal[4]	24	18	4
Spain[3]	26	41	11
Sweden[3]	30	21	6
Switzerland	22	5[5]	2[5]
Turkey	37	12	5
United Kingdom[3]	62	16	10
United States[3]	53	15	8

1. 1997.
2. 14-19 year-olds.
3. 16-19 year-olds.
4. 1996.
5. Subject to high sampling variability.
Sources: OECD labour force database; Switzerland INES Network B special transition collection, 1998.

over twice as high as the Australian rate of 19%, and was the highest in the OECD. Yet because the teenage labour force participation rate in Spain is less than half that in Australia, the proportion of all teenagers unemployed in the two countries was quite similar – 11% in Spain and 10% in Australia.

Two lessons spring from this analysis: quite similar unemployment rates can mask very large differences in the proportion of the teenage population affected by unemployment; and widely differing teenage unemployment rates can mask close similarities in the proportion of the teenage population who are seeking work. Another lesson is that conventional unemployment rates tend to provide an inflated picture of the scale of the unemployment problem within OECD Member countries. For these reasons the teenage unemployment to population ratio – the proportion of the total population aged 15-19 that is unemployed – generally provides a better indication of the relative scale of transition difficulties.

A further problem when using teenage unemployment rates to make international comparisons of young people's transition difficulties is that there tends to be an inverse relationship between labour force participation and unemployment rates (Figure A4.1). Youth unemployment rates tend to be lower in countries where many teenagers participate in the labour force and higher in those where few participate (OECD, 1996b). This arises for two reasons:

– The relatively small numbers of young people who leave school when enrolment rates are high are more likely to be those who, under any circumstances, will have the most difficulty in finding work: those with low levels of educational attainment, behaviour problems, or poor motivation, for example. Such young people will comprise a bigger share of the young unemployed when the proportion of youth in the labour market is low.

Appendix 4: Using Labour Market Indicators of Transition Outcomes

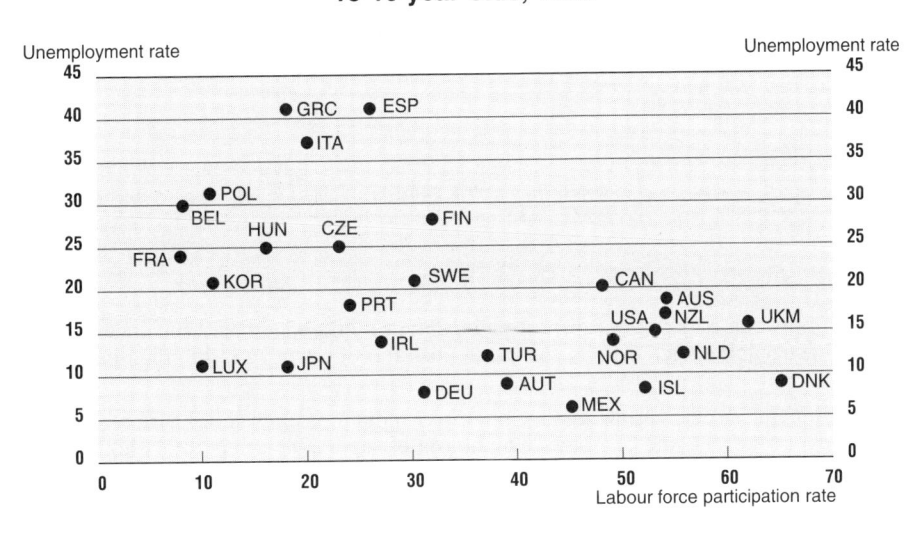

Figure A4.1. **Labour force participation and unemployment rates, 15-19 year-olds, 1998**

Source: OECD labour force database.

– In those countries where few students leave school early but many young people combine education and work, unemployment rates are generally lower among students than among non-students.[2] This is particularly evident in countries with extensive apprenticeship systems, since the apprentices are classified as workers in labour force surveys.

Students or non-students?

When using national unemployment measures as indicators of young people's transition difficulties, the use of unemployment to population ratios rather than unemployment rates will overcome the problems that result from the distorting impact of widely varying national labour force participation rates. But it does not overcome the difficulties that result from the growing overlap between educational participation and labour force participation among young people. This overlap can have two consequences. First, it can make unemployment appear relatively lower through the inclusion of apprentices within the numerator when unemployment rates are being calculated. In the case of Austria, Germany and Switzerland, for example, some one in four or more of all 15-19 year-old students are also in programmes such as apprenticeships, and all of these are counted within the normal labour force survey as employed. In each country those who are both employed and attending education constitute two thirds or more of the total number of employed 15-19 year-olds, and 80% or more of all 15-19 year-olds are participating in education. In such cases both unemployment rates and unemployment to population ratios appear quite different if calculated using only non-students rather than the total labour force or population (students plus non-students) aged 15-19. For example, in the case of Germany the unemployment rate for the age group is 8% when calculated using the total 15-19 year-old labour force, but 21% when calculated using only the non-student labour force (Table A4.2). In all three countries the unemployment rate among 15-19 year-olds is at least twice as high in the non-student labour force as in the total labour force of the same age. In all three countries only 2% of all 15-19 year-olds are looking for work, yet the unemployment to population ratio rises to five times or more this level when only the non-student population is considered.

The second consequence of the overlap between teenagers' educational participation and their labour force participation is that it can make the total number of teenagers who are unemployed appear relatively high. This will be the case where large numbers of full-time students have part-time jobs, and where many of those counted as unemployed in labour force surveys are students seeking part-time work rather than non-students seeking a full-time job. In Norway in 1996 for example, 81% of the 16-19 year-olds recorded as being unemployed in the labour force survey had education as their principal activity at the same time as they were seeking part-time work.[3] Where there is

---

2. Whilst there is minimal variation among the generally fairly low unemployment rates found among teenagers in countries in which labour force participation rates are high (40% or more), unemployment rates among teenagers vary widely among that group of countries in which teenage labour force participation rates are low. On the one hand countries such as Japan and Luxembourg manage to combine low participation rates with low teenage unemployment rates. On the other hand in countries such as Spain Italy and Greece, low rates of teenage labour force participation are associated with high rates of teenage unemployment.
3. *Source:* National authorities.

© OECD 2000

Table A4.2. **Unemployment rates and unemployment to population ratios in apprenticeship countries, 15-19 year-olds, 1996**

	Unemployment rate calculated using:		Unemployment to population ratio calculated using:	
	Non-student labour force	Total labour force	Non-student population	Total population
Austria	12	6	10	2
Germany	21	8	17	2
Switzerland	17	5	12	2

Source: INES Network B special collection on school-to-work transition, 1998. Switzerland subject to high sampling variability.

a positive association between early labour market engagement by teenagers and the chances of gaining employment as a young adult, such job search activity can be an indicator of effective rather than ineffective national transition frameworks.

The impact of student job seekers upon teenage unemployment measures varies widely among OECD countries, and within countries over time. It is the outcome of a number of factors, including total enrolment rates, the extent to which the employment of students arises from apprenticeship-type arrangements rather than from part-time work out of school hours, and whether unemployment rates are higher or lower in the student labour force than in the non-student labour force. In general it appears that teenage unemployment rates are lower than would otherwise be the case when students in the labour force are included in unemployment calculations, as unemployment rates are generally lower among students than among non-students (which can be inferred from Table A4.3, columns B and C). Nevertheless in the case of Greece, Italy and Sweden the two rates are virtually the same, and in Finland the rate is higher among students than among non-students.

Table A4.3. **Impact of student labour force participation upon the measured unemployment rate, 15-19 year-olds, 1996**

	Percentage of students in the labour force	Unemployment rate calculated using:		Unemployment to population ratio calculated using:		
		Total labour force	Non-student labour force	All unemployed as numerator and total population as denominator	Non-student unemployed as numerator and total population as denominator	Non-student unemployed as numerator and non student population as denominator
	(A)	(B)	(C)	(D)	(E)	(F)
Australia	48	20	26	12	6	23
Austria	34	6	12	3	2	10
Belgium	3	23	32	2	2	13
Canada	38	20	29	9	4	22
Czech Republic	3	14	15	3	3	11
Denmark	51	4	10	2	2	8
Finland	26	47	25	16	3	21
France	5	25	58	2	2	39
Germany	26	8	21	2	2	17
Greece	2	41	40	7	6	30
Italy	2	36	35	7	6	22
Spain[1]	6	45	41	12	9	34
Sweden[2]	18	22	23	5	2	14
Switzerland[3]	50	5	17	2	1	12
United Kingdom[2]	53	18	29	11	7	24
United States[2]	37	16	22	7	3	15

1. 14-19 year-olds.
2. 16-19 year-olds.
3. Subject to high sampling variability.

Source: INES Network B special collection on school-to-work transition, 1998. Differences between Tables A4.1 and A4.3 in unemployment rates and unemployment to population ratios are generally due to differences in reference periods, with the Network B pilot collection being limited to the March to May period rather than to annual averages. For example in the case of Finland the period used for the pilot collection coincides with significant numbers of students seeking part-time employment. In the case of Sweden the difference can also be attributed to definitional differences, with the Network B collection conforming more closely to ILO definitions than the data sources used for Table A4.1.

Where significant numbers of students are in the labour force, unemployment to population ratios will be substantially affected by the inclusion or non-inclusion of unemployed students. For example in Australia, where nearly half of all 15-19 year-old students are in the labour force, the unemployment to population ratio is halved from 12% to 6% when unemployed students are excluded from the numerator (Table A4.3, columns D and E). On the other hand in France, where very few students are in the labour force, the unemployment to population ratio is changed very little by a similar exclusion of unemployed students. Where unemployment to population ratios are calculated using only non-students in both the numerator and the denominator (column F), the resulting indicator will again show the relative rankings of countries, as well as the apparent scale of the unemployment problem, quite differently. France, for example, is one of the countries which has the lowest proportion of all 15-19 year-olds who are unemployed of the 16 countries in Table A4.3 (2%), yet it has the highest proportion of non-student 15-19 year-olds who are looking for work (39%). Unemployment to population ratios that are based only upon non-students are highly influenced by educational participation rates, and as such, when educational participation rates are high, are more an indicator of the labour market difficulties of a small group of the least qualified early school leavers than of the transition problems faced by youth as a whole.

It is clear from Table A4.3 that the relative ranking of countries on these various unemployment-based indicators of teenagers' transition difficulties can vary widely according to whether unemployment rates or unemployment to population ratios are used, and according to whether labour force participation by students is included or excluded from the calculation.

What is also clear is that using the number of non-students who are seeking work as a proportion of the total population of 15-19 year-olds as the measure of the scale of teenagers' transition difficulties leads to substantially lower measures of the overall scale of the youth transition problem than does the use of conventional teenage unemployment rates. Greece, for example, has a 41% unemployment rate among teenagers using conventional unemployment rates, but only 6% of the total 15-19 year-old population are non-students who are unemployed. In the United Kingdom a conventional teenage unemployment rate of 18% sits beside the fact that only 7% of that country's 15-19 year olds are non-students who are looking for work.

In summary, if unemployment-based measures are to be used as national indicators of teenagers' transition difficulties:

- *Unemployment to population ratios are to be preferred to conventional unemployment rates;*[4] *and*
- *Unemployment to population ratios that are calculated using only non-students in the numerator and the total population in the denominator are to be preferred to those that use both students and non students in both.*

Youth inactivity rates

Unemployment is only one of the ways in which lack of success in the transition from initial education to working life can be judged. Transitions to insecure part-time work, or to inactivity – engaged neither in education nor in the labour market – are others. Of the two, the second category is often more readily assessable in labour force surveys. A more comprehensive measure of transition difficulties than unemployment might be the proportion of young people who are engaged neither in education nor in employment – in other words the sum of non-students who are unemployed and non-students who are not in the labour market, expressed as a proportion of the age group. Table A4.4 shows this inactivity measure, and compares it to unemployment to population ratios derived by including non-students in the numerator and students plus non-students in the denominator (taken from Table A4.3, column E).

Among the 16 countries shown in Table A4.4, the size of that group of 15-19 year-olds who are inactive (unemployed and not studying or engaged neither in education nor the labour force) is, on average, two and a half times as great as the group represented by non-student job seekers alone. Use of this broader inactivity measure suggests a larger group of young people experiencing difficulties in the transition from initial education than does the use of a measure of the incidence of unemployment among non students. However, it has only a lesser impact upon the relative ranking among countries, with most countries retaining quite similar rank orders whichever measure is used.

While the active engagement of all young people in education, employment, training or job search is a common goal among OECD Member countries, caution needs to be expressed at the suggestion that *all* of those young people who are engaged neither in education nor in the labour force are experiencing difficulties in the transition to work. In some countries – for example in Norway – it is very common for young people to take a period out of both study and work in their late teens and early twenties in order to travel or to undertake voluntary service. These activities are

---

4. However particularly in countries in which few students participate in the labour force the unemployment to population ratio and the unemployment rate can be complementary. The first can indicate the scale of the problem among teenagers as a whole, while the second can indicate something of the labour market difficulties of poorly qualified early school leavers. However even here a better indicator would be the proportion of those who are not full-time students who have employment as their principal activity.

Table A4.4. **Inactivity measures and unemployment to population ratios, 15-19 year-olds, 1996**

	Not in education and not employed as a % of the population	Non-student unemployed as a % of the population
Australia	9	6
Austria	7	2
Belgium	9	2
Canada	8	4
Czech Republic	12	3
Denmark	8	2
Finland	6	3
France	3	2
Germany	4	2
Greece	11	6
Italy	16	6
Spain[1]	14	9
Sweden[2]	7	2
Switzerland	3	1
United Kingdom[2]	12	7
United States[2]	8	3

1. 14-19 year-olds.
2. 16-19 year-olds.
Source: INES Network B special collection on school-to-work transition, 1998.

commonly seen by young people themselves as constructive, allowing the development of resourcefulness, language skills, an international outlook and independence. Such activities are often also recognised as of value in higher education selection. Where countries have strong currencies and high GDP per capita this form of activity can become quite readily available to young people. Data provided in the Norwegian Background Report shows that in 1994 nearly one in four 19 year-olds in that country were neither working, studying nor unemployed, more than seven times the number of registered unemployed. Among 24 year-olds the comparable figure was over one in six.

In the Czech Republic it has been estimated that around a third of education leavers who are registered as unemployed have in fact been voluntarily so in the sense that they are either travelling abroad or prolonging their last holidays after having left education (Kuchar, 1998). The Czech social security system has allowed such people to be registered as unemployed and to collect income support for some period of time.

Australian data provided to the review (Table A4.5) shows that this group of "inactive" young people can be quite diverse in its composition. Home duties and child care make up the largest category (nearly half of the total), and for young women this is the major category. This is of concern to the extent that those included in the category are poorly qualified single parents with few education or employment re-entry pathways available to them. In Australia voluntary activities and travel or leisure account for one in six of the group, and illness, injury or disability account for a similar proportion.

Table A4.5. **Activities of 15-19 year-olds, not in the labour force and not attending an educational institution, September 1997, Australia**
Percentage of group

Main activity	Males	Females	Persons
Home duties, child care	0	73	49
Retired, voluntarily inactive	11	5	7
Disability, handicap	15	0	5
Illness, injury	17	6	10
Travel, holiday, leisure	28	4	13
Unpaid voluntary work	3	4	4
Other activities	25	6	12
Total	100	100	100

Source: Australian Bureau of Statistics, *Persons Not in the Labour Force*, September 1997, Cat. No. 6220.0.

In summary:
- *Inactivity measures can be a useful supplement to measures of the incidence of unemployment among non-students, but should be treated with caution, as some young people encompassed by them appear to be engaged in constructive activities rather than experiencing difficulties in the transition to work.*

Youth to adult unemployment ratios

Unemployment measures express something of the difficulty that young people experience in the labour market when competing with one another for work. But they also compete with adults for the available jobs. The ratio of the unemployment rate among youth to the unemployment rate among adults is one indicator of their success in this competition, and hence of the openness of labour markets to young new entrants. This openness can be a function of a number of factors: the widespread availability of employment and training places in firms, under-pinned by appropriate wage and employment contract arrangements; quality training arrangements that give young people the skills that they need to compete effectively with adults; the availability of part-time employment opportunities for students; and the absence of restrictive employment protection arrangements that discourage employers from hiring new labour market entrants.

Youth to adult unemployment ratios[5] averaged 2.4 among OECD countries in 1996, indicating that on average unemployment rates among youth were two and a half times as high as among adults. However, this ratio ranged from lows of 1.0 in Germany, 1.3 in Switzerland and 1.4 in Austria to highs of 3.6 in Italy and 3.8 in Greece and Korea. The preceding discussion would suggest that the labour markets in the former group of countries are more open to young people than are those in the latter.

Table A4.6. **Standard and adjusted youth to adult unemployment ratios,[1] 1996**

	Derived from unemployment rates calculated using the full labour force	Derived from unemployment rates calculated using the non-student youth labour force and the full adult labour force
Thematic Review countries		
Australia	2.2	2.3
Austria	1.4	1.4
Canada	1.9	2.2
Czech Republic	2.2	1.9
Denmark	1.0	2.0
Finland	1.8	1.9
Norway	3.4	m
Portugal	2.6	m
Sweden[3]	2.2	2.5
Switzerland	1.3	1.6
United Kingdom[3]	2.1	2.4
United States[3]	2.8	2.8
Other countries		
Belgium	2.4	2.4
France	2.4	2.7
Germany	1.0	1.6
Greece	3.8	4.2
Italy	3.6	3.8
Spain[2]	2.2	1.9
Country Average[4]	**2.2**	**2.4**

1. The ratio of the unemployment rate among 15-24 year-olds to the unemployment rate among 25-54 year-olds.
2. 14-19 year-olds.
3. 16-19 year-olds.
4. Based only on those countries for which both sets of data are available.
Sources: OECD labour force database and INES Network B special collection on school-to-work transition, 1998.

There is extensive overlap between teenagers' educational participation and their labour force participation in countries with well-established apprenticeship systems such as Germany, Switzerland and Austria, and extensive involvement of full-time students in part-time work in countries such as Australia and Canada. Given the earlier discussion of the impact of educational participation upon other unemployment measures this might suggest that youth

---

5. The ratio of the unemployment rate among 15-24 year-olds to the unemployment rate among 25-54 year-olds.

to adult unemployment ratios calculated using unemployment rates that include students need to be treated with care. However, the impact of this upon youth to adult unemployment ratios that are based upon unemployment rates for 15-24 year-olds in most cases is not great. Teenagers commonly constitute a fifth or less of the youth (15-24 year-old) labour force, with this share tending to have fallen (OECD, 1996d), and the educational participation rates of young adults are substantially less than those of teenagers

Table A4.6 shows youth to adult unemployment ratios calculated from unemployment rates that are based upon the full labour force, and comparable ratios calculated from unemployment rates obtained in the normal way for adults, but for 15-24 year-olds using only the non-student labour force. On average the ratios rise by only 9% when the non-student youth labour force is used (from a mean of 2.2 to a mean of 2.4), and only in the cases of Denmark and Germany can an appreciable increase be observed. However, even with this increase, Germany remains well towards the lower end of the OECD experience. Except for the case of Denmark there is little change in countries' rank order using either method

In summary:

– *Youth to adult unemployment ratios are a useful indicator of the extent to which young people are able to compete with adults for the available employment, and appear relatively insensitive to the overlap between young people's educational participation and their labour force participation.*

Teenagers or young adults? Employment or unemployment?

The confounding impact of educational participation upon labour market indicators of transition outcomes can be reduced by focusing upon the 20-24 year-old age group rather than upon teenagers. By this age labour force participation rates have risen, fewer young people are students, and a smaller proportion of young people are both students and labour force participants. In conjunction these features will reduce the disparity between unemployment rates and unemployment to population ratios, as well as reducing differences between indicators based upon student and non-student populations. Nevertheless, while educational participation has fallen considerably by age 24 compared to the teenage years, it still remains high among young adults, with one in four or more of 24 year-olds still participating in education in Denmark, Finland, Iceland, Norway and Sweden in 1996. One in five or more of that age were participating in education in Australia the Netherlands and Portugal.

The 20-24 age group has two further attractions. It is an age at which family formation and child rearing are generally having a lesser impact upon the labour market participation of young women than is the case at age 25-29. And it is in the 20-24 age group that the results of foundations laid down by policies implemented in the immediate post-compulsory years (15-19) can be expected to begin to emerge. At ages 15-19 a very high proportion of young people are still the targets of transition policies rather than their beneficiaries. If national transition policies have been effective, a high proportion of those in their early 20s who have left education should reasonably be expected to have a job.

In conjunction these arguments point to the advantages of using transition indicators in the 20-24 age group that focus upon employment rather than unemployment. Such indicators are more likely to capture the benefits of effective transition frameworks, rather than the consequences of ineffective ones, and if based upon the non-student population will avoid complications resulting from the education-labour force overlap. Table A4.7 shows standard employment to population ratios for 20-24 year-olds based upon the total population, as well as, where available, employment to population ratios based only upon non-students (*i.e.* ratios with non-students in both the numerator and the denominator). As will be apparent, employment to population ratios for 20-24 year-olds that are calculated from non-student populations are generally significantly higher than those based upon the total age group. In the same way that teenage unemployment to population ratios suggest that the scale of the youth transition problem is less than is suggested by teenage unemployment rates, non-student employment to population ratios for 20-24 year-olds suggest that the proportion of young people who make successful transitions is higher than is suggested by total employment to population ratios. Of the 16 countries in Table A4.7 for which both measures are available, the employment to population ratio is some ten percentage points higher when the non-student population is used than when the total population is used.

Figure A4.2 gives an example of the use of the employment to population ratio among 20-24 year-old non-students as an indicator of successful outcomes in comparative studies of transition. It shows that there is a strong positive relationship between engagement in the labour market by teenagers and employment among young adults. Those countries such as Switzerland, Austria, Canada, the United Sates, Australia and the United Kingdom, in which high proportions of teenagers are engaged in the labour market, whether through part-time work as students or through apprenticeships, are more likely to have high proportions of their young adults who are employed after leaving education. Conversely, in those countries such as Greece, Spain, France, Italy and Belgium that provide few opportunities for teenagers to become engaged in the labour market, the proportion of non-student young adults who hold jobs is markedly lower. The Czech Republic provides the only significant exception to the latter result.

In summary:

– *Employment to population ratios have many advantages over unemployment-based indicators when assessing the effectiveness of national transition frameworks. They have particular advantages when applied to young adult (20-24 year-old) non-student populations.*

Appendix 4: Using Labour Market Indicators of Transition Outcomes

Table A4.7. **Employment to population ratios, total and for non-students, 20-24 year-olds, 1996**

	Total population	Non-students[1]
Australia	73	78
Austria	64	79
Belgium	56	70
Canada	65	70
Czech Republic	68	85
Denmark	74	74
Finland	62	63
France	59	64
Germany	66	78
Greece	55	60
Hungary	52	m
Iceland	73	m
Ireland	60	m
Italy[2]	40	50
Japan	70	m
Korea	59	m
Luxembourg	59	m
Mexico	59	m
Netherlands	72	m
Norway	65	m
New Zealand	72	m
Poland[2]	47	m
Portugal	53	m
Spain	36	60
Sweden	53	70
Switzerland	79	87
Turkey	48	m
United Kingdom	67	74
United States	70	76

m: Missing data.
1. Percentage of non-students who are employed.
2. 1995.
Sources: OECD labour force data base and INES Network B special collection on school-to-work transition, 1998.

Figure A4.2. **Labour force involvement by teenage students and employment by young adults who have left education, 1996**

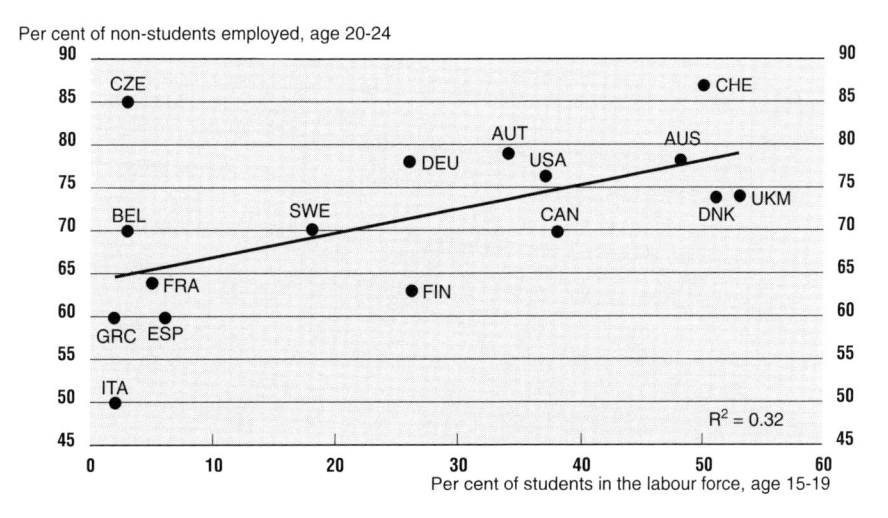

Source: INES Network B special collection on school-to-work transition, 1998.

© OECD 2000

Conclusion

Youth unemployment rates should be used with caution in any attempts to compare the outcomes of national transition policies and programmes. They should be used with particular caution when they apply to teenagers, and in nearly all circumstances unemployment to population ratios are to be preferred for this age group. Those unemployment to population ratios calculated using only non-students in the numerator and the total population in the denominator are even more preferable when teenagers are the focus of the analysis. Inactivity measures can be a useful supplement to unemployment-based measures of transition difficulties, but should be treated with some caution, as some young people who are involved neither in education nor in the labour force appear to be involved in activities that can make a constructive contribution towards their subsequent transition to work. Employment to population ratios have many advantages over unemployment-based indicators when assessing the effectiveness of national transition frameworks. They have particular advantages when applied to young adult non-student populations.

Appendix 5

A COMPREHENSIVE FRAMEWORK FOR INDICATORS OF THE TRANSITION FROM INITIAL EDUCATION TO WORKING LIFE

Purposes

The Thematic Review of the Transition from Initial Education to Working Life has drawn heavily upon available education and labour market indicators. In the process it has become apparent that these address only part of the spectrum of transition issues, and that many gaps exist in any attempt to build a comprehensive framework of transition indicators. Developing better international indicators of transition from initial education is one element in contributing to an understanding of the underlying issues and problems confronting member countries. In common with indicators in other fields, indicators of the transition from initial education to working life should be able to serve three main purposes. They should:

- Inform the process of policy formation and allow key transition policy issues (such as the effectiveness of different pathways, the costs and benefits of extended transition periods, or when it can be said that transitions have been "successful") to be addressed.
- Reinforce public accountability by allowing judgements to be made about the quality and effectiveness of the systems that assist young people's transitions; and
- Provide insight into the comparative functioning of transition systems.

More specifically, a framework for indicators of the transition from initial education to working life should:

- Describe the context, duration, processes and outcomes of transition, as well as the relationships between these; and
- Place transition in a lifelong learning context.

Such a framework would enable the above dimensions, in turn, to be related to individual characteristics such as:

- Gender.
- Educational attainment; and
- Family or social background.

A framework of indicators to describe transition relates to a number of tracks of work taking place within the OECD INES project as well as beyond it. Network B of INES has, in particular, an important role *vis-à-vis* measuring labour market outcomes in relation to initial education and training (type and level) while Network B and the Technical Group of INES together have an important role in contributing to indicators of transition process and pathways especially at the upper secondary level. In addition, the work of the Programme of International Student Assessment (PISA) and Network A of INES in measuring student learning outcomes and that of INES Network C in developing indicators of upper secondary schools can contribute to a better understanding of the transition process. Beyond the issue of the relationship of education to labour market outcomes, there is interest in the social implications of changing transition patterns for young people including impact on family formation. These issues will be addressed in a wider context of on-going work in OECD on social and labour market indicators.

The context of transition

The national contexts of transition vary widely. The duration, processes and outcomes of transition are influenced by factors such as the way in which labour markets are organised, the nature and structure of education and training systems, the ways in which educational and occupational qualifications mediate young people's entry to the labour market, the ways in which labour market assistance and welfare systems are organised, and the organisation and functioning of the social partners and the various levels of government. Typologies have been suggested as one way in which more meaningful comparisons of national transition contexts can be made.

Whilst a range of such typologies have been suggested, work is first needed to:

- Refine the key underlying dimensions of the transition context.

- Reduce complex sets of labour market, educational and social information on the transition context to a smaller number of more clearly understood dimensions, allowing a small number of objective key indicators of them to be developed; and
- Determine how most usefully countries may be described using them.

Clearer and simpler descriptions of national transition contexts will enable them to be related more easily to national transition durations, processes and outcomes.

The duration of transition

Indicators of the duration of the transition should be able to span a period commencing at the end of compulsory schooling (or earlier in those countries in which pathways diverge before this point), progressing to the end of upper secondary education or its equivalent, and extending into the typical period(s) of tertiary education. Single year of age data over the entire 15-29 age span would be of great value in providing a picture of educational and labour force activity over this time span.

The length – and lengthening – of the transition is a key policy issue in many countries, both because of its implications for public costs, and because of its impact upon the supply of qualified labour at a time when populations are ageing. Hence it would be useful, in addition to simple descriptions of the length, to have indicators that were able to shed light on the varying reasons for the length, as these reasons will have different policy implications. These could include:

- Extended full-time participation in education, arising both from movements between courses and programmes at the same level as well as from progression from one level to another; or
- Unsuccessful attempts to enter higher education; or
- Extended periods of joint participation in both education and the labour market; or
- The incidence and duration of military/national service; or
- Delay in obtaining work upon leaving full-time study, both as the result of extended periods of job search and as the result of periods of educational and labour market inactivity for reasons such as travel.

A comprehensive framework of transition indicators would be able to describe the periods that young people typically spend in different forms of activity – for example the periods spent in education, in unemployment and in full- or part-time employment, or in various combinations of these.

Longitudinal data sets are essential for describing many of the key features of the transition process: for example the proportion of time that young people spend in the first five years after initial education in employment, unemployment and out of the labour force. They are also important in helping to relate many features of the transition context to transition outcomes.

A comprehensive framework of transition indicators would also allow many of the features of the school context that are important in the transition to working life to be described: for example the nature and quality of career information and guidance services; and the relationships between the school and its community, including its community of employers.

The transition process

A comprehensive framework of transition indicators would describe the nature of the pathways in which young people participate during upper secondary education or its equivalent. A simple framework would separately describe:

- General education pathways.
- Vocational education pathways that are school based.
- Vocational education pathways of the apprenticeship type; and
- Participation in labour market programmes or other safety net programmes.

It would also be of value to separately describe:

- Vocational and technical pathways that differ by level of educational attainment.
- Those vocational pathways that are intended to qualify young people both for work and for tertiary study, and those intended to qualify them for work only, whether these are school-based or of the apprenticeship type; and
- Vocational and technical pathways by field of study.

Indicators of the extent and nature of young people's involvement with work places during the transition period should be seen as essential. These should separately identify involvement in:

- Apprenticeship type arrangements.
- Part-time employment whilst a student; and

- Unpaid or paid periods of workplace experience as part of educational programmes such as those characteristic of US and Canadian co-operative education, Swedish APU periods, and Australian school-industry programmes.

In a policy sense it is as important to know about continuation from one level of education to another or to know about continuation in second programmes of study at the same level as it is to know about movements from education to the labour market or otherwise out of education. Thus transition indicators should be able to describe flows at key points in the transition process (the end of compulsory schooling; the end of upper secondary education; the end of tertiary education), not simply at the point at which young people leave school (or its equivalent). Longitudinal data sets are of great value for such purposes

Transition outcomes

To date work on outcomes has largely focused upon labour market outcomes. But it is important to see transitions also in educational terms, and to provide indicators of qualifications gained:

- By type.
- By level.
- By field of study.

Labour market indicators of transition (from whatever point the young person leaves education) need to be richer than simply employment or unemployment rates (taking account in both instances of the importance of presenting indicators separately for students and non-students). There is a need also to look for the elements of "successful transitions" and define a set of indicators which could appropriately describe these transitions.

- *Employment indicators* need to be able to describe the characteristics of the employment that those leaving education enter and how these characteristics relate to their educational background, *i.e.* level of education and field of study. Such indicators could describe:
  - part-time, casual, temporary and other insecure forms of employment separately from employment that is full-time or permanent;
  - earnings; and
  - the occupation or industry of employment.
- *Unemployment indicators* need to separately describe the qualitative nature of unemployment: for example the extent of long- versus short-term unemployment; and periods spent in searching for a first job after leaving education.
- *Inactivity indicators* are needed to supplement employment and unemployment indicators. There would be a need to separate out family responsibilities from other reasons for inactivity.

© OECD 2000

Appendix 6

LOW EDUCATION LEVELS AND LABOUR MARKET DISADVANTAGE

The apparently rising disadvantage of those with low levels of education as the number of early school leavers falls is a common policy concern in OECD countries. It formed a substantial theme in the discussions that took place at the joint OECD-US Departments of Labor and Education conference on "Preparing Youth for the 21st Century" held in Washington in February 1999 (OECD, 1999b). This Appendix explores the relationship in more detail, and is directed at the question of whether the relationship is an inevitable one: in other words is it possible at the one time to reduce the numbers who leave education early, with low qualifications, and to ensure that these early leavers do not suffer unduly in the labour market compared to those who have completed an upper secondary education?

The incidence of low qualification levels is here measured by the number of 20-24 year-olds with less than an upper secondary education as a per cent of the population of the same age. (Note that this leads to inflated estimates in countries such as the Netherlands, Denmark and Switzerland where substantial proportions of 20-24 year-olds are still enrolled in upper secondary education.)

The relative labour market disadvantage suffered by those with low qualification levels is measured by the ratio of low qualified 20-24 year-olds' share of total unemployment to their share of total employment. A score of 1.0 indicates that their share of unemployment is the same as their share of employment. A score of 2.0 shows that that their share of unemployment is twice their share of employment, indicating significant labour market disadvantage. A score of 0.5 shows that their share of unemployment is half their share of employment, indicating a comparative labour market advantage for the poorly qualified.[1]

Table A6.1 shows these values for 23 countries in 1996. These include 13 of the Thematic Review participants, with only Japan missing.

The proportion of 20-24 year-olds who have not completed upper secondary education ranges from a low of 5% (Korea) to a high of 71% (Portugal). It averages 25%. Countries falling within the lower range of OECD experience include Korea, the Czech Republic, the United Kingdom and Norway. Countries falling in the upper range of OECD experience include Portugal, Turkey, Spain and Italy.

The relative disadvantage that poorly qualified young adults suffer in the labour market ranges from the Czech Republic at the upper end, where their share of unemployment is almost three and a half times their share of employment, to Greece and Turkey at the lower end, where their share of unemployment is slightly over half their share of employment. Countries in which the disadvantage is greatest include the Czech Republic, the United Kingdom, Ireland and the United States. The disadvantage is lowest in Greece, Turkey, Italy and Portugal. In each of these countries the index is less than 1.0, showing that poorly qualified young adults in fact have a positive advantage in the labour market when compared to those who have completed an upper secondary education.

Figure A6.1 plots the data in Table A6.1. It shows that there is quite a strong inverse relationship between levels of under-qualification and labour market disadvantage among young adults (R^2 = .42). Where few young adults are under-qualified, unemployment tends to be relatively higher for the under-qualified. Where many young adults have poor levels of education, the penalties associated with being poorly qualified are fewer.

Nevertheless there are significant exceptions. Among countries participating in the Thematic Review Norway and Sweden have comparable incidences of low qualifications to the Czech Republic, the United Kingdom, the United States and Canada, and all six are below the OECD average. Yet the labour market disadvantage suffered by under-qualified young adults is lower in the Norway and Sweden than in the other four countries. This suggests that it is by no means inevitable that as the incidence of early school leaving falls the labour market disadvantage of the low qualified need rise.

While the data by themselves do not explain these differences, among Thematic Review participants both Norway and Sweden are characterised, compared to the Czech Republic, the United Kingdom, the United States and Canada, by safety nets that actively attempt to reintegrate young early school leavers into education so that they can complete an upper secondary education (see Section 4.4). Both Norway and Sweden also make substantial efforts to ensure that unemployed young adults can access labour market assistance – education, training or subsidised employment.

---

1. Using the ratio of the unemployment rate among those with less than an upper secondary education to the unemployment rate among those with an upper secondary education but not tertiary education leads to an index with almost identical values.

Table A6.1. **Low qualification levels and relative labour market disadvantage of the low qualified, 1996**

	Low qualified as a proportion of 20-24 year-olds	Relative labour market disadvantage of low qualified 20-24 year-olds
Australia	26	1.8
Austria	18	1.9
Belgium	22	1.7
Canada	15	2.1
Czech Republic	7	3.4
Denmark[1]	32	1.6
Finland	21	1.8
France	22	1.6
Germany	22	1.7
Greece	25	0.6
Hungary	20	1.9
Ireland	22	2.3
Italy	37	0.8
Korea	5	1.3
Netherlands[1]	30	1.4
New Zealand	28	1.6
Norway	12	1.7
Poland	13	1.3
Portugal	71	0.8
Spain	39	0.9
Sweden	14	1.7
Switzerland[1]	21	1.8
Turkey	66	0.6
United Kingdom	11	2.6
United States	14	2.2
OECD Average	**25**	**1.6**

1. In Denmark, the Netherlands and Switzerland significant proportions of 20-24 year-olds are still enrolled in upper secondary education.
Source: OECD education database.

Figure A6.1. **Incidence of low qualification levels and labour market disadvantage of the low qualified, 20-24 year-olds, 1996**

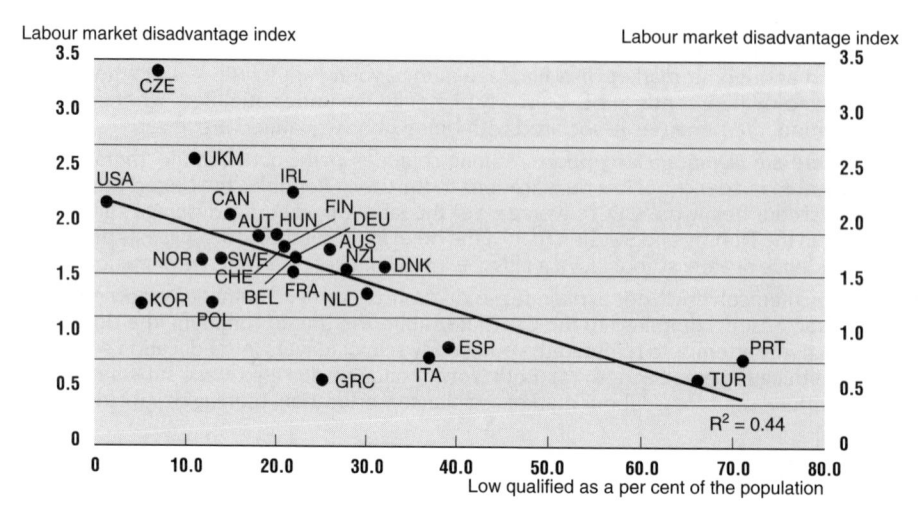

Source: See Table A6.1.

Appendix 7

THE AVAILABILITY OF INDICATORS OF KEY TRANSITION GOALS

Section 2.1 sets out seven basic goals that all transition policies should aim for. Here we describe the availability of data for a number of indicators of each of these goals, with particular reference to countries participating in the Thematic Review.

High proportions of young people completing a full upper secondary education with a recognised qualification for either work, tertiary study or both

- OECD (1998*a*) reports 1996 apparent upper secondary graduation rates at the typical age of graduation for 12 of the 14 countries taking part in the Thematic Review, with data for Australia and the United Kingdom being missing. These estimate the proportion of a cohort who complete an upper secondary education, but do not indicate whether or not they have obtained a qualification either for employment or for tertiary study. Where significant numbers of graduates are outside the "typical" age of graduation, the index can be markedly skewed. For example in Norway it exceeds 100%, as many adults return to upper secondary education after the "typical" age.
- The proportion of 20-24 year-olds whose educational achievement is below upper secondary level is another indicator that can be used to assess this goal. It is available from the OECD education database for 13 of the countries participating in the Thematic Review and is missing for Japan. It is misleadingly low in countries such as Denmark, the Netherlands and Switzerland where significant numbers in the age group are still enrolled in upper secondary education.
- The proportion of young people who are not in education one year after the end of compulsory schooling is a indicator of early school leaving that helps to shed light on this goal. It can be calculated for all 14 countries taking part in the Thematic Review (see Table 2.4).

High levels of knowledge and skill among young people at the end of the transition phase[1]

- The International Adult Literacy Survey provides data on literacy levels among 16-25 year-olds in 12 countries, but for only five participants in the Thematic Review: Canada; Switzerland; Sweden; the United Kingdom; and the United States.
- The proportion of 25-29 year-olds who achieve tertiary qualifications is available for all Thematic Review participants other than Japan.

A low proportion of teenagers being at the one time not in education and unemployed

- This is available for 1996 for 15-19 year-olds for 16 countries from the INES Network B 1998 special transition collection, and is reported for 15 of these in OECD (1998*a*). It is available for 10 Thematic Review participants, and is missing for Hungary, Japan, Norway and Portugal.
- The unemployment to population ratio for 15-19 year-olds can be used as a proximate indicator of this goal, but is influenced by rates of student participation in the labour force, as discussed in Appendix 4. It is available for all countries taking part in the Thematic Review. For Switzerland it is available from the INES Network B special transition collection rather than from the standard OECD labour force data base, and is subject to high sampling variability. This high sampling variability is a result of the very small numbers aged 15-19 who are unemployed in Switzerland.
- The proportion of 15-19 year-olds who are either unemployed or inactive (neither in education nor in the labour force) is a related indicator of this goal. However its meaning can be ambivalent to the extent that those in the inactive category can be involved in activities potentially able to make a positive contribution to the transition such as voluntary work or travel abroad.

---

1. See Caspi *et al.* (1998), Marks and Fleming (1998*a*, 1998*b*) and OECD (1997*b*) on the relationship between literacy levels and labour market outcomes.

A high proportion of those young adults who have left education having a job[2]

- This is available for 1996 for 20-24 year-olds for 16 countries from the INES Network B 1998 special transition collection, and is reported for 15 of these in OECD (1998a). It is available for 10 Thematic Review participants but not for Hungary, Japan, Norway and Portugal. OECD (1999b) reports this for 17 countries, 13 of which are included in the Network B collection, for 22 year-olds for 1997.
- The employment to population ratio for 20-24 year-olds can be used as a proximate indicator of this goal, but is influenced by rates of student participation in the labour force. It is available for all countries taking part in the Thematic Review.

Few young people remaining unemployed for lengthy periods after leaving education

The proportion of those unemployed 15-19 and 20-24 year-olds who have been unemployed either for six months or more or 12 months or more is available from the OECD unemployment duration database. It does not separately report students and non-students, but the great majority of long term, as opposed to short-term, unemployed youth will have left education. Using six months or more of unemployment as the cut off point seems sensible in view of the European Union's use of this as the recommended point before which unemployed young people should be offered assistance (European Communities, 1999a and 1999b). This indicator is available for all Thematic Review participants except Canada and Japan.

Stable and positive employment and educational histories in the years after leaving upper secondary education

- For this goal to be assessed a consistent comparative approach to longitudinal surveys is required. OECD (1998b) attempted part of the task in analysing employment and unemployment rates over the first three to five years after leaving education. It was able to report results for only five countries, only two of which (Australia and the United States) were Thematic Review participants.

An equitable distribution of outcomes by gender, social background and region

- This is the most difficult of the goals to assess. All standard education and labour market indicators are available by gender, including the 14 key indicators that appear in Table 2.1a. However data on their distribution by social background and region is rare. Some countries monitor some equity indicators,[3] but consistent comparative data is rare.
- The relative labour market disadvantage of those with low levels of education sheds some light on the goal. This indicator is measured by the ratio of the share of total unemployment among an age group of those with less than an upper secondary level of education to the same group's share of total employment. It has been calculated for 20-24 year-olds and is available for all Thematic Review participants except Japan. It is shown in Table A6.1.

---

2. It can be argued that this goal should encompass the nature of the work held by young adults (full-time or part-time; permanent or temporary; low-paid or high-paid). The meaning of this will vary widely, depending upon the extent to which part-time, low-paid or temporary work is associated with education and training and is a stepping stone to better quality work. Comparative data on the type of work held by non-students of this age is available for only a small number Thematic Review participants. OECD (1998b) reports data on 16-29 year-old school leavers in temporary and part-time work for five Thematic Review participants. It shows that in many countries – notably Austria, Finland, Denmark and the United Kingdom among Thematic Review participants – this type of employment is very likely to be associated with school-based education and training. OECD (1996b) and OECD (1999b) provide data on low pay among full-time workers aged less than 25 in eight Thematic Review participants in the mid 1990s. This shows that the incidence is highest in the United States, Canada and the United Kingdom. However this in part reflects the overall incidence of low-paid jobs in these countries. When corrected for this, the likelihood of young people being concentrated in low-paid work is highest in Finland and Sweden among the eight countries, and lowest in Austria. Australia, Canada, Japan, the United Kingdom and the United States fall between the two ends of the distribution.
3. For example Hungary has consistently monitored achievement in basic skills by geographical region during the 1990s. Longitudinal studies of youth in transition such as those conducted by the Australian Council for Educational Research and Statistics Canada also allow trends in equity outcomes over time to be assessed.